LAMBADA COUNTRY

LAMBADA COUNTRY

A Ride Across Eastern Europe

Giles Whittell

CHAPMANS

Chapmans Publishers Ltd
141–143 Drury Lane
London WC2B 5TB

BRITISH LIBRARY CATALOGUING IN PUBLICATION DATA
Whittell, Giles
Lambada country : a ride across Eastern Europe.
I. Title
914.7

ISBN 1–85592–591–5

First published by Chapmans 1992

Photoset in Linotron Bembo by York House Typographic Ltd, London
Printed and bound in Great Britain by
Butler & Tanner Ltd, Frome and London

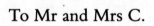

To Mr and Mrs C.

Acknowledgements

For their help and hospitality, without which I would have gone bankrupt within days instead of months and would have returned from Eastern Europe with nothing to write about, I would like to thank Jörg and Heike Schröder, Iain Frater and Thomas Fuchs in Berlin, Jan Vild and Maria Holubova in Prague, Slawek and Ewa Ponichtera in Warsaw, Janos Karakas in Budapest, the Szimas in Transylvania, and Bojidar Marinov and Peter Popov in Sofia.

I would also like to thank Megan Meredith, Marilyn Warnick, Bill Hamilton and Mark Crean for their advice and encouragement in London, Nick Crane for recommending a traditional bike over a 'mountain' one, my grandparents for the cottage and David Rowan for his boat.

Contents

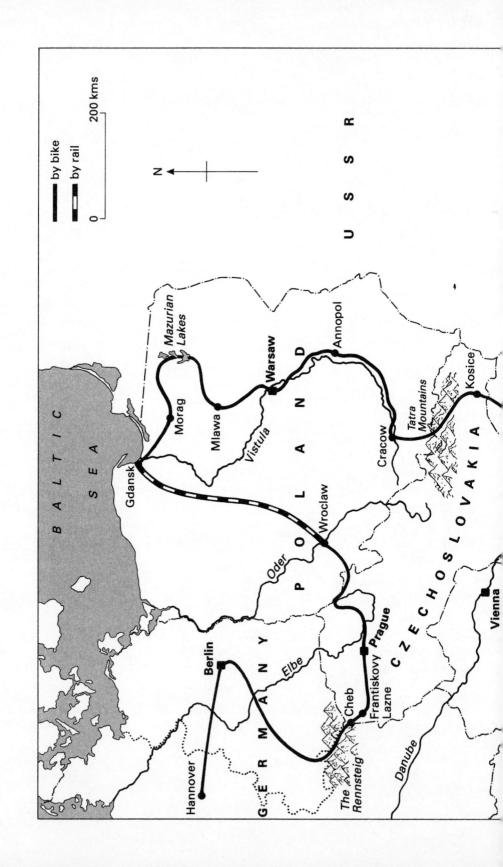

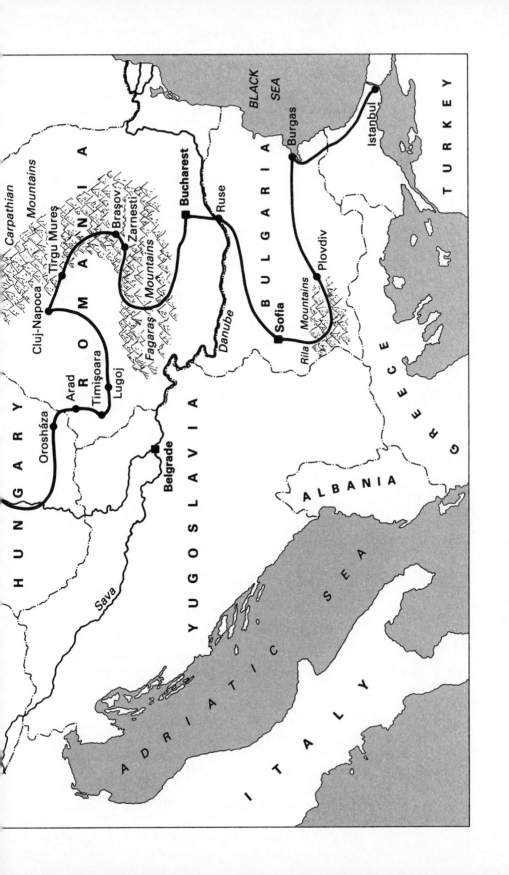

Preface

You could say this journey started in Somerset. On Christmas night, 1989, Ceauşescu was shot by a firing squad in Bucharest and I began to wonder about riding a bicycle across Eastern Europe. That was in Somerset, under some damp blankets in an aunt's unheated attic.

But it would be more accurate to say Cambridge. In Cambridge I spent £500, no less, on a bicycle which I then rode to the station, wobbling at traffic lights because of the toe clips.

Or even Hammersmith. I was aiming for the 5.18 from Victoria to Dover Western Docks, but panicked at the last moment and bought some extra socks and T-shirts from King Street Marks and Spencer's in Hammersmith. In the end I got the 5.38.

None of these really counts, though. The first place which really counts is Hannover, towards the eastern side of old West Germany. The bicycle went to Hannover by train, but from then on it was just me and it as far as Turkey.

Like thousands of others, I wanted to see Eastern Europe before it disappeared and became a mere annex of Western Europe. In particular – and this was as close as I got to what you might call a line of enquiry – I wanted to go to those parts which other forms of transport might not reach. That is, down minor roads, up steep roads, along dirt roads. Once there, the idea was to ask whether the revolutions had made a *difference* – to the beer, the newspapers, the prospect of going to work on a Monday morning, the way policemen spoke to you, the availability of bicycle spares – or whether, when the television crews packed up and returned to the West, the revolutions would pack up too.

Then there were the grandchildren to think of. ('Yes, Tom, what your father says is true. Many years ago I rode a bicycle to Istanbul . . . .')

This being a bicycle trip, there was also, for the first time in my life, the prospect of developing some real muscles.

And finally, if I'm honest, I had nothing better to be doing.

Giles Whittell,
London,
September 1991

Route 188

Document-naked, I approached the Central European front on the afternoon of Easter Sunday 1990. The East German frontier guards conjured a visa out of their hut and said that for all they cared I could camp where I liked.

Behind the checkpoint two empty watchtowers faced each other over a ditch and a quarter of a mile of green space, which this summer would be farmed again. In front of me there was a different sort of tower, part of an old granary. It was built with a mixture of brick and stone. The pointing was gone and strips of iron strained to hold in the bulging walls.

Route 188, which I had picked up in Hannover, curved away to where the road to Madgeburg forked right. A few cars, mostly West German, were using it to avoid queues on the transit motorway. A small boy rattled past on a bicycle called Freedom. From a ground-floor window an old woman in a tall brown hat surveyed the crossroads through one eye while a cataract crept across the other. She beckoned me over and delivered a sad monologue about life under the eye of the *Grenztruppen* and the exodus of the young people since last summer.

Between cars, the place was bewilderingly quiet.

I pedalled on towards Berlin – and the Urals and Siberia for all the sea that stood in the way.

This was Saxony-Anhalt, the poorest of Germany's poor new eastern *Länder*. It is flat farming country, inclining hardly at all to the slow, brown streams which drain it. Poplars shade the streams, but most trees here are conifers, bands of pine forest which stripe the map and darken the horizon.

Lifeless villages started and stopped abruptly, defined by the cobbles which turned Route 188 into their main streets. One village introduced itself grandly with a duckpond. There followed a bus-stop, a grocery and an avenue of timber-frame houses. There was not one splash of advertising colour to undermine the sense of having indulged in a gentle spot of time travel.

Half-way down the main street a stone arch led to a farmyard. Straw straggled out over the pavement. Farmyard smells mixed with lignite smoke, the national smell of East Germany.

A stiff westerly breeze bowled me along, which seemed appropriate. It also kept four gliders aloft near the town of Gardelegen. Fathers and sons in Trabants and Wartburgs puttered up a sand track to watch them swishing in to land. A tractor plane hammered backwards and forwards between a short grass landing strip and the cloudbase. It was the bare minimum required for powered flight: two wheels, two overworked pistons and a cockpit slung beneath a pair of wings. On its tail were the hammer and dividers of the German Democratic Republic.

On the other side of town were garrisoned – still – the forces of the hammer and sickle. Behind a wall and a line of pine trees there were barracks and volleyball courts for thousands of Russian soldiers.

They seemed well and truly ensconced, as permanent as anything else about the town. It would surely take more than a Cold War thaw to move them. But across the Elbe the Russians were already pulling out.

The only bar in the village of Steckelsdorf was empty except for Rudi and the landlord. Rudi was cadaverous and small, and older than he looked. He had no wife and he drank and smoked to fill his time. He had grey stubble and sat in a black greatcoat fingering a bottle of *Sekt*. Wolfgang, the landlord, was humouring Rudi but concentrating on the telly. They were winding down after the Mandela Concert.

Was there food? In principle there was not, but Wolfgang brought some goulash. It was a splash of brown, salty nutrient containing strands of meat.

Rudi introduced himself and asked if I was Russian. Wolfgang
came and sat with us. He tucked his belly under the table and
explained that this was his first night in fourteen years as landlord
that the place had not been packed with Russian soldiers. The
local base had emptied for good this morning. Hardware had been
trundling out of the forest towards Berlin all day. Wolfgang
blinked, and laughed through his moustache.

We discussed dictators. Rudi reckoned Hitler was a better sort
than Stalin, but he was still undecided about Churchill and
Gorbachev. Wolfgang explained amiably that Rudi was a Fascist.
Rudi asked my opinion of Gorbachev and I said he seemed to have
been good news for East Germany. We all knew about the Sinatra
Doctrine, and Wolfgang hummed 'I Did It My Way'.

Wolfgang, it turned out, had lit a fuse calling Rudi a Fascist, and
Rudi began to shout at him about Brezhnev. Wolfgang didn't
rise. There was a personal aspect to this. He kept a proportion of
the bar's takings even though the State owned it. Russian soldiers
had been good business, and he'd learned their language. Now he
was going private along with the rest of the country and would
have to survive on summer custom from a nearby caravan site.

Rudi finished his tirade and asked me again: 'So, are you
Russian?' Wolfgang was putting on his coat. He turned off the
television and the light, and herded Rudi and the Englander into
the street.

He asked where I intended sleeping and I said something about
camping. He wouldn't hear of it. Camping started on May Day
and we were still in April, so I followed him to his house. (He
drove a Dacia; a Renault 12 built under licence in Romania.) It was
a modern house with two bedrooms, and he owned it.

He introduced his charming wife and daughter, and a dog, a cat
and a parakeet. We drank English tea and French cognac while
watching a Swiss cop thriller in a living-room crammed with
souvenirs from trips to Yalta (before the revolution) and Stuttgart
(after). Heat poured off a huge tile-covered briquette oven which,
once lit, could not be turned down. But Wolfgang was confident
that oil and gas central heating would be along soon. In the
meantime he opened the patio doors to keep the birds warm.

The trip to Yalta had clearly been as memorable as any revolution. Next morning the details were recounted over a breakfast of

boiled eggs and home-made liver paté in blue fat. Freddy Mercury sang 'Crazy Little Thing Called Love' on West Berlin radio.

They had flown to Sebastopol with Interflug – German airline, Russian plane; very modern, very comfortable – and then driven over the mountains to the Black Sea in a bus. The hotel had been grand, right on the beach. Out came the postcards. Their balcony was ringed in biro, on the fourteenth floor of a massive silver rectangle of people's holiday accommodation. It was, as they said, right on the beach.

Of less consuming interest, but definitely quaint, were pictures of the nineteenth-century hotel where Roosevelt and Churchill bargained away East Germany to Stalin in 1945, and of the Swallow's Nest, the Rhineland castle on a crag above the bay from where, between 1912 and the October Revolution of 1917, the German oil magnate who built it enjoyed spectacular views inland towards the Massandra vineyards.

'It was beautiful,' said Wolfgang. He popped another Nutrasweet into his coffee. But next year, if they managed to get a new car, it would be England.

The crucible of two world wars lay over the next hill. Through a few more fields and woods, on the outskirts of modern West Berlin, stood the villa where Hitler and his specialists settled on Zyklon B for use at Auschwitz. Inside the orbital motorway, four miles ahead, the city of the Reichstag, the bunker and the airlift into Tempelhof would shortly be coming into view. The 1940s have been called 'a cataclysmically active decade' and Berlin was always the centre of the action. Before that there was Bismarck and the Kaiser; afterwards, the Wall . . . and the end of the Wall. The whole blur of modern European history passes through Berlin like sand through an hourglass.

It was raining hard. The approach to Spandau checkpoint was through a Soviet military zone. Army lorries thundered past sending up curling sheets of water. The view to the right, behind barbed wire, was of trenches and low brick turrets. A graded mountain of rubbish slid by on the left but I concentrated on the road because the traffic had dug tyre-width grooves along the tarmac. Lightning crackled down towards a queue of cars – Audis, BMWs, and Trabants half their length – beyond which lay no man's land. It was the width of a football pitch and lined with watchtowers and floodlights. The East German edge was a ten-foot fence. The West German edge was the Wall, made of the same prefabricated sections that bisect the city. Everything was still in place.

The new cross-border traffic crawled, blasé already, back to East Germany. Peter Stuyvesant provided the first advertisement since before Gardelegen: a poster of a beautiful Bedouin girl and the caption 'Come Together'. Up ahead I could see the silky-smooth West German cycle lanes beginning.

Someone was honking his horn. I heard my name shouted and saw a car window being lowered. Where had I seen that car before? It was Wolfgang and his wife.

'What took you so long?' he yelled, but the queue rolled them on before I could answer. Weird. Steckelsdorf was in another world.

Berlin was full. Every hotel, youth hostel and campsite was full. The benches by the Europa Centre in West Berlin and the snugger corners of Friedrichsstrasse Station in East Berlin were full.

I found this out on a bicycle tour of the city which took from dusk to midnight. First I bought a Snickers and a street map at a petrol station. They cost four times the price of a slap-up meal in East Germany. The route to the Wall passed Siemens' colossal headquarters, which has a street named after it, and an Osram factory from which clouds of noble gas for making light-bulbs wafted across the road.

I went to the wrong crossing point. The Brandenburg Gate was for German pedestrians only, and besides, was being renovated.

'After all the people in November,' explained a smiling woman from under an extravagant perm.

'Use Checkpoint Charlie,' said a policeman. 'Follow the Wall.'

The avenue through the Tiergarten to the Brandenburg Gate had been decorously lit. (This is Strasse des 17 Juni. It commemorates the failed workers' putsch of 1953 which started with a strike in East Berlin's Karl Marx Allee. There is a move to rename it Strasse des 9 November, after the day the Wall was opened.)

But along the Wall the arc-lights which used to burn all night at East Germany's expense were switched off. A hundred yards away the backs of East Berlin apartment blocks were dotted with low-wattage orange squares. The Wall itself was gone, leaving a murky view across a swathe of grit which used to be a minefield but is now prime real estate. The grit got in my brakes. A rabbit bounced away into the Tiergarten. The lozenge that runs on West Berlin's experimental magnetic levitation railway emerged from its glass-walled station in the wasteland of Potsdamer Platz and glided overhead like a spaceship. It was ten o'clock. I passed the Golden Nugget Amusement Arcade, left the American Sector through Checkpoint Charlie, and plunged up Friedrichstrasse and across Unter den Linden into the final scenes of *The Ipcress File*.

Two months later, Barry D. Wood was able to write in the *Financial Times*: 'As darkness falls on the Linden, rich and fashionably attired West Berliners descend from their Mercedes and enter Frederick the Great's magnificent 1743 opera house through three polished wooden doors . . . The enforced greyness of the Stalinist past diminishes daily.' The only Mercedes I saw was the one whose driver beat me to the last room in a Christian Hospice in Oranienburgerstrasse. The greyness of the Stalinist past – looming, grubby buildings and deserted streets – seemed extant and oppressive. I recrossed the border, took the S-bahn to the end of the line, and slept in a wood.

Berlin

When I woke up, my expensive Gore-Tex bivvi bag was dripping with cold dew and my toothpaste was almost solid. It had been a knobbly night. Now dogs were being walked through the wood along a tarmac path towards a pond. I didn't want their owners to think I was homeless, so I rolled up the bivvi bag before it had dried and took the S-bahn back into town.

The tourist office fixed me up with a private room at three times what I could afford to pay, then I returned to the Wall to look at it in daylight.

'Hammer and chisel for rent. 10 minutes. 5 Deutschmarks.' Or you could bring your own. Or you could buy prequarried, authenticated Wall from one of the displays on trestle-tables and car bonnets along Zimmerstrasse. There was Wall in all sizes, from tiny chips to heavy chunks for mantelpieces, polished and mounted. (This was in April. By July the resource was scarcer and heavies were keeping freelance diggers away.)

Museums, eat your heart out. Likewise galleries, beautiful buildings and all standard tourist fare. The Wall was why Berlin was full. It had been a gripping physical presence for that slippery terror, poached almost out of existence by fiction, known as the Cold War. Now it stood for 1989 as well. No wonder it sold.

On the corner of Charlottenstrasse and Zimmerstrasse a boy was renting out ironmongery with a silhouette in rifle sights on the back of his sweatshirt. Beyond him, East German frontier guards were letting people through a hole to go up their empty watchtower. I squeezed through the hole. Two Americans followed and one said to the other: 'You know, that was symbolic what I just did.'

On the no-man's-land side, the Eastern side, there was a message for Peking in thick red spray paint: CHINESE GOVERNMENT YOU DIRTY MURDERING BASTARDS. Also: ROCK 'N' ROLL IN EAST BERLIN, I LOVE JULIE SHOGAN, and ULTRAVOX ARE BEST. In small, fading letters, low down: DESTROY CAPITALISM. Fat chance.

A mile further north, the famous stretch of S-bahn which crossed the Wall and no man's land between Friedrichstrasse and the Zoo had become a desperadoes' trading shuttle. East Germans thronged around the bank under the railway bridge buying black market Deutschmarks. Poles queued in their hundreds outside the pawnbroker across the road. They bought video machines, ghetto-blasters and trays of beer in cans to sell on pavements back east, and hauled them up and down the station steps on folding luggage carriers. West Berliners clucked with exasperation, elbowing past, missing their old island existence.

My room was in Giesebrechtstrasse, just off the Ku'damm in West Berlin. It was quiet, with a high ceiling and a narrow window filled by a tree in a courtyard. You reached it via a dark corridor lined with dark original portraits. The landlord, Herr Jahnko Jahnke, was unmarried and didn't seem the marrying sort. He was tanned and sinewy with prominent veins on his hands and feet. There were books on male modelling in my room, published by *Playgirl* magazine, and a signed photograph of Mikhail Baryshnikov.

Jahnko worked bizarre hours and spent the rest of the time with his hand down his tracksuit bottoms in front of the television. There were enormous ferns in the bathroom, and the bath and lavatory were made of white marble streaked with blue, like stilton. Very Berlin, I thought.

Jahnko spoke good, clipped English, but his manner was so brisk as to imply conversation would cost extra. He was measly about the breakfast the Tourist Office obliged him to provide and unsympathetic when poisoned grapefruit juice prevented me

from cashing enough traveller's cheques to pay him in advance.
Quite quickly, I decided I disliked him.

I had a contact in Köpernick, the Richmond of East Berlin. The
name was Schroder.

At eight o'clock one Friday evening I called at the Schroder
family's apartment, unannounced. They lived in a dark cul-de-sac
a few feet from the River Spree and had written to the British
Embassy saying they were hoping to meet an English family,
now that they were allowed to. They got me instead, asking to
interview them.

Mrs Schroder asked me in and sent the children to bed. Mr
Schroder produced chocolates and cognac, and we sat and talked
for four and a half hours, seriously at first, about the world they
had lost, uproariously by the end, about having the doorbell rung
by an Englishman on a Friday evening.

Mr Schroder, Jorg, was a lecturer in law and economics and
was having to relearn all his law and all his economics. Mrs
Schroder, Heike, was an engineer working in a factory which
made power stations. She had been told to find out all she could
about advertising. That seemed to say it all. Any sense of unrea-
lity about the television revolutions of autumn 1989 evaporated.
Here was the follow-up, the bottom line. A man with nine years
of higher education and two degrees was having to accept that
everything he'd learned was 'wrong'. He had been praised as a
student for his *Marxist-Leninist Klassenstandpunkt* (class-based
viewpoint). Now he had a day off work each week to forage in
libraries in West Berlin for material on market economies and
independent judiciaries. Heike had given up looking for books on
advertising. They were all signed out for months ahead.

Heike Schroder had awesome energy and cheerfulness, which
was why she was so despondent. She would almost certainly be
unemployed within the year because her company had to fold or
shrink to half its size to be attractive to investors. She dreaded
housewifery. 'There were good things as well as bad about our
country,' she often said, but she would scold me if I said she was
nostalgic about Communist East Germany. The truth is she was a
natural stalwart. Her instinct was to make the best of bad jobs;
anything less would be a stupid waste of time and life.

'The good things' about her country had been guaranteed

employment, free health and education, token charges only for rent, heating, bread, milk, potatoes, and *Wurst*, and a year's paid maternity leave for each child. Shortages were rare. The Stasi question had been sensationalized by the Western press. There had been time for friends and family, holidays in Hungary and Czechoslovakia. She had been a Party member and always declined her mischievous mother's invitations to meet Westerners. 'Everyone wants to do their job well,' she said, and foreign contacts would have jeopardized hers.

Now there were new times to make the best of. She wished she'd thrown away her Party card before the end, but was ashamed of nothing. Her new dreams were a holiday in Denmark and a management traineeship. Since foreign contacts were allowed, she'd started looking for them, and hey presto! Was this not a foreign contact seated before her?

She asked where I was staying and I explained about Jahnko. I painted him really black.

'You can stay here,' she said.

I pretended not to hear. I wanted nothing more than to stay here. It was warm. The Schroders were interesting, interested and friendly. But I was calling myself a journalist and journalists look after themselves. I talked on. I said that Jahnko spoke English if he spoke at all, which was a problem because I wanted to improve my German.

'You can stay here, and speak German with us. You can stay as long as you like.'

I gave in. I went with them to Sans-Souci Palace in Potsdam on the Sunday and moved in on the Monday for a month.

On the long haul back to West Berlin that night, a man with a big, ragged circle of blood on his white sweatshirt was taken off the train by police. It was the end of 20 April, Hitler's birthday, and the skinheads had been celebrating.

Next morning I telephoned Thomas Fuchs, freelance journalist, to ask if I could ask some basic questions about Berlin. For a book. Fuchs came on the line. It was a classic voice, slow and rasping. He spoke English with a strong American accent and a crackle on the line made him sound like the world-weary pilot of a jumbo:

'I must tell you, I don't have much time. An Australian who said he was a journalist ripped me off last month.'

If I was not a 'twilight' journalist he could give me half an hour. Thomas Fuchs is now a friend of mine, but it was not a hopeful start.

He lived near a bar called The Golden Egg up Greifswalder-strasse, which sweeps north from Alexanderplatz at right angles to Karl Marx Allee. It is very long and wide and, except for a showpiece housing development called Ernst Thalmann Park, grey. Fuchs had a one-room flat on the third floor of a big bland block with a yard.

He shook my hand at the door. His little finger was badly skewed, pointing up at his thumb, but I never dared ask why. He was slim, with thick stubble and black hair which stood tall on his head. One wall of his main room was a fold-away bed which he had devised himself. Along another was a black desk with a black typewriter. Opposite them were two black shelves, one support-ing a black cassette player, the other supporting books: *Catch 22*, *Huckleberry Finn* (in English, printed in Russia), two volumes of Hemingway short stories and three P. J. O'Rourke paperbacks. We sat down in black swivel chairs and he started smoking, and talking.

About Communism: 'I always thought Communism, as a reality, ridiculous. I couldn't take it seriously, but I accepted it as a power.'

About Erich Honecker: 'He was ridiculous even as a dictator. That's his personal tragedy.'

About dissidents: 'The opposition was even more ridiculous; often just sons and daughters of die-hard bolshies fighting the generation gap.'

About political parties: 'I was always very sceptical of political parties. They wanted my passion.'

About Chancellor Helmut Kohl: 'Kohl is a bimbo.'

About military service: 'What really made me hate the system was military service. Till then Communism was a joke. A bad joke, but a joke. Then we were entrusting our lives to complete fools. Being in an army is very useful to see how a dictatorship works. I thought: it may be brutal, but it will last.'

About Poles: 'They're very nationalistic but I don't know what they're proud of.'

About Germany, in the light of increasing violence against Turks, Vietnamese and Poles: 'It's a nation in boots and sometimes they kick other people's ass. Basically, the Germans are not too fond of foreigners and never were.'

He spoke in a stream of sound-bites and needed little prompting. After about an hour, during which he must have decided I was not like the Australian who had ripped him off (by pretending to collaborate on a story about East German rock bands, and disappearing once he had milked Thomas for his expertise), he put a cassette in the cassette player and got me a drink. As he loosened up he began to talk about himself.

'Yeah. I'm sort of exotic,' he said.

Freelance journalists had not officially existed before the revolution, but he had been allowed to call himself a publicist, and had got his own telephone by claiming he looked after an ailing grandfather and needed it to contact the hospital in emergencies.

He had written about films and pop groups, and he suggested that one reason for the demise of Communism was its guarantee of employment: by the early 1960s there were already more people than jobs, so the State connived at those who did not want to work. Not working became the safest way of expressing dissent, most popular among young people who didn't mind the insecurity and hardship. By the mid-1980s the wilfully unemployed included valuable young professionals. They made ends meet by selling home-made leather clothes and jewellery at flea markets (and by forming rock bands, which was how Thomas met them). So in November 1989, when the word went out that demonstrations would be held in Leipzig and Berlin, there was a Bohemian and rebellious – in other words, unGerman – core to give them life.

East Germany's first punk band was born in 1983. It called itself Rosa Extra, after a brand of tampon. It was outlawed and played its concerts in cellars and churches, but found a fan in the relatively enlightened director of the Berlin Centre for Workers' Culture, Wolfgang Friedrich. He got a female colleague to persuade the band to change its name, and then broadcast some of its tamer tracks on local radio. It was a breakthrough, said Thomas.

But there was nothing special about Rosa Extra any more. It was just another primitive East German outfit struggling to make it against overwhelming Western competition.

The same applied to Thomas Fuchs, in fact, said Thomas Fuchs. He didn't expect to survive as a freelance in the new Germany. He would need unimaginable things like a fax, and a phone which didn't sound like an intercom, and decent reference books.

So what did he want to do?

'OK. Let's dream. I want to be a staff writer on *Der Spiegel*.' (He had a box of treasured copies of the West German magazine. 'It was easier to get pornography than *Der Spiegel*.') 'I'd like to do that for ten years and then write some great novels.' In the meantime, like Heike, he was looking into advertising copy-writing. He did occasional short news stories for the *Berliner Morgenpost*, which paid Deutschmarks – not many, but real money. With them he was gradually buying all ten hardback volumes of the *Grosse Duden,* the definitive German grammar. Writing, after all, was a craft.

I asked if he had heard about officers from the East German army going AWOL and offering their services to NATO. It was a story with which I hoped to keep my own creditors at bay. No, he had heard nothing. But he said: 'I think a better story for you is former Stasi men becoming private eyes.'

'Would they talk?'

'I think so. I could . . .'

'Could you help?'

He paused and then laughed. 'I have to ask, how much would I get?'

Thomas Fuchs was wearing full financial battledress for his entry into the capitalist jungle.

'That depends if I can get a commission.'

'If you do, I will arrange the interviews and translate.'

I had a partner.

The Schroders' flat had seven rooms, including one for each of the two children. Robert, who was nine, had a big bunk bed reached by a ladder. On his wall there was a poster of a caribou-humanoid hybrid which Heike hated. He had stacks of toy cars but with all his soul he desired more. There was a blazing, chunky, soft-top-hard-top, GTi new world of model cars out there. How could he possibly take a Lada to school when friends were turning up with General Motors jeeps?

Julia was seven. Except when there was company, she slept in the playroom under a wall covered with Walt Disney characters painted by her mother. I was company, so Julia moved in with Robert and I slept in the playroom. Cupboards along the opposite wall were filled with children's clothes which Heike had bought over the years because they were available. Most had never been used and never would be, now that the era of scarce children's clothes had passed.

There was only one tap in the bathroom, to be swivelled between bath and basin as required, but there was hi-fi and a colour television in the sitting room and a rotary bread-slicer and coffee machine in the kitchen.

Before November 1989, the Schroders did not want and they did not worry. Now they could not help but want a Western holiday and a Western car. 'We are hot to travel,' they said. Meanwhile they were worried stiff about jobs, schools, prices, rent, and status.

There must have been a good deal of wrong-headed thinking to have brought them from the soaring hopes of November 1989 to this morass of *Angst*. In consequence, one word that positively bounced around the flat was *Kwatsch*, meaning 'nonsense'.

It was *Kwatsch* that Gregor Gysi's new Socialist Party was in fact the old Communist Party, as the Christian Democrats had claimed. The West German finance minister was talking *Kwatsch* on a TV phone-in when he denied that currency union would bring inflation. Chancellor Kohl, above all, was a *Kwatsch*-monger to set currency union for 1 July and allow a one-to-one conversion only for the first 4,000 ostmarks of East Germans' savings. As it was, Jorg would be earning less than a third of his West German counterparts.

Here were the hard, cash contours of the imminent East–West status gulf. Whose fault would it be? Democracy's fault. That is, the fault of the Saxon Germans; the aspiring businessmen of Dresden and Leipzig who had voted overwhelmingly in March for Chancellor Kohl and the Christian Democrats, the party of rapid reunification. The Saxons, to be honest, were a load of *Kwatsch*.

But then, later, there was Axel, a Thuringian builder who belched and dismissed Berlin as Red. There was Jan, a Czech law student running for Parliament in Prague, who could only dream of an entry as swift as East Germany's into the EC. There was Peter Popov, a Bulgarian hang-gliding champion, who thought East Germans 'spoilt'. For the record there was the *Economist*, calling a one-to-one conversion rate for the currency union 'highly generous'.

In the spring of 1990, East Berlin was a hole compared with West Berlin but it was nirvana compared with much of Eastern Europe. And it never occurred to the Schroders to compare themselves with anyone but their capitalist countrymen. Why should it? They were all German. It was the obvious comparison to make. Comparisons with the rest of Eastern Europe were irrelevant. Eastern Europe was *Kwatsch*.

Contrasts

Jorg and Heike Schroder were extending their sociability into West Berlin. One evening we drove out onto the Ring, turned south towards Potsdam and entered the American Sector at its south-eastern corner, to drink beer with some new friends.

Axel and his wife Claudia lived in a neat little house with a garden and a veranda. From the smell of it, Claudia was cooking something chocolate, which I very much hoped we would be able to eat. Instead we drove in Axel's new Volkswagen Passatt, via his parents' house – they followed in a silver Audi – to a fashionable walled *Biergarten* in the grounds of a converted brewery.

It was a Friday night and the garden was full. A pair of gleaming 1,000cc Kawasaki Ninjas were tethered in the cobbled yard. The brewery's old stonework had been repointed and inside there were banisters and bars of hardwood and polished brass. The Schroders were used to the contrasts, or pretended to be, but I wasn't. After a mere three weeks of East Berlin I was reeling even at the branded pavement parasols and the faces round the oil lamps underneath them; fashion faces; tanned ones; fat, pink faces; and haggard burnt-out rock star faces. Above all, animated faces. We walked through the *Biergarten,* failed to find a table, and sat down in the brewery.

The beer kept coming. To stop it you had to cover your glass with your beermat. For each round the edge of Axel's mat got a tick from the waitress's Biro and it was tacitly understood that he would pay. It wouldn't break him. Oliver, his four-year-old, had just learned to ski on a three-week holiday in Bulgaria. My journey to the Black Sea reminded Axel of his 3,500-kilometre ride as a student to France via Denmark and John-o'-Groat's. Meanwhile, the Schroders were hoping for a week in a holiday cottage in Denmark, to prove to themselves that this freedom to travel was real, and to see, for the first time, a tidal sea.

Heike's parents had a summer house on the Oder-Spree canal and one Saturday we went to lunch there. Her brother Willy brought an enormous ex-convict friend with a goatee and tattoos and an embarrassing willingness to talk about prison life without saying what he'd been put away for. (The question Heike and her mother hissed at each other over washing up was, did Willy know?)

After lunch Jorg and I went on a short bicycle ride up the hill away from the canal to visit a former Stasi holiday home which had three swimming pools to Kopernick's one. (Kopernick was the biggest borough in East Berlin.) When we returned, Heike's parents and brother and the ex-convict had all gone, and she was beginning to relax. She suggested staying overnight at the summer house, which was how Jorg and I found ourselves returning to the apartment in Spreestrasse for pyjamas and toothbrushes.

It was not far back to Kopernick; a pleasant drive – even in the Trabbi – through the forest between Muggelsee and the Spree.

There is a slight rise on Muggelheimerdamm, the forest road, and on its crest we got a fat Mercedes in our sights. We had a clear shot, downhill, with the wind on our backs and the sun at six o'clock.

'Do I take it?' asked Jorg.

'Take it,' I said.

The bogey was a soft-top, top down, cruising in from the West. Metal blue, custom tyres, hadn't seen the bandit. We closed to 50 metres, 40, 30, 20. The bogey had a foxy babe on board. She turned, wind in her hair. Jorg checked the rear-view, swung straight out, and we took the sucker slowly, engine screaming.

The end of Muggelheimerdamm was looming fast. Time to turn and burn, but with a cool hit scored. Tinny Trab takes Mighty Merc.

Thomas Fuchs had a contract with a post-revolutionary East Berlin cultural weekly called *Das Blatt*. He won my life-long friendship by interviewing me for it. We needed a picture, so I lent him my camera and stood with my bike in front of the statue of Frederick the Great in Unter Den Linden while he agonized over the split-ring focusing. There was a food shop nearby where I had previously bought some very good East German chocolate, with nuts, called Block. After the photo session I suggested eating some chocolate.

'OK. But all East German chocolate is disgusting,' he said. Since my first visit, the shop had started stocking Ritter Sport, the Porsche of West German chocolate brands, and Thomas bought Ritter while I bought Block. He declined my offer of a piece of Block.

'You think I don't know what it tastes like?'

I accepted some Ritter, however. The two were very different, but it was not that the Block was disgusting. It was partly that the Ritter was obscenely smooth and rich, partly the packaging. The Block was wrapped in a piece of paper. The Ritter was wrapped in a patented survival blanket called the Knick Pack designed to be broken open in a carefree, TV ad sort of way, and then re-closed to preserve the very wonderful flavour of Ritter Sport Trauben Nuss chocolate. Its ingredients and the advice to consume before April 1991 and to keep cool were printed on the Knick Pack in six languages.

Marlboro Light

There was a man at large in East Berlin trying to marry up bits of the two Germanys, and finding it difficult. He lived in the Grand Hotel, drove a Mercedes sports coupé with automatic seat belt slides which saved passengers the strain of twisting to strap themselves in, and he smoked Marlboro Lights. He was very tall, with black hair and white skin. He wore a white shirt and a dark suit which looked as if it covered a gym-trim body.

Marlboro Light worked for one of the world's big, fast, straight-talking, result-getting management consultancies. I had seen his partner representing the arrival of capitalist know-how on a television chat show, and had phoned to ask for an interview.

('When?'

'Um. As soon as possible.'

'See you at five.' Click. Brrr.)

The partner, in all important respects, was a clone of Marlboro Light, but being the senior of the two his suit was less deferentially dark and his face less workaholically white. They would have made a good second row, except that there is not enough raw glamour about a second row. Marlboro Light and pal were archetypal whiz-kids. They had been whizzed here from the Frankfurt office to size up the new market within days of the opening of the Wall. They had been whizzing ever since.

('Where will you be this evening?'

'Stuttgart. Back in the morning.')

If they happened to be standing still they whizzed verbally with phrases like 'production synergies' and 'chemical smellies'. If they were stuck in a traffic jam they whizzed down the car phone.

And they were kids. Marlboro Light was twenty-eight and his partner was thirty, which is young to have a nation hanging on your every televised word.

The partner didn't have time for me because of Stuttgart, which was how I ended up with Marlboro Light, in a bare borrowed room in the Berliner Commerzbank, Bülowstrasse, West Berlin. He was instantly likeable, and obligingly slowed down the verbal whiz.

East Germany's economic future seemed to lie in privatizing big old state enterprises and setting up small new private ones. But it was impossible to help the big old ones until someone found out what, if anything, they were worth. So Marlboro Light had accountants billeted in hotels across the country valuing the *Kombinaten* and privatization teams standing by in London, where they had learned their trade during Mrs Thatcher's reign. They worked on a 'fly-in' basis; the Red Adairs of the inexorable triumph of the market. That is, they flew home at weekends to be with the family in Woking.

There was a glitch, of course: in practice it was impossible to help the small new companies because they could not afford Marlboro's consultancy fees. At the Leipzig spring fair 'people were running in off the street with our advert in their hands,' he said. 'But we're not a charity.'

ML was likeable because he was honest. He said of the Grand Hotel, East Berlin's poshest: 'If we stayed in an ordinary East German hotel that would be considered pretending to be something you're not.' Hell, that would be spying.

He was riding the new wave. The Cold War was history now and time was money.

'Is Berlin the new gateway to the East?' I asked, hoping I was keeping up.

'All this talk of gateways to places is very antiquated. Stay an extra half hour on the plane and you're not in Berlin, you're in Budapest. OK, Berlin's not bad. You can use your fax and your portable phone and your portable computer without any problems, and get them serviced.'

A Greek-born American millionaire who wanted to invest in East Germany was waiting for Marlboro Light at the Grand. We piled into the Mercedes. 'We used to call the hotel foyer Sell-out City,' he said. In the euphoric weeks after 9 November the Grand was where the two besuited business Germanys had met and dealt.

We crossed the Wall at Potsdamer Platz, sunroof open. The frontier guard laughed at Marlboro's passport because sixteen pages had been filled with East German visas. Marlboro talked expansively about the bold architectural schemes already competing to turn this minefield into the centre of the New Germany. It seemed a world away from the flat in Spreestrasse to which I then returned by clattering S-bahn for an *Abendbrot* of bread, wurst, East German brie, and beer.

State Security

Thomas Fuchs had spent the long May Day weekend tracking down former Stasi agents and he telephoned on Tuesday evening to say that Thomas Sindermann, whose father Horst had just died after thirty years in the politburo, would talk. So would Herr Dieter Strunk of Plonzstrasse 31, Berlin-Lichtenberg.

Lichtenberg was always a rough part of East Berlin, incorporating the main station, the skinheads' squats, and the Stasi headquarters. The entrance to Plonzstrasse was arched, like the entrance to a mews. Inside it there was a heap of old bedsteads and washing machines. At the far end, by one of the bells at number 31, there was the name D. Strunk. We knew from the *Berliner Morgenpost* that when the Stasi was disbanded Strunk had set up a private detective and security agency called Abacus, and that he worked from home, but there was no trade name by the bell. Just D. Strunk.

Behind Strunk's block ran a wall and barbed wire surrounding East Germany's erstwhile generator of State fear. It covers two blocks and contains 3,000 rooms. Net curtains filled every window. At one point on the wall someone had asked in letters three feet high: 'How Many People Have You Destroyed? 20,000? 50,000? 85,000?'

Reports were appearing at the time of new evidence of guillotining by the Stasi in Dresden in the 1960s, but its main task seems to have been the distribution of fear by meticulous surveillance rather than by gory example. 'The Stasi was not brutal,' Thomas said, but it was very Prussian.'

Der Spiegel began researching a three-part dissection of the Stasi as soon as its headquarters was stormed by an incredulous mob in December 1989. 'Big Brother was everywhere and forgot nothing,' said *Der Spiegel*. 'A critical word about Walter Ulbricht in 1964 could mean the refusal of permission for a foreign trip twenty years later.' There were five million names – a third of the total population – on the Stasi's central computer.

With a payroll of 85,000, the Stasi was the country's second biggest employer. To rise up its hierarchy you had, first of all, to recruit informers. This was how most East Germans came into contact with the Stasi, if they did at all. For a Stasi operative to recruit fewer than twenty-five new informers in a year apparently raised eyebrows in personnel. And to recruit that many required up to sixty meetings a month with potential informers.

Thomas had been approached once. The Interior Ministry had

telephoned and asked him to attend an interview in a yellow
Wartburg in a nearby park. It had been raining. The driver in the
Wartburg never quite came to the point but he did say something
like: 'Of course, I can't promise that you'll go to America, but
you never know' – and Thomas had understood. He was given
time to think, and instructed not to talk about the interview.

At the second Wartburg session, fearing he risked being called
up to the army after admitting that he loathed national service,
Thomas told the driver 'no': 'I'm not the right person,' he
explained. 'I'm a computer whiz and we must win the computer
war with Japan.' The driver wished him luck and drove away, and
the call-up never came.

The interview with Mr Strunk was to be held at his partner's
office in West Berlin. Thomas and I planned to meet at the Post
Office under Friedrichstrasse railway bridge, but we were both
early. The combination of nerves and coffee sent us both, independently, to the lavatory in the International Business Centre.
We met at the washbasins there, and Thomas was a touch
embarrassed. 'She'll think we're queer,' he said as he tipped the
janitor.

Strunk's partner's office was in a big house in a quiet residential
street.

'Are you ready?' asked Thomas. We were at the garden gate.

'I'm ready,' I said, and that was about as frightening as the
whole Stasi thing got; it was soon clear that ex-Stasi men do not
necessarily exhale contagious evil. They were mostly recruited
for their competence and reliability and for not being given to
independent thought. In Western countries they would probably
be accountants.

Dieter Strunk was actually apprenticed as a locksmith. And the
ante-room leading to his partner's plush office, in which Herr
Strunk himself looked ill at ease, was full of safes and locks.

In a gurgly voice he delivered his first preamble. We were to
understand that the bulk of his and his partner's work was the
installation of security systems . . . that is, locks. Private detective work was a sideline. Secondly, he hoped that we had not
expressed an interest in his current work only to question him,
once granted an interview, on his career in the 'Ministry of State
Security'.

We promised not to ask about the old days, and broke the
promise. Strunk had worked in Department VII, tracking smug-
gled Russian caviare, computers and antiques.

But wasn't it Department VII that broke up the last big
demonstration in Berlin before the Wall was opened?

Yes, said Herr Strunk. He had been there. He said nothing for a
while, then continued.

'You think over the past. You chew it over, and in doing so you
reach another point of view. But while I was working for the
Ministry of State Security, if I had problems with my conscience I
told myself I had no other choice – except to quit.'

After his apprenticeship Dieter Strunk studied philosophy at
Dresden University. In the Stasi he had earned twice the average
wage for working double average hours. He had a wife, a
daughter and a son, enjoyed sailing and Verdi, and counted
himself lucky to have had a holiday in Cuba.

On the way back to the station Thomas suggested that Herr
Strunk was not a villain in the drama of the end of East Germany
but a private man whose world had fallen in.

The next day we went to interview Thomas Sindermann. He
lived with his wife and daughters and dogs in a comfortable house
which he had built himself in the northern part of East Berlin. The
wife worked as a receptionist in one of the hard currency hotels.
The daughters, about as tall as the dogs, played round the edge of
the swimming pool licking lollipops. Sindermann sat at a table by
the pool wearing football shorts and nothing else. His partner,
Thomas Lorenz, sat beside him wearing only jeans. Both had soft
torsos; Sindermann's was actually podgy. Their office was in the
cellar but this morning they were taking advantage of the sun. A
mildly controversial Peugeot 305 stood in the garage. Sindermann had bought it before the revolution when for East Germans
without fathers in the politburo there was a ten-year waiting list
for a Trabant. It was to this house that the father had moved from
Wandlitz when the old regime collapsed, and in this house that he
died.

Thomas Fuchs was in cowboy boots today. Again, he had been
pointedly relaxed on the way to the interview. He had talked
laconically about being tear-gassed, beaten up and fined fifty

crowns by the Czech police for singing dirty songs at the Brno motorbike Grand Prix in 1979. 'So yes,' he sighed. 'I'm a victim of the Communist system.'

Sindermann, as well as being his father's son, had been head of the homicide unit in Berlin's Volkspolizei. Lorenz had been Sindermann's opposite number in the Stasi. Now they were Sindermann and Lorenz, private detectives, and life had slowed right down. They had traced a runaway wife to Bavaria for her husband and were looking forward to proof-of-adultery jobs as the strains of revolution and reunification began to tell on East German marriages. But most of their work involved digging up East Berlin title deeds for dispossessed West Berlin landlords. Business was beginning to pick up as a result of media interest in young Sindermann's career, and long-term prospects could only be improved by the breakdown of law and order in Berlin, of which the skinhead troubles were a symptom and 1989's political changes a cause.

When Sindermann's name had become an embarrassment to his employers at the end of 1989 he was sacked from the Volkspolizei and began to nurse a grudge against former colleagues. He considered buying into a grocery store but then realized he could make use of his experience and contacts as a private eye. Lorenz was both a contact and a friend. Vilified and almost unemployable as a former Stasi man, he wanted in.

Lorenz looked a bruiser, but turned out to be the thoughtful one. He had short grey hair and didn't speak for the first hour except to confirm for the benefit of potential English clients that he could handle 'dangerous' as well as divorce and property work.

I asked how they had voted in the elections on March 18.

'Liberal,' said Sindermann.

'I am a convinced Marxist,' said Lorenz. 'My attitude has not been changed.'

'My attitude has not changed either,' said Sindermann. 'The market economy has won over the socialist one. In the end people decided the important thing was what you could get in the shops.' He paused. 'But we are both called Thomas. That's why we get along so well.'

'I'm glad the frontiers are open, but they did not have to be closed,' Lorenz said, looking as if he meant it. He believed that a

one-party Communist state could have been created from which
no one would have wanted to escape. I was baffled. Did he mean
East Germans should always have been free to go to West
Germany? He did not mean that. The frontiers should have been
open, but East Germany would still have been a police state.

'It has to be that way,' he said, and I caught the merest glimpse
of a wholly different way of thinking; what some people call a
different set of values. 'Besides,' he continued, 'East Germany
was no more a police state than any other European country.'

'Than any other East European country, you mean?'

'No. European.'

In the West, he said, secret police were just as omnipresent,
only more secret. He granted that the Stasi had been overzealous
running dossiers on every 'Other-Thinking Person' in the
country, but that was all he would concede.

'We needed a different understanding of democracy under
socialism. But the Stasi was far more tolerant than the system as a
whole. Look,' he went on, 'a teacher who disagreed with the
government's policies in his locality would probably be in trouble
with his head-teacher before getting into trouble with the Stasi. It
might be the Stasi that the head-teacher feared, but unless he was a
known dissident himself this fear would usually be groundless.'

Even dissidents were treated reasonably, said Lorenz, reasonably. 'I've interrogated them myself. We always had a tape
recorder on the desk so that interrogations could be recon-
structed.' This, apparently, was to prevent the use of torture. 'It
was basically a conversation. A loud one sometimes, but there
were no threats. Many Other-Thinking People we interrogated
said afterwards they wished they could talk so freely with
someone in the government. We let them let off steam.'

I asked which other secret services he most admired.

'Mossad and the CIA,' he said wistfully, as if he were talking
about football teams.

Valedictory

When I phoned Thomas to say I was finally leaving town he put
aside an afternoon. We had lunch and ducked under arcades

afterwards to get out of the rain. If he hadn't been with me he
would have been trying to write a radio play, but he had dropped
the fiction that he was really too busy to waste time like this, and
laughed grimly about it.

The restaurant was his choice, a place called Niquet Klause
right up against the western end of the city, in the shadow of the
Interior Ministry. It had been a haunt of East German journalists,
said Thomas. But then Axel Springer and his rival West German
press barons had mobilized their sales forces, stretched their print
schedules to make room for Eastern Editions, and moved in from
Hamburg blazing with full colour and full frontals to woo their
miraculous windfall of ten million new readers. The old East
German press had more or less caved in, and there were tables free
at Niquet Klause.

The speciality here was a kind of reconstituted steak with peas
and stale tinned mushrooms. Beer made it bearable. Afterwards,
Thomas smoked and described how he saw himself in this time of
barely resisted anarchy: he was the ultimate mobile writing unit.
One brain, one phone, one typewriter. No roots. No commit-
ments, marital or financial. Ready to jump whichever way the
racing political and economic seismographs indicated. 'When I
was eighteen I was always complaining about what a boring
country I lived in. I'm twenty-eight and I feel old already.'

We walked east to Friedrichstrasse, then north towards Unter
den Linden, and had coffee opposite the Grand. I had been reading
a book called *The Germans: Rich, Bothered and Divided*. I asked
what the Germans would be bothered about when they were no
longer divided.

Their place in the world, said Thomas. 'When it was unified in
1866, Germany embarked on a never-ending quest to know
where it stands. It has an inferiority complex but it always wants
to be number one. The vital thing now is social and economic
security – house, car, spending money, bringing down the price
of guitars, biannual bonking trip to Bangkok – then the Germans
will be tolerant. All they will lack is style.'

Over another coffee, before I left him to get on with his radio
play, Thomas delivered a chirpy parting shot: 'Two paths
face East Germany. To become like West Germany and be

disappointed; or to fail to become like West Germany and be disappointed.'

He exhaled and shrugged ruefully behind the smoke, but he also grinned.

Himmelfahrt on the Rennsteig

Czechoslovakia was to hold its first free election since 1948 on 8 June, a fortnight away. I swapped Bohemia and Poland round on my itinerary in order to be in Prague on polling day, and decided to spend some of the intervening days in Thuringia.

Thuringia has a high profile in old East German coffee-table books. Here, they trilled, was a land of lush deciduous forest, of hill-top medieval castles and mist floating in valleys. When the mist cleared on sparkling winter mornings the lucky children of the German Democratic Republic could ski, toboggan, skate, and point enraptured with bemittened hands at horse-drawn sleighs.

The books called this the Green Heart of Germany, though during its forty-year sojourn in the south-western corner of East Germany Thuringia was more borderland than heartland.

I had been warned that there would be drunkenness on the Rennsteig – good-natured but extreme. It was Himmelfahrt (Ascension Day) and for the first time in forty years it was a public holiday. And, one other thing, I would have to push my bike the first kilometre or so. Russian panzers had turned the Rennsteig into a row of ponds.

The Rennsteig is 160 kilometres long and 650 years old. It started life as a frontier between ducal domains and is punctuated by standing stones which mark where they began and ended. Nowadays it is Germany's answer to the Pennine Way, meandering through the higher reaches of the *Thuringer Wald*, sometimes on the watershed itself, sometimes sheltered by a ridge or secreted by a groove of forest. Villages which straddle it incorporate it in their names: Neustadt am Rennsteig, like Kingston upon Thames.

I pushed my bike up through a meadow to the Rennsteig and turned east. It was true about the panzers. I slalomed through the trees beside giant puddles and rutted mud left by the tanks that used to patrol this, the first high ground behind the Iron Curtain.

At the point where the tank tracks joined the path there was a skipful of empty Honduran banana boxes. Did the panzer crews eat bananas? The Kremlin could ill afford their boots, which was why it had called off the Cold War and ordered them home. Perhaps the local inhabitants had thrown a banana party to celebrate their going.

I rode into Neustadt am Rennsteig at five o'clock on Ascension Day, and meant to do another twenty kilometres before eating and sleeping. But some red-eyed men in overalls beckoned me to their barbecue and strongly recommended putting up in Neustadt. They pointed to a large grey clapboard house which seemed to be propped up by a lean-to on one side and a conservatory on the other. Pension Sonne.

Nine men in the overheated conservatory were, in terms of beverage consumption on this special day, entering the home straight. The youngest of them stumbled out and ordered me to join them. This was Axel. He was tall, with a down-turned black moustache and a working knowledge of German. The rest spoke only the Thuringian dialect. Their massive beer-filled trunks strained their T-shirts. Beer, brandy and home-made apple wine were arranged in front of me. The landlady put her head round the door and advised against drinking it, but the men won me round.

It was a leisurely journey into stupor, not a blitz. The man sitting next to me said he drove a Massey Ferguson tractor. His neighbour put in that it was built thirty years ago in Yugoslavia. One of them wore dungarees, but they were ripped to shreds. This had been a hunting accident, Axel said. They weren't that poor. No one went hungry in Neustadt, he said, and the landlady came in on cue with two baskets of bread and an unlabelled tin of slaughtered pig: Neustadt's finest, a fertile mulch of guts and trotters, under an inch of fat.

A convoy of eleven BMW motorbikes roared past. Everyone turned to watch and then there was silence for a moment. I asked Axel whether he thought reunification was going to mean second-class citizenship for East Germans.

'Berlin is Red,' he said. 'There will be four or five hard years and then we will have forgotten all this panic about union. We will be like them.' He waved down the street, where the convoy had gone.

There was a disco on the edge of town, outdoors. The victim of the hunting accident turned up in a natty cream-coloured outfit but most of Neustadt's youth sported the acid-washed denim that poured over the Wall when it opened. Three girls were dancing to the Communards. This was London music. As it belted out I sat on a bench a safe distance away trying to sober up, and pictured close-cropped Jimmy Somerville doing his patented squashy box-step and yelling his falsetto over the chill Thuringian slopes.

The following evening, at dinner time, a white-haired woman from Hannover came blustering into the conservatory with news of an opulent former Stasi guesthouse on the road to Ilmenau.

The Berghotel Gadelbach has thirty-eight spacious suites. There is an indoor swimming pool and garaging for eight limousines. The forest has been cleared for an acre or two around to make space for lawns, staff quarters, a tennis court and an enormous barbecue area in the Wild West style. Neither the hotel nor the private road which serves it is marked on the map. But an old hunting lodge by the perimeter fence is marked, because Goethe used to study natural history there. The Berghotel is now open to the public; it needs the money.

East Germany is peppered with former Stasi holiday homes, and some of their gardens are being turned into nature reserves. This one, according to the woman from Hannover, was a favourite retreat of Honecker himself. The *maître d'* rolled his eyes towards the ceiling when I walked in at lunchtime wearing shorts and asked for a coffee. Six months ago he had been serving ministers and generals.

I was seated next to a solitary Frankfurter with a hearing aid.

Like every West German I had met in East Germany, this one was here because of roots. When he was a boy, Ilmenau had been beautiful, its only factories porcelain factories whose owners lived in enviable houses along the river. The Berghotel had been Hermann Goering's hunting lodge. (Honecker, who was imprisoned by the Nazis for ten years for being a Communist, presumably knew this.) Now Ilmenau stank, but at least the Berghotel was in good nick.

East of Route 281 from Neuhaus to Saalfeld, tourism stops abruptly. This is where the East-West frontier zone began. For forty years you were allowed here only if you lived here.

Would-be escapers who got past the checkpoints on Route 281 then faced, after ten kilometres, a floodlit electric fence which triggered alarms in the watchtowers above it; the frontier fence itself, patrolled by teams of troops and dogs; and three kilometres of no mans's land, densely forested but planted with mines and automatic firing devices. Local people would be unlikely to help.

'You would be playing with your life,' one of them said. This was Heinz, in the only bar in a frontier village called Zopten.

'The military were everywhere,' said the landlord. 'They were in here every night, and friendly enough. But they had a job to do and they watched us all the time. The frontier was taboo. To talk about it . . . even to look at it was practically taboo. All we could do was live.'

Life itself had been an unnatural business. Heinz was a builder by trade but there had been no new building in Zopten since the early 1960s. So he had worked for the local agricultural collective. The collective was told what to grow and paid according to acreage sown. Zopten was decreed a strawberry area even though strawberries do not grow there – late frosts tend to kill them. But Heinz had planted them anyway, year in year out, and had been paid for planting them.

It was eleven o'clock on Saturday night and we were the only three left in the bar. Heinz had been in earlier for a schnitzel with his wife. He had overheard me asking about accommodation. There was none. What could you expect? Zopten was a railway's width from the frontier. Heinz had wanted to offer me his spare room, but the wife had said no. Meanwhile I had arranged to camp in a field behind the village.

'Whom did you ask?' said Heinz.

'I asked at the house nearest to the field. They seemed worried. The grandmother said I'd frightened the life out of them.'

The landlord explained why. That was Thomas's house. He lived there with his wife and mother-in-law, but his father-in-law was dead. He'd been in trouble with the Stasi. Thomas didn't talk about it and Heinz didn't know the details, but he drew a finger across his throat and changed the subject.

'What are you doing for breakfast?'

I breakfasted with Heinz. His wife couldn't complain because she'd been at work since 6 a.m. at Saalfeld hospital. Breakfast consisted of coffee and slaughtered pig. Heinz had kept two pigs under the house and got 150 jars from each, not to mention a mountain of pork steaks and sausages in the freezer.

After breakfast we went on a tour of frontier installations. The wiring had been ripped out of the watchtower and charred newspaper was stuffed into the frames of its windows. But the searchlight was intact and you could swivel it like a periscope with a handle that came through the roof.

It was a beautiful morning. As we walked along the cleared strip beside the rusted frontier fence we agreed that no man's land should become a nature reserve.

I was stuck for Sunday lunch. The roads and villages along the old frontier were still unusually quiet. But at half-past one a crowd was walking out of Lichtentanne as if after a pied piper, and I followed it. Lichtentanne is on the crest of a hill, with a splendid view of West Germany. Its burghers had already carted away most of the local frontier apparatus, and now they strolled down past the scar through a field and a wood. They gathered on a forestry track where food was clearly going to be cooked because a man in an apron was fanning charcoal. A priest shook my hand and I saw a purple cross on a white altar cloth hanging from a tree. Below it, choir stalls had been improvised from logs. It was the first Sunday after Ascension, and the neighbouring parishes of Lichtentanne (East Germany) and Schweinbach (West) were getting it together in an old minefield.

The priest spoke in his sermon of a dark chapter in the history of the Fatherland, and of the Second World War finally coming to an end. But he was scarcely audible in the breeze and late arrivals were piling up behind me. It seemed the moment to ease back towards the gently hissing Bratwurst.

Bohemia

Albrecht Wallenstein was one of history's boldest traitors, and one of the first people I encountered in Czechoslovakia. From a distance, his career resembles that of General Jaruzelski. But whereas Jaruzelski worked for a declining empire and judged acutely when to turn his back on it, Wallenstein worked for an expanding one, and allowed this fatally to inflate his already towering ambitions.

On the eve of the Thirty Years War he was a Protestant colonel in the army of the Czech Estates. But when two Catholic counsellors were defenestrated in Prague by his compatriots, Wallenstein predicted Hapsburg reprisals and nimbly converted to Catholicism. The reprisals lasted three centuries, according to the Czech view of history; three centuries of Austro-Hungarian bondage. But the first thirty years were the bloodiest, thanks in no small part to Albrecht Wallenstein.

Hapsburg forces defeated the Czech nobles at the Battle of the White Mountain in 1620, and confiscated their property. Wallenstein undertook to keep an eye on one or two ex-Protestant estates for the Emperor Ferdinand, and began killing off their erstwhile owners. Wallenstein's expropriation enabled him to run a private army. He defeated the Danes, the Saxons and the Swedes, and Ferdinand loved him for it. He made him his generalissimo and gave him the title Duke of Friedland. Wallenstein converted twenty-six houses and three large gardens into his Prague *pied-à-terre* (he based his duchy round the Bohemian town of Jicin) and commissioned a portrait of himself as Mars, god of war.

It was only natural for his thoughts then to settle on the vacant throne in Prague Castle, a short walk up the hill. The hitch was Ferdinand, who took a less than sanguine view of attempts to dismantle his empire. So Albrecht clandestinely sought support from his mortal enemies the Swedes, but in doing so counted not with the Austro-Hungarian secret service. Ferdinand was alerted to his protégé's treachery and had him stabbed to death in Cheb.

Cheb is the westernmost town in modern Czechoslovakia. Its main square is in fact a triangle; a long, cobbled triangle with a cluster of leaning thirteenth-century shops in the middle. The sides of the square glow with stuccoed façades painted in pastel shades of orange, yellow, pink and blue. They slope down towards the eastern edge, where the house in which Wallenstein was assassinated has been turned into a museum of local history.

After the requisite half-dozen rooms of ceramic fragments and maps of palaeolithic Bohemia you come to the master bedroom. Here, on 25 February 1634, the deed was done, by a man named Deveroux from the local Hapsburg garrison. Previous curators crammed the room with Wallenstein memorabilia – armour, banners, pistols and engravings – but the current one has left it almost bare: a four-poster and side table in dark polished oak, a chair, a pair of thigh-length boots, and a Van Dyck portrait of the man himself. He looks a dandy.

Here is a chance to be thrilled – thrilled! – by a museum. Deveroux, dagger drawn, would have entered right behind you. His quarry would have been . . . pulling on his boots?

Deveroux's thoughts: I have to kill the tyrant of the Czech Estates. I must not botch this job. He will not look kindly on me if he survives.

Wallenstein's: Why didn't this fellow knock? Mother of God, he means to butcher me. On whose orders? How much does Vienna know?

However it happened, it happened right here. Under these very beams. Real, documented gore.

I had crossed the border into Czechoslovakia that evening after a brief trip to Hof in West Germany. My first action had been to get

out the map and sit on a bench, which had collapsed. It seemed an
almost choreographed re-entry into the post-Communist bloc.

The elections were eight days away, and Bohemia was smothered in posters of Vaclav Havel and his cronies in Civic Forum,
the anti-Communist popular front that had emerged from the
heady days of the Velvet Revolution. Havel, in epaulettes, was
looking shattered but enlightened. Vaclav Klaus, his finance
minister, was on the phone and looking smooth. There would be
twenty-three parties but no contest. The Civic Forum would take
Bohemia and Moravia, and its Slovakian partner would take
Slovakia. The Communists were saying that every percentage
point over 10 per cent would be a major achievement.

From Cheb I rode north to Frantiskovy Lazne. Dark green hills
rose towards the German frontier behind the town. Below it,
three underground lakes were fizzing gently and attracting ill or
hypochondriac or idle Czechs much as they had once attracted
aristocrats from most of Europe.

Frantiskovy Lazne is one of Bohemia's most important spas,
blissfully undeveloped since the drinking pavilions and sanatoria
were built in the first half of the nineteenth century. It is more
park than town, and tranquillity is carefully preserved; even
cyclists must dismount and walk.

There were no spare mugs under the pillared cupola which
dignifies the Frantisek spring. You had to bring your own or wait
for someone else to finish. A white-coated woman who was
dispensing the water gestured to another, bigger, building and I
followed her arm past middle-aged Czechs sitting on benches in
the sun, their soft thighs spreading out from shorts and hitched-
up skirts.

The bigger building housed the Kaaba, the nerve centre of the
spa. Beyond a pair of heavy doors between Corinthian pillars,
mineral-rich water bubbled up from the earth's crust into three
sealed chambers of thick glass and polished brass. The middle
one, tapping the deepest lake, skulked at the bottom of a circular
marble pit guarded by twelve naked figures in bronze. The other
two released a faint rumbling into the muggy pavilion, but when
you pressed your ear to the glass the sound turned to a roar. This
was the last stop before Valhalla, nothing less. Two rows of
orange vinyl armchairs added psychedelia to metaphysics. A

dough-faced employee of the State Spa Authority spun a stainless steel tap and handed me a steaming plastic cup.

'Outstanding results have been achieved here in the treatment of cardiovascular disorders, gynaecological diseases and diseases of the motory organs,' says the handbook for visitors.

Thus fortified I took the high road to Karlsbad.

It was late afternoon and hot. Cut grass striped the fields. A shrivelled old man with a blackened face and a pipe a foot long emerged from behind a barn. Down in the valley of the Eger a blue metal sphere glinted on top of a water tower. I stopped to lose a bladderful of gynaecologically beneficial mineral water, and two cyclists in racing kit cruised past.

'OK?' they asked.

'OK,' I said to their backs, and sprayed my bike. Five minutes later I heard a shout: '*Ahoy! Mineralwasser!*' ('*Ahoy*' means 'hello' in Czech.) It was the two cyclists, down a short track by a spring. The water welled up from a muddy hole but tasted exactly like the stuff in the pavilion at Frantiskovy Lazne. That is, like carbonated brine.

One of the cyclists was broad and spoke no German but spoke nevertheless. The other was narrow and spoke some German but was taciturn. Like dogs, we eyed one another's equipment, then Broad suggested we ride on together.

'*Kamerad!*'

'*Kamerad,*' I agreed. '*Aber langsam.*' They had no luggage to carry.

Their concession was not to go slower but to avoid the steep bits. We came down out of the hills and pounded along the main road. My crotch burned.

It was half-past seven when the ravine which holds Karlsbad came into view. Broad and Narrow suggested leaving sightseeing till the morning. I thanked them for the ride and headed for the campsite, standing up on the pedals to let the wind circulate.

By Czech standards, Karlsbad's modern name is well-endowed with vowels: Karlovy Vary. You can practically caress it. Its campsite is above the town and I approached it from the west with the sun on my back. The tarmac radiated the heat it had absorbed during the afternoon. The road was winding and overhung with boughs and blossom. It was a sultry evening.

In the campsite a group of East Germans were grilling *Bratwurst* on a barbecue and singing. Two young couples sat in long grass by a pair of low tents listening to a car radio. Three girls, tarted-up, monitored new arrivals from a bench. In the campsite café I met a merchant seaman who had left Rostock the previous October on a five-month voyage through Suez to Karachi, Madras, and Vietnam. He had missed the revolution, but it wouldn't make much difference to him anyway – unless he lost his job. He could have defected a hundred times. He knew Le Havre, Bilbao, Hamburg, Tower Bridge . . . .

He came here every year with friends from Magdeburg; a hair stylist, a barman and a teacher – and one thing was for sure, the place was *empty*. East Germans used to come in droves, and as if by chance they would find their Western relatives had had the same idea. Karlsbad Autocamping had been an institution, packed right through the summer.

I went for a walk towards the town, past a deserted tennis centre and the Toscana disco. Two dancers came out of the disco onto an elegant but unlit terrace for a session with each other's mouths and buttocks. I went back and arranged my sleeping bag on a pile of hay and got into it. At three in the morning the tarted-up girls whom I had noticed on my arrival woke me to ask if I was cold. I said I was warm and very comfortable. At half-past three they asked again and jangled a set of keys in my face.

'*Cabana, cabana!*'

I said OK.

'Bordello!' declared one of them, and I smelt Bekerovka, the delicious Czech herbal liqueur, on her breath. Four pairs of flannel knickers were drying on a night storage heater. Music started. I asked if they had been at the Toscana.

'The Toscana? You kidding? We were at the Pupp.'

They laughed and began to swing their abdomens around. Wherever the Pupp was, they were still there. I accepted the offer of a shower but couldn't get the chain oil off my legs. When I came out, two of the three were preparing to go. The one who stayed had orange fingernails and short black hair. She introduced herself as Laura and there is no doubt that I would have slept better on my pile of hay.

Leibniz, Bach, Goethe, Schiller, Beethoven, Metternich, Paga-
nini, Chopin, Wagner, Gogol, Marx, Dvořák, Freud, and Janáček
have all visited Karlovy Vary, roughly in that order. But so has
Yuri Gagarin, the first man in space, and it was in his honour that
the centre of the town was rebuilt in 1975.

For millennia, two tons of water a minute from a mile and a half
below the earth's surface have gushed forty feet into the air at
72.2°C through the most powerful geyser in the Tepla valley.
Now it all happens inside the Yuri Gagarin Colonnade, and it is
switched off at night. Outside, there is an extremely sinister statue
of the cosmonaut himself. He is larger than life, in a plain-cut
black marble space-suit; an alien come to drink alien waters.

Down the road the Karl Marx Museum had been turned into
the local Green Party headquarters, which was good for the local
Green Party but hard on Marx, whose standing as a central figure
in nineteenth-century thought is little altered by the events of
1989. Gagarin is a far more potent symbol of the misguided
spending of unearned money which made such a mess of Eastern
Europe. Gagarin must go!

He probably will. De-Russification is the trend. Down the road
the other way I found the Pupp. The Grand Hotel Pupp, in fact
(Laura and co. danced in ritzy places). It was marked on my map
as the Grand Hotel Moskva. I bought a beer there and a copy of
the *European*, and read about nuclear testing in Soviet Central
Asia.

Behind Spring 8, Knize Vaclavi, a sad man in dungarees was
arranging music stands in an alcove. A choir called Belcanto was
due on at half-past two.

They wore white shirts and purple ties and their star turn was a
tenor, six-and-a-half feet tall with long, curly hair and a moustache. A friend with a tripod was getting it all on video. They
started with Pergolesi, and the tall tenor waggled his eyes in
boredom at the camera. Then they raced through three centuries
of music in an hour. Around the 1920 mark, by which time the
tenor was enjoying himself, it began to rain. Water-takers
crowded in for shelter. The basses started up a deep, wordless riff.
The sopranos floated in on a hum and a soulful rhythm from the
Deep South stole over the Colonnade of Czechoslovak-Soviet
Friendship. The boys from Belcanto clicked their fingers down by

their thighs. The girls began to sway and sing 'Oh Happy Day' ('. . . When Jesus washed/ All our sins away./ He taught me how (clap) –ow (clap) –ow/ To walk, fight and pray'). A cagouled section of the audience joined in with the clapping. Then the tenor stepped to the front, filling up with air, and let rip with an ululating 'Happy Day', over and over again. It cut through the steam rising off Knize Vaclavi, leaped out between the pillars of the colonnade and bounced off the sanatorium Astoria, where I should hope the invalids were stomping in their bath chairs.

The rain intensified. Up Zamecky Street a big fibreglass fist made a victory sign, the sign of the Velvet Revolution. Two Socialist Front activists under pavement umbrellas tried to offload election news-sheets onto scurrying voters.

I ducked into a second-hand bookshop which boasted an English section of half a dozen volumes – half a dozen volumes from another era. First there was *Pioneering With Fruits and Berries* by George D. Aitken, 'dedicated to the old Sweet Greening Tree whose hundred years of humble usefulness reflect the ruggedness and vitality nurtured by the hills of Vermont' (New York, 1936). Then I took down a thick blue volume and read the frontispiece. '*A Warning To Wantons* – A Fantastic Romance, setting forth the not undeserved but awful fate which befell a minx', by Mary Wantage. Published and reprinted twice in 1934, it must have been a hit. The disclaimer insisted that the minx's name, Renée de la Vaillière, made 'no reference . . . to any actual person living or dead'. But there was a handwritten dedication in this copy, dated 30.1.1934, to 'Dear, sweet Renée!'. Was this pure coincidence? The shop owner said the book had come from a private library in Karlovy Vary.

I found a room in a hotel near the station and spent the evening swimming in the period prose of Mary Wantage, wondering if the real Renée was even now, at eighty-odd, taking a cure at the Astoria.

Next day I meant to cover some ground towards Prague but got a drawing pin in my front tyre soon after breakfast. My pump had been stolen in Cheb. I had bought a Czech pump but it turned out not to fit my valves. I was in a forest. There was no view but there was a log, which I sat on, and plenty of air. I just needed to squash some of it into a tube. I contemplated my crippled steed for an hour or two and sympathized with Richard III. Unlike him, I got lucky. Around lunchtime a passing cyclist rescued me with his Western pump.

At lunchtime I had goulash and dumplings and a litre of beer, and telephoned Jan Vild in Prague. Jan was technically a law student but his life had been solid politics since the revolution the previous November. He had represented Charles University's law faculty at a crucial meeting on the night of 17 November which produced a decision to strike in protest at the beatings of peaceful demonstrators in Wenceslas Square that day. During the revolution Jan had slept two hours a night and founded a non-Communist international department for the Students' Union. When Havel announced free elections for June 1990, Vild announced he was standing for parliament. Today he was on hunger strike to show solidarity with Chinese students. Tomorrow, Monday, he would meet me at 14.30 in the strike committee room.

It was three in the afternoon and Prague was a hundred miles away. I attacked the pedals.

Central Bohemia is practically free of cars, but the town of Touzim compensates with a full-size Ilyushin airliner parked in a housing estate. There was no one about to ask how it got there.

I pressed on to Rabstein, a forested nipple surrounded by gorges in the middle of an undulating plateau. On top of the nipple, peering over the trees, there stood a church, a manor house and a cluster of lesser dwellings. All of them had, for the time being, given over their garden fences to Civic Forum posters.

In Zdeslav, a couple loading up their Skoda by a fishpond said they would be voting for Havel but were worried that he still had Communists aboard. The wife hoped that her son, who was fifteen, might be living like a Western European in ten years. But she had no great expectations on her own account.

They were going home to Most, in industrial North Bohemia, where a church had been moved and a mountain half dug away to make room for flats. Zdeslav was their weekend bolt-hole, with a permanent population of forty-two. There was no running water, but the air was clean. The pond was home to carp which you could eat in the café, but during emergencies the fire brigade would suck it dry.

The countryside took on a special aura in the discriminating evening light. Shambolic golden haystacks brooded over the fields like ruined castles. Wherever the land fell away into forest the faded red roofs of villages no bigger than Zdeslav nestled in its dark cleavage. I surprised a deer in the valley of the Rakovnicky River, and rolled into a campsite thirty miles from Prague at ten o'clock.

There was not much of a sense of discovery on arriving in Prague. There was, instead, a strong feeling of others having got there first.

Wenceslas Square, the Old Town Square, Charles Bridge, and every museum, monument and restaurant were seething with handycam-touting Western tourists. There was even a letter waiting for me at the British Embassy from my ex-girlfriend, describing her recent visit to Prague with her new Czech boy-friend and thoughtfully recommending various lesser-known churches and culinary specialities – the kind you only find out about if you are with someone who speaks Czech.

None of this was Prague's fault, of course. It was simply living up to its reputation as the best-looking city in the new Europe, 'the prettiest gem in the stone crown of the world'. On top of that it had hosted 1989's most stylish revolution. A really classy one; started by students, picked up by a playwright with something near a cult following abroad (but not in Czechoslovakia), run from a fringe theatre, and given the name 'velvet' because it killed no one.

As I freewheeled down to the Moldau river a red Porsche shot past on the other side. An executive jet whistled overhead, in and out of low clouds. Was this the New Prague, post-Communism's bright young thing, darling of international bankers? I was suffer-ing from heightened awareness – a common affliction on long-anticipated arrivals and one conducive to rampant speculation.

I crossed the Moldau and waited for Jan Vild in the Law Faculty, Room 23. The students' strike which Vaclav Havel took as his cue to found the Civic Forum and confront head-on the government of Milos Jakes was run from this room. It was tall and bare except for some British university prospectuses and a typewriter. There were also stickers advertising, or warning against '*Le Cache-Sex Socialiste*'.

Jan blew in a little late in grey flannels, brown suede brogues and a pin-stripe shirt. He had failed to get the Chinese ambassador to accept a petition protesting at the massacre of students in Tiananmen Square a year before. But he had talked to the press and hoped to be on the news that evening. This marked the end of his forty-eight-hour hunger strike. Yes, he was hungry. But two imminent pre-election speaking engagements left no time for food.

On the metro, heading for Jan's first meeting, he explained that he and his fellow law students had had most of the year off. Apart from procedural law, in which they would be cursorily examined at the end of the week, the revolution had scuttled the syllabus. New degree courses in law would follow the new constitution, to be drawn up by the Federal Assembly after the election. If he was elected to that Assembly, Jan wanted to be involved in drafting the constitution. Either that or in the formation of Czechoslovakia's new foreign policy. (Jan Vild was twenty-one.) His mother, herself a lawyer, and father, a film director and owner of a soon-to-be-privatized film studio, were anxious that even as an MP he should continue his studies. But they recognized that for a law student in these extraordinary times there was no better place to study law than in parliament.

Jan was good-looking. He was very clean-cut, laughed easily and walked with a boyish stone-kicker's gait. We arrived early at what seemed to be a school hall and met a friend of his, also a law student. He would be describing the physical process of voting to the meeting. During the revolution the two of them had helped set up a legal clinic next door to the strike committee room. Frightened Czechs could come in off the street and learn about their rights to demonstrate and withhold labour, as enshrined in existing law but never exercised for fear of police batons and knocks on the door in the night. Now the legal clinic was supplying the Civic Forum with instant experts on the secret ballot. It seemed that the new Czechoslovakia was going to be run by fresh-faced law students. This particular law student was not fresh-faced because a falling wardrobe had cut his forehead and cheekbone. He was reserving the right to raise a laugh by blaming it on the Communists.

No laughs were needed. The audience, which filled the hall, was serious and rapt. The voting ritual was performed. A woman ringed the number 7 on a ballot paper (Civic Forum was seventh on a list of twenty-three parties), walked behind a large flag, called out over it that she was folding the paper and putting it in the box, and re-emerged. A man craning to see and holding a bundle of aluminium rods between his legs beamed with delight.

When Jan stood up to speak the hall went quiet. This was one of the faces on the Civic Forum posters, and a hero of the revolution. He slouched a bit and spoke briefly, without notes, about why Prague's students supported the Civic Forum. The reasons were simple. The other parties were either Communists calling themselves Socialists, or interest groups fighting not so much for a democratic Czechoslovakia as for a slice of power. The Civic Forum was the only contender with a comprehensive programme for the future.

To outsiders, a more interesting question was perhaps why the students' support mattered. To Czechs this was obvious. Many, Jan said, believed they owed their freedom to the students.

For his own part he was confident that student MPs would not be token MPs. Their contributions would be taken seriously in parliament. After all, they would not be the only ones with no experience of government.

The Civic Forum guaranteed students representation within the Party, and, if it won enough votes, within parliament. The system of proportional representation being used required the Forum to win 55 per cent of the Prague vote for Jan to get a seat. He was fifth on the party's slate and there would be nine members for Prague, each representing 11 per cent of its electorate. Optional preferential votes could push popular personalities up the slate if they got enough of them. Jan said that only the film stars on the slate were in the running for preferential votes. From the number of adoring mothers plucking at his sleeve as he left the hall I doubted it.

A driver had arrived as Jan was speaking and as soon as he sat down had whispered in his ear. There was a car waiting outside to take him to his next engagement. We drove fast across the city to 'the Prague foreigners don't want to see'; Jan apologized for the blocks. The second meeting was deep in the heart of a complex of grey monsters, in an amenities building serving maybe a thousand households. Television aerials sprouted from every balcony and satellite dishes from a few.

Despite the setting of this second meeting, there was carnival in the air. Behind a long high table sat speakers, committee chair-people, wise old men, a master of ceremonies in sandals who went on too long but was forgiven, and a small fat boy shuttling between them all with messages. The evening sun had found its way through the windows behind them and was causing the applause-prone audience to squint. There was a screen between the entrance and the body of the hall. Jan caused a hubbub by putting his head round the end of it. He spoke, they loved him, and a trio in the corner played 'We Shall Overcome' during the interval.

An actress called Daniela Kolarova standing for the Czech National Assembly arrived for the second half in grey culottes and a shimmering waistcoat and was received like a rock star.

It was happening in dozens of halls all over Prague, and Skodas were racing between them bearing the haggard harbingers of democracy, Civic Forum-style – and the cool young masters of the universe, the Jan Vilds.

He and Ms Kolarova signed autographs afterwards and he said over his shoulder that this truly had been a good meeting.

On the way back across Prague I said it felt strange to plunge into the wake of a political powerboat after a hundred miles on a bicycle. I hoped he might be just a little impressed by the 'hundred miles'. He said nothing, and probably couldn't help thinking, 'Big deal, kiddo. I made history. I started a revolution. I delivered my country from forty years of dictatorship. *How* many miles did you say?'

The centre of Prague has three main foci: Wenceslas Square, Staromestske Namesti (the Old Town Square), and Malostranske Namesti (The Little Quarter), which is across Charles Bridge under the Castle. In June 1990 Wenceslas Square was still the place to go to breathe history-in-the-making. The latter two, and perhaps above all the bridge in between them, are where one generally goes to swoon over Prague.

Wenceslas Square was originally a horse market. It is notable not just as the scene of the crushing of the Prague Spring by Soviet tanks in 1968, and of Havel's historic balcony speeches in November 1989, but also for not being square; it is a dual carriageway. In the central reservation there is now a memorial to Jan Palach, the student who in 1968 doused himself in petrol which he then lit. A memorial to Palach was inconceivable under the regime which caused him to do this. Now there was not just a memorial, but a rampart of candle wax round it, and more candles burning and building it higher.

At the northern end of Wenceslas Square is a plaza. It is where crowds start to form – crowds of Americans nowadays, among others. ('Which way to the old town?' '*How* much did you pay to get to Berlin?' 'I'm so excited to be here.')

There was a vehicle parked nearby called the Vixen. It was as long as a stretch limousine and as high as a minibus, with tinted windows, Oregon plates and a bumper sticker saying: IMPORTS SUCK. JOBS ★ MONEY ★ FUTURE ★ USA.

It was a proud time for Americans, in a backward-looking sort of way; a time to remember that Americans as well as Russians liberated parts of Czechoslovakia after the war. By May 1945 General Patton's troops were stationed along a line from Karlsbad to Budejovice, some of them within an hour of Prague. Now the American and British flags and the dates 1945–1948 adorned banners across the street which leads away from Wenceslas Square towards the old gunpowder tower. 1948 was the year the Communists outlawed other parties.

(Historically-minded Americans might have been less than proud to remember that Eisenhower refused to let Patton liberate Prague even when begged to do so by Czechs involved in an insurrection against the occupying Germans; he was sticking to a 'spheres of liberation' agreement reached with Stalin at Yalta.)

On the western side of the plaza there is an elegant white building of about six storeys, acquired by the Civic Forum as its headquarters. Inside it there was an exhibition of black-and-white stills from the revolution. They were arranged chronologically. The first photograph was of a group of students' faces on the

evening of 17 November; faces drawn with exhaustion and fear.
The last was of Vaclav Havel in a black coat inspecting a guard of
honour after being sworn in as President of Czechoslovakia on 29
December.

Outside the headquarters on the white wall behind a long-
haired man selling Civic Forum badges was a sticker: 'Better both
feet in NATO than a cold ass in Siberia.' Underneath, someone
had written: 'I say fuck 'em both.'

I walked past a spread of 'fresh foreign newspapers' on the
pavement, and under the banners commemorating 1945–1948.
On the left, sealing off an empty plot, there was a hoarding the
length of a cricket pitch. It was topped with the heads and
shoulders of the Communist contribution to world leadership
since the war. All the big names were there, all the great dictators,
from Stalin to Ho Chi Minh, Brezhnev to Kim Il Sung. Honecker
and Ceauşescu had had their heads knocked off and Stalin had
been removed. (He was to return a few days later twice as big as
the rest; the dictators' Big Daddy.)

There is a black lump in the middle of the Old Town Square. On
it stands a black statue of Jan Hus, whose reformatory religious
teaching in the fifteenth century made him a symbol of Bohemia's
struggle against the Catholic Imperial yoke of the Hapsburgs.
Hus was burned at the stake and the Hapsburgs were not
shrugged off until the First World War, but his name lived on.
Now the word 'Peking' was strung out across the black lump in
bold red letters on a strip of black cloth. First Prague, next Peking;
second time lucky! Jan's friends had been collecting signatures
here the day before. It was a time and a place for youth to believe
itself invincible.

The Party

The talk of the town was a French slide projector up on Castle
Hill. For two nights only it was throwing giant images of the
French and Velvet Revolutions onto the walls of St Vitus's
Cathedral in the Castle courtyard. Designer revolutionary after-
math; this must have been a first.

The great courtyard was jammed solid and detachments of the Castle Guard were having to hold back crowds of latecomers at the gates in the outer wall (I was a latecomer).

The Castle Guard is Prague's ceremonial élite. They wear old-fashioned blue-black jackets with red and gold piping. They tend not to be the skinny or the spotty sort and on this occasion they were enjoying being glamorous. Infectious good humour seemed to spread back through the crowd from them and from a group of girls contriving to be pressed against them.

Eventually they let us through to jockey for a view through the stone arches on the eastern side of the courtyard between the Cathedral and the residence of the Head of State.

I caught a few glimpses of stylized Delacroix juxtaposed with the faces of ecstatic Czech students. The slides were tinted with the colours of the tricolour, which are also the colours of the Czech flag. Swathes of red, white and blue fell across the heads of the enraptured audience. The voice of Marta Kubisova welled up into the space above it. This voice had inspired crowds in Wenceslas Square in 1968, had been silenced for twenty-one years, then had done it again in 1989. You could almost hear the swallowing, the lump in the communal throat.

Somewhere in the crowd there was a tennis team from Wheaton College, Chicago, Illinois. They had arrived that day from Moscow via Minsk and Warsaw. Like me, they were billeted a long way up the hill behind the Castle in halls of residence belonging to the university. I met them there after the show. They had kind of been expecting lasers. But yeah. It had been intense.

The Wheaton boys were good, clean company, with names like Geoff, Kent and Blake. I said I'd cheer for them in their match against Prague Technical University. They said 'Good night and God bless'. I smelt a rat, a holy rat.

Next day Geoff gave me the whole picture. They weren't here just for the tennis or even mainly for the tennis. They were in the East Bloc to glorify God – through sport, through 'sharing', through any which way God chose to be glorified.

'Tell me Giles, do you go to church?'

Geoff seemed a straight-out, up-front kind of guy so I told the truth. No. That was cool. We continued to get along fine.

But Geoff didn't give up. A few days later, on Saturday evening, after I had seen the Wheaton boys with their Nikes and their enlarged-head Heads get beaten by a yawning team from the Technical University, I walked past Geoff's open door. He was playing cards with 'Coach' and the other guys.

'Hey Giles! Busy tomorrow?'

Tomorrow was Sunday. I ummed really hard.

'We're going to church and we'd like you to come.'

'Come on big guy, make a commitment.' (Coach was joining in. He seemed to be spiritual coach too.) 'You got two choices. Either you wake up yourself or we do it for you. We leave at nine.'

Geoff was kind enough to wake me at half past eight. I drew back the curtains and one of God's beautiful mornings filled the room. Geoff sat on my bed in the warm, clear sunlight and said he had been called aged five.

'Called?'

'Yeah. Our Lord called me.'

It was too early in the morning to ask if five wasn't too early in life to commit your future to the great tele-salesman in the sky.

Geoff said he wanted to be a youth pastor after graduating, and left me to get dressed.

At a quarter to nine he returned with Kent, both now resplendent in crisp white shirts, silk ties, pressed beige chinos and Italian loafers. They carried bibles. I had one collared shirt, far from clean, and was putting it on.

Coach video'd his team leaving the hall of residence and we drove into town in their hired Austrian minibus.

There are scores of breathtaking baroque churches in Prague but we shunned them all. It was denomination that counted. We parked in Klimentska Street, which runs at right angles to Revolucni, and filed through what could have been a domestic front door. We walked up a broad white staircase and into a chapel which was full except for two rows near the front reserved for the guests from Illinois.

Heads turned, and politely turned back, as we entered. This was a Brethren church, Kent said. The congregation smelled of soap. It wore simple sober suits, or skirts and blouses, and its hair was neatly parted. In front of us were the children, feet swinging

way above the floor, big sisters with hearts of gold keeping them
in order.

Our visit was to be more than a terrestrial gesture of solidarity.
The idea was to surmount the language barrier and commune
together with the Lord. To this end interpreters squeezed in
among us as the minister, with a muscular and kindly face but no
ceremonial silk, walked to the plain wooden lectern. The inter-
preter who sat between Kent and me seemed to have mastered one
phrase of English, 'We must ask forgive', which he repeated
through the whole address, interspersing it with a low growling.
He sweated. Afterwards we thanked him very much.

Then it was Coach's turn.

'Usually we all share,' Kent whispered as Coach approached
the lectern.

'Share what?'

'We . . . well, we share; with the others, with our hosts.'

'Right.'

'We share our personal testimonies,' Kent said.

Coach was in position, with the minister at his shoulder to
translate for the congregation.

'You don't use that word?' whispered Kent. He wanted to get
this sharing thing straight.

'We do, but we usually share *something*. I don't think we just
share.'

Coach said it was good to be back, and by way of introducing
the team, said:

'These young men I'm travelling with are all fine young
athletes. But I want you to know that the main reason we came on
this trip was to glorify God.'

He read the team verse, or a descendant of it. It was supposed to
be 1 Romans 16: 'For I am not ashamed of this Good News about
Christ. It is God's powerful method of bringing all who believe it
to heaven. This message was preached first to the Jews alone, but
now everyone is invited to come to God in this same way.'

'It's on our team shirts,' said Coach.

The first line was familiar because Geoff had introduced me to it
on his early-morning visit. 'I am not ashamed . . .' It had got him
through the taunts of High School.

Coach, actually, turned in a fine performance. That is, despite its content, it did not make one squirm. He was not given to the querulous tone, the crescendos or the tears of televangelists. He was a god-fearing college coach with a sensible voice and a manly chin which would have looked fine beside Abe Lincoln's on Mt Rushmore.

The service was truly memorable for none of this, but for a violin solo by a member of the congregation. It was a simple but apparently flawless rendering, from memory, of a largo and allegro by Handel. The violinist had a lean and serious look until he closed his eyes, and then he seemed to be transported. His mouth and eyebrows began to move, and during the allegro his thick black hair trembled. He turned out to be Cenek Pavlik, Czechoslovakia's leading concert violinist. Being in church we did not clap, but perhaps, in the ringing silence that followed his final flourish, he was hearing the usual thunderous applause in his head.

'Don't come to Prague for the music!' So said my Lonely Planet guidebook, probably the least inaccurate of all the guidebooks made obsolete by the events of 1989. But on Prague and music it had been comprehensively overtaken by events.

There was music everywhere. On a scaffolding stage sponsored by Civic Forum in front of their building in Wenceslas Square, in open-air concerts in the Old Town Square, in smoke-filled jazz cellars, in every concert hall and church, and by every one of the thirty statues along Charles Bridge, you could hear the Velvet Revolutionary groove. (You could get amorous to it, too. I was very aware of this. Prague 1990, snog city.)

Charles Bridge is the second oldest in Central Europe, according to the State English-language guide to Prague. Building began in 1357 and local magistrates took to lowering delinquents from it into the Moldau River in wicker baskets. By 1990 it was a busking strip, with an air of innocence about the busking. The music for the most part was comically bad, played more for fun and friends than money.

Election rallies had ended on the Tuesday to leave a cooling-off period before voting on Friday. Jan Vild's girlfriend studied medicine and was working for exams, which left Jan on his own, biting his nails and dreaming secretly of preferential votes. We met on the Thursday and walked through the Old Town towards Charles Bridge, past the Student Theatre where the meeting of the night of 17 November had been held. Jan had been scared almost to death that night.

A girl had arranged herself and her guitar on the statue of St Vincent Ferrarius on the far side of the bridge. Her partner was sitting on St Procopius with a tambourine, and they were singing ballads while swans drifted down the river behind them.

I was not the only one who found it impossible to take his eyes off the girl with the guitar. Two Japanese men stepped forward at the end of a ballad and asked her to be in their film about beautiful women. The girl spoke no English and simply smiled down at them like a mermaid. One of the men wore an emerald green headscarf tied in a thick rope to create, it seemed, a buccaneering look. Jan thought the Japanese were up to no good. He told the mermaid what they wanted and advised her not to believe them. The buccaneer told me they were making a series of commercials for Japanese International Telecom. They had to find a beautiful woman from every country in the world. 'Nice work,' I said, not believing him either. Jan said they should give the mermaid their hotel number and let her think about it.

Two days later, in a crowded Staromestski Namesti, I saw the mermaid again; in half-repose, just as she had been on St Vincent Ferrarius, only this time without her guitar and at the foot of the tall black figure of Jan Hus. At the base of the statue, creditably serene himself in the midst of a chattering film crew, the buccaneer stood behind a silver movie camera under the same emerald scarf and gestured at the mermaid to swing her long hair once more across her bewitching face.

I gained an entrée into the hitherto exclusive world of live classical music in Prague through a student of Physical Education who specialized in downhill skiing but was also an accomplished rock climber and had contributed to the revolution by abseiling down tall buildings and industrial chimneys to remove Communist slogans and red stars.

Matthew Holub was hip, and more of a doer than a talker. We met in Malostranske and had a beer in a cellar under the Wallenstein Palace gardens. I asked what he thought of the old regime.

'Bastards, fucking bastards.' And he liked to call them Bolsheviks. He didn't much care for Greens either. They protested that climbers harmed cliffs – can you believe it? – while quarrying companies went on blowing cliffs up and carting them away unchallenged.

We walked south, past the Museum of Musical Instruments and the Church of our Lady Victorious, to the PE faculty. Matthew bumped into a friend, a hulking fellow-student with red hair. Afterwards Matthew said: 'This time last year his father was a swimming teacher. Now he is Minister of Education.'

We had another beer, over which Matthew said that if I liked classical music his mother could get me tickets to concerts because she worked for a concert agency. But if I was into reggae I ought to hang loose with him and his girlfriend at a gig on an island in the river that very evening.

We took a tram towards the eastern edge of the city, where town planners seemed to have celebrated the further-flung reaches of the Marxist–Leninist world: the tramstop was in Cuba Square and Matthew's family lived behind it in Omsk Street.

It was election day and Matthew had come home to join the family voting expedition. He left me with his parents and went next door to fetch his Granny. ('We have to make sure she votes right.')

There was a certain *gravitas* in the schoolroom across the road which had become the polling station. Matthew's family, at any rate, said it felt significant if not exciting to have twenty-three parties to choose from. They all voted for the Forum and gave their preferential votes to Jan Vild.

I tried and failed to find the island reggae concert, which probably meant Matthew and his babe could hang looser than they would have done with me around. But a few days later I kept a rendezvous with Maria, Matthew's mother, on the steps of the Smetana Hall. This cavernous 1,300-seater box is Prague's leading concert venue and was built in the style of the Secession. Maria was dressed in the style of the Secession, in a diaphanous cotton *combinaison*, red and black. I fancied myself a guest of the proud new Czechoslovak bourgeoisie as we took our seats in a box and listened to Dvořák's *Stabat Mater* performed by the

Prague Radio Symphony Orchestra and Choir. It lasted an hour and a half with no breaks and nothing sprightlier than a Que Quasi Allegretto. Everything else was largo or andante. It had to be said that it was a programme for Dvořák devotees. Afterwards, drinking wine downstairs in a cross between the Café Royal and a *fin-de-siècle* hall of mirrors, I told Maria I had very much enjoyed the concert. She smiled and said she didn't believe me.

She described the night the wizard Rafael Kubelik had returned from exile to conduct Smetana's *Vltava* in Smetana Hall. It was the opening concert of the 1990 Prague Spring festival, and Vaclav Havel, the man who chased the philistines from power, had processed into the hall beneath the gilded flags of old Bohemia. Oh yes – Maria drained her glass – that had been an evening and a half.

Kubelik was back in town for the election, with the same tune in his head. On the day the votes were counted he filled a huge stage in the Old Town Square with the symphony orchestras of Prague, Brno, and Bratislava. The crowd was in shadow, the orchestras in sun. The dark twin towers of the Church of Our Lady Before Tyn rose behind glinting massed french horns. There was rapturous applause as Kubelik took the podium, and then quiet as the soft, rushing notes of the opening passage of *Vltava*, which is the Czech word for Moldau, sent sensuous shivers down a thousand spines.

The concert was Kubelik's gesture towards amity between the country's three historic lands – Brno being first city of Moravia and Bratislava of Slovakia. For this reason, but probably also because he liked the music, Havel joined Kubelik when it came to taking bows, and the Square erupted like a football stadium.

Havel was everywhere that day, and loving it. Soon after the provisional election results were scribbled on a blackboard outside the Civic Forum's headquarters there was a surge up Wenceslas Square towards an opening car door. News cameramen surfed along with the crowd, trailing their sound recordists. Havel walked fast from the car towards the headquarters, grinning liberally. He didn't bother with a walkabout. There was champagne to be drunk and laughter to be had with friends. He looked too healthy for a chain-smoking President and wore a yellow V-neck under his blazer. The blackboard gave the Forum 52 per cent. The Communists were on 10. For Jan Vild, needing 55 per cent to get a seat, it was an anxious afternoon, but the movement as a whole was home and dry.

A crowd waited for hours below the white building, craning up at all its balconies for twitching curtains – any sign of an impending victory speech. There was no speech, but Havel did step out briefly, three floors up, to grin some more and wave. The moment he appeared I found myself yelling deliriously with everybody else.

There was non-stop music on the scaffolding stage below the balconies: A flatulent euphonium ensemble, a quartet of scary-looking women playing Czech country and western, a bearded balladeer whose lyrics drew the biggest crowds of all, and an unstoppable rag-tag human dance machine led by a pianist in a caveman outfit. With him on stage were two saxophones, a tuba, a trombone, a flute, three trumpets, some drums, a marimba and a bass guitarist with a compact disc for an earring. An all-female camera crew from Visnews prowled the stage for close-ups and a press photographer tried to dance and take pictures of the marimba man at the same time.

Meanwhile in the Old Town Square, under a giant yellow awning supported by two cranes, an Elton John lookalike who was also a member of the interim government was rocking against apartheid.

This was the evening when Paul Simon jetted in to be with his friend Vaclav. As it grew dark, spotlights began roving over the crowd to make us feel special. (Slick producton came courtesy of Europe II, an FM station.) Mr Simon had to borrow a guitar for his surprise appearance, and when he sang 'The Sound of Silence' he raised a roar with almost every line.

'Narrow streets of cobbled stone . . . ' We liked that; narrow streets of cobbled stone are the only kind that lead to Staremestska.

'Ten thousand people, maybe more . . . ' Oh more, definitely more.

'Silence, like a cancer, grows . . . ' There was sudden hush as the significance of this line sank in, then a smooth wave of applause and the return of the roar as Mr Simon put down the guitar and bowed.

The Hangover

When the music stopped, people were still worried about the secret police. For example, there was a big fellow with a pigtail who wanted to start a business importing oriental carpets when he graduated. He was another friend of Jan's and he wore a menacing scowl on his face all that jolly day the votes were being counted. I bumped into him by a tableful of Havel's plays in Wenceslas Square.

'We've got to clean up this society,' he snarled. The StD (the secret police) was alive and dangerous and in league with the surviving Communist politicians. He wanted a purge. Dancing in the streets was for air-heads.

At the time he seemed paranoid. Prague felt singularly un-oppressed.

But Jan was bothered too. I met up with him again after the election. He had got his seat in parliament and later that summer he would be inter-railing on a 'diplomatic' parliamentary pass-port. But the StD worried him. He had been thinking back over the revolution. How had they got away with it?

In the corridors of power there had been powerlessness, because of the sheer decrepitude of the old regime, and because of the Gorbachev factor; Gorbachev had said the tanks would not roll. The great red rug had been pulled. Meanwhile, on the streets, idealism, youth and courage had received their share of credit, and deserved it.

But the blunt-faced men with revolvers could have snuffed out youth and idealism at any of a hundred moments. So the question remained, why didn't they? Well, they chose not to. But why?

A journalist called Anastasia had been pondering these things too. I had arranged to meet her outside the Hotel Europa in Wenceslas Square. We both arrived just as a fight was starting between a punk and a Turkish man. The Turkish man broke a heavy glass ashtray over the punk's mohican and was drawing blood with punches to the face by the time the two were pulled apart. Anastasia and I watched the fight, then introduced ourselves to each other and sat down to lunch.

She worked for *Young World*, a Czech weekly heavily quoted by Western journalists during the revolution because it got all the scoops. Anastasia's patch had been the hospitals. On the night of 17 November she had seen about forty people being treated for injuries inflicted by police, but the doctors had been too scared to talk or give the patients' names.

After that the StD had let the demonstrations happen. And *as* they happened, 'while the crowds were ecstatic on Wenceslas Square,' a list of 24,000 secret policemen and informers was quietly destroyed. A new regime could destroy the old secret police only if it knew who the old secret policemen were.

It was, suggested Anastasia, an extreme case of reforming to survive: the secret component of the old regime secured its future as a secret component of the new one, and then allowed society to think it was having a revolution.

Anastasia was cogent, beautiful, and half Russian. She said I should get in touch if I needed any help, but I never dared.

In a restaurant in the castle one evening, I heard a less glamorous view of how the old men might be staying on.

I had locked myself into the lavatory in a café near the castle. I had not locked myself in on purpose, nor in a way that could easily be unlocked. While hauling myself through a narrow gap between the top of the door and the ceiling to get at the outside handle I got covered in cobwebs and strained my groin. I had a concert to go to in a church behind the castle, but needed a few minutes to peel off the cobwebs and massage my groin, before taking my seat.

I headed for St Vitus's Cathedral. There are usually tranquil corners in cathedrals. But mass was in progress and the side pews were full. I hung around in an aisle, sniffing incense and admiring gothic tombs. A short man in a smart suit was doing more or less the same as me, and I realized I recognized him: the head of a well-known international polling organization. I had once analysed his data on students. He left the cathedral, crossing himself with holy water at the door, and I followed him. We were going to the same concert so I caught up with him and he invited me to join him for dinner afterwards.

The pollster said many things over the course of the evening. Things like: 'Number Ten was asking my advice on . . .,' and: 'You *must* go to Vilnius. *Do* try.'

He moved fast about the world, scything through red tape with hard cash and blue-chip contacts. ('Raisa got this card to get me into Lithuania . . . a fiddle with some Moscow friends of hers.') It was Brussels yesterday, Budapest tomorrow. He loved to whip out his Sharp IQ electronic personal organizer between arias (sung by a pregnant soprano in white muslin) and had spent the afternoon at the Queen's birthday party at the British Embassy teasing the East German air attaché about Mig 29s.

'They've just bought nineteen of them – you know, the ones that stand on their tails at the Paris air show and then crash. And what are they going to do with them? Give 'em to NATO?'

But the most useful thing he said was: 'Take my advice. Get the low-down from your interpreter.'

His interpreter was a prophet of doom called Nadia. She had a smooth, white face, wore glasses, worked for the Institute of Commerce, and said Czechoslovakian industry was in the grip of Communists.

'Seventy per cent of Czech companies are uncompetitive. All the managers from the old regime are still in place, and fifty-five-year-olds don't change. All the good people have gone. Only the stupid ones – like me – have stayed.' Her sister had emigrated to Canada twenty years before and Nadia had not been promoted since.

We were in the Castle Restaurant. The pollster was drunk and enjoying life and pouring wine and Bekerovka down his inter-preter in an effort to make her enjoy it too. I told her I had witnessed some cheerful scenes in Prague, and surely that meant something? She rounded on me.

'Don't be naive, young man. Nothing has changed. We will go the way of Poland.'

Poland. Still the country the rest of Europe couldn't bear to be compared with.

To Poland

You hear things about Poland, like you hear things about Romania. These seem to be the two live yoghurt countries of Eastern Europe; the unpredictable ones. Places of tragedy, passion, beauty, desolation, hope, exasperation, despair. Places of abstract nouns. History says Poland has been almost continually partitioned, occupied, or threatened with invasion by greater and certainly more arrogant powers. Foreign correspondents were saying Poland was desperately poor and that the Pope was arguably its most influential leader. Many East Germans seemed to think Poles constitutionally incapable of working.

I expected to be exhausted and depressed by Poland; to ride across an endless grey-green plain under drifting palls of industrial smoke. I was expecting barely-controlled anarchy, cavernous empty butcher's shops, bushy moustaches, grubby blue overalls, residual gratitude for the British guarantee of Poland's frontiers in 1939, and hunger.

I wanted to cross the border into Poland in the Giant Mountains and rode there via Kutna Hora, forty miles east of Prague.

Kutna Hora stands on high ground south of the River Elbe, which eventually disgorges its water, its heavy metals and its other toxins into the North Sea at Hamburg. But it flows south, not north, from the Giant Mountains. It seems to want to meet the Danube, for it flirts with the Moravian uplands looking for a way through. But they resist it and it turns slowly away in its own peaceful green basin.

A headwind blew across this basin from the north and I tacked into it along roads which hardly ever see a car; roads which give way to fields and follow streams where they can, under natural avenues of willows.

(It is much less fun riding into the wind than up hills. Hills are honest. They stand up and are counted, and they give views. Wind is silent and magical when it is behind you, but deafening, exhausting, infuriating and everything else that is bad when it is against you.)

Up a cobbled rise on the north bank of the Elbe the town of Tynec was preparing for school prize-giving on a sports field. The head-teacher, in a beige suit, seemed pitiably nervous. Alternately he bossed the band around and stood like a potential suicide at a corner-post overlooking the river, rehearsing his speech. An express train to Ostrava swept past on the opposite bank. Two muscular lads out of uniform were dragging mats onto the pitch for a gym display and being watched by the older girls in leotards. They looked away when the lads came close.

I continued to Jecin, once the seat of Albrecht Wallenstein, and failed to find his palace there.

A funambulist had set up in the square. Customized bicycles and unicycles hung upside down from tightropes between two portable pylons. The pylons were secured by cables attached to things like the caravan's wheels and a statue of a local saint.

There was nowhere cheap to sleep in Jecin, so I unrolled my bivvi bag in dew-drenched grass beside the road north of the town. Mosquitoes homed in on my head, which I covered with my shorts. It was a moonlit night, and through one leg hole I could see the forested foothills of the Giant Mountains.

A few weeks later a Polish ecologist described the area north-west of here, around the junction of the Polish, Czech and East German borders, as the 'triangle of death'. Even the pre-revolutionary official Czech tourist guides admitted that its spruce forests 'have been substantially damaged due to the influence of exhalations from numerous industrial works'. Exhalations have no doubt also damaged the countryside along the route I chose from Jecin to the border. The trouble is, it looked idyllic.

The little road was thrown about by the jumble of hills, disgorged one moment by forest, to follow a narrow, twisting strip of farmland, switching back the next to link a lonely homestead to civilization.

Vaclav Havel has a farmhouse in these parts. Timothy Garton Ash defied the police by visiting it in 1984, when for Havel's sake he could not be more specific about the address than 'northern Bohemia . . . up narrow lanes towards the Sudeten mountains, through the damp Bohemian pine woods'. That was all I knew, which made every farmhouse a potential monument.

The wind was kind when it mattered, blowing me up a long climb beside the infant Elbe towards the ski resort of Spindleruv Mlyn. The Giant Mountains rate 'mountain' status for their bulk, not their shape. They are smooth and grassy except along the frontier ridge which is enlivened by granite outcrops and which I reached around teatime, in drizzle. The road slipped under a single red barrier and down into Poland.

However, the barrier was not to be passed. This was not an official crossing point. Frontier guards with Kalashnikovs gave me and my visa the blank stare which means 'Try anything you like. You are not getting through.'

I spent the evening up there on the border in a turn-of-the-century lump called Chalet Spindlerova. It rained outside.

At eleven o'clock I left the chalet, rolled a short way back towards Spindleruv Mlyn, pushed the bike off the road into some stunted pine and went to sleep.

Soon after four I was woken by a growling noise. It could have been distant thunder or, rather closer, wild boar. I heard it again, and some hoof-steps. Not thunder. I was zipped into a sleeping bag and a bivvi bag, blind and immobile as a slug. So like a slug, I hardly moved or breathed. After a few minutes' silence the noise came again, loud, angry, and very close. Did boar have horns? Then it moved away. In a minor frenzy I tore open the zip and sat up, to see a young deer trotting off into the dawn.

There was no getting back to sleep after that. I freewheeled back through Spindleruv Mlyn and rode along the south side of the mountains to the official crossing point.

I rode gingerly into Poland trying to notice things. Passport inspection: a formality. Customs: none. Money change: private (American Express traveller's cheques would do nicely). Road: smooth. View to the right: two articulated lorries in a lay-by. View to the left: haymaking. Ha! Haymaking, not with tractor but with horse and cart. So this was Poland.

Beyond the fields on the left there was a steep scarp to which trees clung where possible. Tucked under the scarp there was a town called Kudowa Zdroj.

There was little evidence of destitution in Kudowa Zdroj. A display of fresh fruit and vegetables on the pavement outside the police station made the head swim after Czechoslovakia. There were peaches and bananas, peppers, cauliflowers, kohlrabi, leeks, baby cucumbers, and big, firm tomatoes. For those with zlotys to burn there was chocolate, fruit juice, and *Vin du Pays de l'Aude* imported privately from West Germany. There were two night-clubs and Mercedes as taxis. The police station looked like a well-endowed Ivy League frat house.

Six scouts were pooling resources to buy chocolate. A vodka-soused National Serviceman snored, horizontal, on a bench. On the upper edge of town, where the high road to Wroclaw set off up a cleft in the scarp, three generations of a farming family were engaged in mowing a meadow, while a fourth, too old to move, watched from a deck-chair in the porch of a log cabin.

It felt good to be in Poland, but then a swarm of flies began to follow. The steep road made it impossible to pedal faster than they could fly. Any slowing brought the flies whining in for a lick of sweat. Eventually the slope eased. Clunk. Up a gear. The ounce of extra speed created a breeze out of the hot, still air. The flies were struggling, receding gradually in a furious little cloud. I hit the apex of the climb, flicked the chain into top and with a sense of triumph which Trajan himself probably never knew, left the maddening pests for ever.

The road had wound up onto a plateau of pastureland which turned out to be a National Park. There was one village up there, called Karlow, where the locals milked cows and chopped wood.

It was half past four. England was playing Belgium at five in the World Cup quarter finals, and there was no television in Karlow.

'Kudowa Zdroj,' said a woodcutter. '*Televizia* Kudowa Zdroj.' I didn't want to go back the way I'd come.

'Nowa Ruda,' said the woodcutter's wife. That was an hour further on.

'Radkow?' I asked. Radkow was half-way to Nowa Ruda.

'*Nie. Radkow niema televizia.*'

Very well. I would press on. The road climbed a little out of Karlow, snaked along a gully to the plateau's edge, then plunged diagonally down a cliff. Oh man. I must have been doing sixty.

There were fleeting views of the countryside round Radkow: Fields of yellow and orange, fields striped green and brown, woodland in random blobs and slivers, not a pylon in sight but the spires of many churches.

Mostly I watched the road, though, for this was Donald Campbell stuff. The slightest unseen ripple in the tarmac would have sent me hurtling off the cliff to certain death.

Radkow did have a television, in the ale-house. The ale was *pisswasser* compared with Czech Pilsener. The women serving it were irritated by the stranger who couldn't understand how much it cost. The television was black and white with loose vertical hold, and the whole place looked decrepit after the swanky frontier town of Kudowa Zdroj. The other drinkers got the message that I was English and football-mad and made a huge fuss about positioning me directly opposite the screen.

At half-time a select group of us repaired to a private sitting room with colour satellite TV for the higher-quality Austrian transmission. The score was nil-all. My host was a heating engineer named Richard who had obtained his television and satellite dish through Marek, also present. Marek made furniture as a *Gastarbeiter* in Austria; three weeks on, three weeks off. In two days in Austria he could earn a month's Polish wages. Richard's wife, who worked in the Town Hall and spoke French, believed Lech Walesa should be content as leader of Solidarity and not stand for president. She produced grilled sausage, coffee, and Polish export vodka for the second half, which ended with the score still nil-all.

(In the penultimate minute of extra time, responding to a

desperate shout from Bobby Robson on the touchline, Gazza floated the ball into the box from just forward of the half-way line, and David Platt turned in the air to volley it home. The rest is history.)

There was more anti-Walesa talk at breakfast.

'You can't have an electrician as a President,' said Jacek, one of four eighteen-year-olds camping in the same field as me. Mazowiecki, the then Prime Minister, had more brains.

Jacek's girlfriend made me a picnic lunch which included some wicked jam sponge.

It was very hot, that day and the next. Outside the farmhouses along the road north-east from Radkow, milkchurns waited on wooden stands for their milk to be collected. Most front gates were guarded by Madonnas or paintings of Jesus in his crown of thorns. Fat white hens snoozed on the verges in the sun and heavy bunches of redcurrants hung over wooden fences.

On a terrace overlooking a lake near a place called Sobotka I met a Fascist. His name was Heinrich, and he had a vodka problem. He was a big man with a diploma in cartography, he claimed, but no job and no confidence that Lech Walesa as president would get him one. Walesa was a worker – a mere worker.

'You need *kultura* in a president,' Heinrich said.

The concept of *kultura* figured prominently in Heinrich's pickled consciousness. He much admired German National Socialist *kultura* and intended to rat on his wife and go and work for the West German Republican party as soon as he obtained his passport in September. Ten years. Ten wasted years he had been waiting for his passport.

In Heinrich's view you either lived under one lot of extremists or you lived under another. The Communists had wrecked his life so far. It was time to try Fascism.

'*Fascismus*, that's the thing . . . *Fascismus!*'

We drove to Heinrich's house in his red Lada and chased down vodka with raw eggs sucked from their shells. Heinrich introduced his poor wife as 'a good Catholic', and volunteered his opinion of Jews by miming the wringing of a chicken's neck. He invited me to stay the night and I declined. He said at any rate I should visit his cherry orchard in the morning, and I agreed.

Heinrich was a dot on a hillside when I turned up to go cherry picking. He was twirling hay onto a cart with a pitchfork, and his rustic half-brother was sprawled on the growing pile to keep it from collapsing. His seventy-six-year-old aunt brought up the rear, raking. They were helping a neighbour. When the cart reached the end of a line of cut grass we left it and walked down to the cherry trees. They bore superlative cherries, more purple than red and some as big as plums. The trees were as big as oaks, with deeply gnarled black bark. Heinrich left me to climb them, gorge myself and fill my pockets.

As a parting gesture he gave me a five Reichsmark coin and some notes, from his collection of Third Reich currency.

Wroclaw (pronounced Vrotswav)

It was raining midges in the centre of Wroclaw. They came out of a lowering, humid sky in their millions, probably their billions. They smothered everyone and everything, turning the dark brick of the town hall darker. People ran for cover, spitting out midges and wiping them from their eyes. It made an apocalyptic vision. It was an act of God or the Devil and it would take another one to rid the city of this plague.

The heavens duly opened. Billions of raindrops bombed the midges out of the sky and washed them down the storm drains. I watched it from a window seat in a cocktail bar opposite the town hall, slurping beetroot consommé.

Pavement enterprise was rampant. It was rampant all over Poland, providing everything shops did not provide, clogging Polish trains and West German supermarkets with its extemporized supply system, and giving Polish towns an incongruous mediterranean air: Phil Collins tapes, Bic razors, neon knickers, Tonka Toys, depilatories, pain-killers, curling tongs, chocolate hazelnut spread, wine in boxes, beer in cans, accountancy textbooks, dark glasses, tennis shoes, cigarettes, aftershave, endless trashy radio cassette recorders . . .

What I wanted was a good book.

My Lonely Planet guide recommended 'an excellent Russian bookstore at Rynek 14,' promising that 'many of the books are in English or German'. I had very high hopes of this bookshop, but it turned out to be a relic. The Russian greats were still disgraced and the only English-language book in stock was *The Hills of Vilnius* by a Soviet People's writer from Lithuania.

But another bookshop had some Penguins and other English books. I bought a collection of American short stories and, from the Marxism-Leninism section for the equivalent of 1p, a collection of essays entitled *New Problems for an Old World*.

I had failed to find a youth hostel and was on my way to the station to take the night train to Gdansk when the rain began again. I sheltered under a flyover. By and by, so did another man on a bicycle. He had a fat face and a flowing gut, but he had a big frame to carry it on. He combed the rain out of his black hair and offered me a cigarette. I offered him a Jolly Rancher. (The Wheaton boys had given me two bags of American boiled sweets called Jolly Ranchers before leaving Prague. 'You'll *love* Jolly Ranchers,' they had said. 'They last like *ten hours* an' we brought forty-eight packs.') The fat man declined. He tapped his shoulder. I was learning that this meant 'I usually wear epaulettes'. He was a policeman and he wanted me to follow him.

We splashed for a mile or two along a dark brown river of rainwater mixed with soot to the policeman's apartment building. He had the use of a cellar, which was flooded, but we still parked the bikes there. Upstairs, no one else was home yet. The policeman introduced himself as Tadeusz, or Tadek, and apologized for not speaking English. He lit a flame under a vat of soup and put an electric heating element in a large tin mug, for coffee.

The apartment was spotless and relatively spacious. But it was on the fourth floor. The stairs, in combination with his smoking and his surplus flesh, seemed to be torturing Tadek's heart and lungs.

When his wife got in from work she put soup, bread, ham, tomato salad, coffee, vodka, soda water, and meat stock jelly on the table and bade me eat.

At their insistence I slept in their bedroom while they slept on sofas in the sitting room.

Tadek took the next day off work to show me what he called
the Polish Vatican, a group of churches on an island in the Oder
River. He had been holding back the crowds here when the Pope
had helicoptered in and gone walkabout on his historic tour of
Poland in 1983. It had been worth being a policeman just for that.

In a Russian Orthodox church on the island we found a priest
who spoke English.

During the siege of the city by the Red Army in 1945 this
church was destroyed, and with it 500,000 books from the
university library which had been stored in the crypt. The books
were of course irreplaceable but the church had been rebuilt. Only
now, in 1990, were the finishing touches being put to the ceiling
frescoes. The faces of the twelve apostles still needed, theoreti-
cally, to be painted in, but a visiting Catholic had thought it a
deliberate and wonderfully ghostly depiction. The priest was
debating with his colleagues whether to leave the apostles face-
less. Tadek was delighted to see me writing all this down. '*Gut
Reportage!*' he wheezed as we left the church. '*Gut Reportage!*'

Tadek's son and his son's girlfriend both faced their final school
exams the following week but abandoned revision to show me
the second biggest painting in Europe, the *Panorama Raclawicka*. It
is a painting of Cossacks by Cossacks; a continuous canvas
designed to fill all 360 degrees of the circular inside wall of a
rotunda. When its first rotunda was damaged in 1944, the painting
took two months to roll up.

I had a final coffee at home with Tadek before catching my
train. He was smoking, of course, and looked profoundly miserable. He was resting his chin on his fists and his jowls poured
down over his knuckles. He said he earned 1.3 million zlotys a
month (the equivalent at the black market rate, which was the
only rate of any use, of $130). How much did an English
policeman earn? About ten times that, I said, guessing, but
confident I was not overestimating. I droned on about correspondingly higher costs of living but he just put his head in his
hands and shook it, slowly.

Weekend in Gdansk

My weekend in Gdansk would have been nothing without Miro-slaw. He was outside the shipyard when I met him. Behind him the shipyard cranes climbed into the sky like preying mantises. Beside him a group of Australians asked questions about the photographs in the Solidarity souvenir kiosk.

'What's this, Miroslaw?'

'This: part of Solidarity Monument. High: forty-two metres. Constructed by shipyard workers.'

The picture was of three giant steel crosses inching through a crowd on a low-loader, one night in 1980. The crosses were erected later that night by the entrance to the shipyard and Jaruzelski never ordered them to be taken down. Miroslaw pointed at two more photographs.

'This: Jan Pavel Two, the Papa. Here, George Bushy, Margaret Tatcher. They all famous people come to Gdansk. Here, Henryk Jankowski, Spirit Father of Solidarity. Now follow.'

Miroslaw led the way to the Church of Santa Brygda, spiritual home of Solidarity. Henryk Jankowski, confidant of Walesa and the Pope and one of Poland's most powerful and political Catholics, is the padre here. Against the north wall of the church there is a shrine to Father Jerzy Popieluszko, murdered by the secret police in 1984. The shrine is centred on a lifesize bronze statue of the martyr – if 'statue' is the word for a bound, gagged, drowned and horizontal figure.

Miroslaw had been showing the Australians around for two days. They were travelling with a group called Bamtours. Bamtours consisted of an old Bedford bus with a crew of twelve and 2,000-watt sound system. They planned to spend two months playing recorded Belgian acid music at various venues across Eastern Europe.

We had tea and buns, then the driver woke up and it was time for them to go, destination Budapest.

Miroslaw said his goodbyes and led me jerkily across Gdansk towards his flat.

'Crazy people, but good people,' he said. 'They are my English friends. I make many friends with foreigners.'

Miroslaw was strong on statements and instructions but it was difficult to talk back.

'Don't you want to ask me anything?' he said, so I asked if he could show me round the shipyard.

'Take it easy. I will arrange it. And maybe you want to meet some famous people? I know many people in Gdansk. I think you want to talk to them.'

Miroslaw was an unemployed journalist left behind by one of the great, bold brushstokes of contemporary history: Solidarity. He was short, with a thick orange beard and greasy hair. His sunken eyes were usually behind tinted glasses. He wore brown trousers, a brown jacket with corduroy shoulders which gathered dandruff, and a green safari shirt with epaulettes. When moving around Gdansk he would sweep back the wings of his jacket, plunge his hands into his pockets, and press back on the tops of his thighs so that each step was a jerk forward, an acceleration.

I think he wished above all to inspire respect. But he didn't, and he didn't inspire much trust or affection either, though these would have been more useful to him. Most people seemed to say goodbye to Miroslaw with a sort of numb gratefulness. I probably would have done too, if he'd given me a chance.

We entered the old town through the Golden Gate and weaved through the tourists in Dlugi Targ, showpiece of the city's post-war reconstruction. It is lined with seventeenth-century burghers' houses which were mounds of rubble by the end of 1945. Now they're back, down to the last leering gargoyle, and air pollution has ensured they don't look new. Miroslaw said that Barbara Johnson of Johnson and Johnson had fallen in love with the Artus Mansion and pledged money for the city in order to get her hands on it. And the building next to the Artus Mansion was once a *Bierkeller* where Hitler drank when in Danzig.

I caught only a glimpse of it. We were already jerking under the Green gate at the eastern end of Dlugi Targ, and over the old harbour bridge towards modern Gdansk.

Beyond the bridge the stub of an abandoned urban freeway project was surrounded by apartment blocks standing on gravel and mud.

Miroslaw shared his flat with his mother, but had a meeting there with her estranged husband, his father, a veteran of the 1944 Warsaw Uprising. He arrived at three in a dark suit with medals on the lapel. His head was like an ostrich egg. He was diffident towards the Englishman but clearly still a fighter underneath. He had saved the lives of some London-based Polish partisans, also in 1944, and believed this had earned him a medal and some money. Would I look up this address in Hammersmith when I got home?

Miroslaw left me with his father and took a shower in the shower shared by all five flats on his floor. He had spent the previous night in his clothes on the Bamtours bus, and the safari shirt was dark with sweat round the armpits and neck. The father smiled but didn't talk. Miroslaw's room was about ten by eight feet. Crammed into it were a divan, a big black-and-white television, two armchairs, a desk and a bookcase. Load-bearing concrete struts lowered the ceiling to caravan height. A lamp-shade hung from one of the struts and an autographed pennant from the Netherlands' national handball team hung from the lampshade. On the bookcase there was an expired press card with a picture of a beardless young Miroslaw. Also, an autographed Johnny Cash LP.

When Miroslaw returned, towelling himself, I saw flat pink growths on his white stomach and earnestly hoped they were only birthmarks. He put the safari shirt back on and dictated a list of topics on which he wanted to write for English newspapers, if I wouldn't mind putting him in touch with the right people. These included the life and times of a Jewish doctor called Janos

Korchak, and Witkacy's theatre of the absurd. Then he talked jovially into the phone for five minutes.

'Come. We go. I have arranged a meeting with Anna Walenty-nowicz, mother of Solidarity.'

Anna Walentynowicz was a crane driver in the Lenin shipyard. On 14 August 1980 the management tried to sack her for trade union activities. This prompted a strike whose committee came to be chaired by Lech Walesa, who founded Solidarity and nine years later toppled Poland's Communist government. That is Walesa's story. Anna Walentynowicz, in a friend's flat next to the shipyard entrance, had a different version.

She sat on a sofa flanked by the friend whose flat it was, and another woman. The hostess was called Alexandra. All three seemed remarkable for their good complexions, but a French Trotskyite whom I later met in Cracow said Anna had been seriously ill for much of the '80s. She had thick grey hair and wore a cream-coloured blouse and a tweed skirt. She started her discourse in 1970, Miroslaw translating.

(Miroslaw sat opposite them, straight-backed and excited. He barked confident nuggets of English at me, but was clearly paraphrasing like crazy in his head to get round to words he knew. In the same brittle tone he exchanged Polish pleasantries with the three women while I scribbled.)

Anna first stepped forward from the proletariat in 1970 when soldiers were brought in to control crowds protesting in Gdansk and elsewhere about food price rises. It was a literal stepping forward: two shipyard workers were shot dead outside the gate and there, backed by a huge crowd, she pleaded for twenty minutes with the soldiers to stop shooting. They did, and wages and the price of bread levelled off again, and Anna went back to driving cranes.

Her dismissal in 1980 is said by many to be the pretext for the birth of the first free trade union in the Communist bloc. In fact that union was born in 1978, and Walentynowicz's involvement was the pretext for her dismissal. Between 1978 and 1980 she was intermittently arrested and detained for agitating for better pay and working conditions in the shipyard. Hence the depth of her support in 1980: 17,000 dockyard workers.

Anna said proudly: 'Until 1980 the demonstrations were about economic questions. This was the first one about human rights' – *her* human rights.

She dwelt on August 1980. Specifically, on the exact sequence of events in the shipyard on the second weekend in the month, for these were Gdansk's days in the spotlight of history. It has not been as heady since. Those were the hours when people like Walesa who knew about manoeuvring and deals and urgent phone calls could fix their reputations as in stone, while simpler folk, more honest perhaps but anyway less multifaceted, were outmanoeuvred. In Gdansk the middle weekend of August 1980 is like the day of Kennedy's assassination for Americans or 9 November 1989 for Berliners – 'Where were you when . . .?'

Anna was at home in Grunwaldska Street, out of a job. But the first demand of the 17,000 was that she be brought to talks with the shipyard management. These were conciliatory times, pre-martial law. The invitation to the shipyard conference room arrived. Only then, said Anna, did Lech Walesa appoint himself spokesman for the 17,000. He was taking no risks.

'He says he jumped over the wall, but that's not true,' she said. 'The authorities let him in. He had contacts in the Party.'

Nevertheless, Anna handed Walesa the chairmanship of the strike committee: 'I thought a man should lead it. With a woman in charge it would not be taken seriously.'

Three days later, Walesa called off the strike.

'To this day I do not know why he did it,' Anna said. 'Maybe it was because I had my job back so he thought there was no more reason to strike. Maybe he did a deal with the Communists.'

Ten years on she regretted letting him back onto the strike committee, and claimed she could have prevented it.

'I had the power. *I* had the power. It was only a question of whether to use it, and I did not.'

During the years of martial law Anna joined hunger strikes in Cracow, laid wreaths at the tablet by the shipyard gate to the dead of 1970, and went three times to prison. She also tried three times to meet Solidarity's national committee, which was at that time underground. Three times Walesa ensured that the meetings did not happen.

'Walesa descredited other organizers of the strike so that he could claim it was his strike only. When the state of war ended, Jaruzelski said he would talk only with Lech Walesa as a spokesman of Solidarity.

'I'll never work with him again,' said Anna. 'The trust is gone.'

Miroslaw was getting fired up. With pride in the fame and eloquence of his acquaintances, he broke off to tell me: 'Your editor will pay you well for this. The mother of Solidarity says the trust is gone with Lech Walesa.' I was not so sure. Editors tend to be concerned with the mainstream, and I had the feeling that this sitting room had been relegated by the rush of history to the status of a valiant eddy. 'Yes, I hope he will,' I said.

We had a picture session. Anna performed a wistful gaze from the balcony towards the shipyard cranes. She also posed in front of the Solidarity monument. She has a better right than most to pose in front of it, since it commemorates the workers who died in 1970, in the shootings which she risked her own life to stop.

Miroslaw was dripping more sweat into his safari shirt when he arrived for our rendezvous the next day. We took a tram up the coast to the suburb of Oliwa, where northern Poland's principal cathedral forms the edge of a botanical garden. I didn't want an earnest tour of a cathedral and I didn't get one. Miroslaw had come here to talk to someone else about a murdered friend. The murder, a year ago, had now produced a trial at which Miroslaw did not want to appear as a character witness. It had been a 'mafia job'. The dead friend had been buying and selling abroad. If Miroslaw knew what commodities and for whom he did not say.

An organ concert was about to start. Miroslaw left me in a pew and scurried off.

The cathedral was soaring thirteenth-century Gothic; the real thing. The weather had been turning gothic too. The air was heavy, and thick clouds were poised to drench the botanical gardens. As the organ's huge bass pipes filled the nave with the first ponderous semiquavers of a fugue, thunder started.

Miroslaw's contact didn't show and by the end of the recital there was a downpour in progress outside. We waited at the great west door with a coachload of elderly East Germans for a pause in the rain. None came, so we got soaked looking for a bar. 'At least we aren't made of sugar,' Miroslaw said.

It was mid-afternoon, but very gloomy. The only bar in the neighbourhood was a Class III tourist establishment; top of the range. A disco ball sent circles of reflected light round the room, over pink napkins and red candle-holders.

Miroslaw talked about himself. He was thirty-three. He had been twenty-four when Solidarity was founded. At that time he had been working for a manufacturer of electrical equipment for the shipyard. The firm provided two of Solidarity's early Vice-Presidents and Miroslaw had wanted to get involved – but he was a Party member. The local Party committee had convened a meeting with Miroslaw and a secret service representative (in Miroslaw's world the secret service was everywhere). The inconsistencies of simultaneous membership of both Party and trade union were pointed out to the young Miroslaw.

He had left the Party and busied himself with Solidarity ('I was in charge of Solidarity's own secret service'). He had been in and out of work ever since. In his last job, in a building materials factory, he seemed to have improvised a little rashly around his job description. He said: 'I wanted to make a little *perestroika* but my boss don't agree. I am sacked.'

He leaned across the table and said with complete conviction: 'Wherever I go I take success. I have always been a revolutionary. I want to see what is wrong and make it correct. I never break.'

Unemployment benefit in Poland is about ten dollars a month. It would be easy to break in Miroslaw's shoes, but he used the phrase itself like a mantra, or rosary beads: 'I never break. I never break.'

Loud Europop filled the bar.

'Tell me about the mafia, Miroslaw,' I said. He looked right through me, uninterested, and didn't reply. After a while he said, 'Sorry, I must go outside.'

I sat and read Edgar Allen Poe's 'The Fall of the House of Usher'. After half an hour I went to look for Miroslaw.

He had been just outside the door the whole time, watching the rain fall and talking with the waiter. Now he turned and said: 'You want to see the mafia? I know the hotels where they play cards. It will be interesting for you.'

We splashed along a soggy, unpaved sidewalk to a tramstop. A drunk old man missed his footing on the crumbling edge of the road and fell into a brown puddle.

'Have you ever had trouble from them?' I asked.

'No. Just my friend, the one they killed. But it would be dangerous for me to be a witness at the trial. I will ask my doctor for a sick note.'

The tram took us out onto a green tongue of land in the bay between Gdansk and Oliwa. We walked for five minutes from the end of the line through a dripping wet arboretum, then through a carpark of Western cars, to the Hotel Poseidon. It was cheaply constructed , boringly designed, and very tranquil.

'So, um, Miroslaw. Are we going to *talk* to these people . . . I mean, do you *know* them?'

We were approaching the hotel entrance. Coolly, I thought, Miroslaw didn't slow down to explain the game plan.

'Of course I know them. I know who they are. No, we don't talk, we have a look. If they are there I show them to you . . . and we go.'

You would need some reason like illicit cards to come to the Poseidon. Dead, it was. And not even any illicit cards.

'Are they here?'

'A minute, please. I look around.'

I left Miroslaw to look around and used the pristine lavatories downstairs beside the Hades nightclub, whose door hung open. It was black and silent. Presumably it would be less like Hades after dinner, with a few pairs of semi-erogenated thighs flexing to an electro-pulse.

Back upstairs Miroslaw was triumphant. He had found a prize contact – in the jewellery boutique. The contact wore Docksiders, carefully-faded jeans and a suede blouson with a sew-on Harley Davidson badge. There was an unobtrusive knot of scar tissue on his upper lip. He sat on a chrome-plated armchair with his right foot on his left knee as if he owned the place. He handed me a catalogue with the name Zbigniew Swiatecki on the front, and said in smooth American English:

'That's me. I own the place. Miroslaw says you want to know about the gangs.'

I said yes, anything he could safely tell me.

'I am not a member of a gang, you understand.'

I understood. It seemed from the catalogue that he was a jewellery designer. He opened the catalogue for me at the English page.

'Mr Zbigniew Swiatecki, Gdansk, constantly seeks the unique solutions, bold, sometimes even eccentric shapes. Does not forget about the basic function of jewel-proof finery.'

'It is my hobby. I like to be creative . . . and if I can sell my creativity I like that also.'

He smiled at a salesgirl standing behind a glass counter and she dispensed free smiles all round. I said the jewellery looked very fine, and asked what his main business was, if the jewellery was only a hobby. He produced a card.

Richard Z. Swiatecki, President, American Music Federation, Polish Department.

The man on the card was a promoter of Polish pop talent and was not to be confused with Zbigniew the designer. Richard was buddies with Johnny Cash and Leonard Cohen. Miroslaw contributed: 'You saw my Johnny Cash LP? Mr Swiatecki gave it to me.'

Mr Swiatecki managed not to look indulgent and asked whether I frequented clubs in London. He was interested in making contacts, serious contacts. I dropped the names of Ronnie Scott's and the Town and Country Club – casually, in case they were the wrong scene. They were. Richard Swiatecki promoted country music.

We were veering away from the mafia. Perhaps Mr Swiatecki responded to direct questions.

'How does the mafia make its money here?'

'Cars. They steal them in West Germany, smuggle them to Poland and sell them – cheap for you. I could get you one in half an hour, but luxus, only luxus. BMW 7 Series, Corrados, a Corvette Stingray even.'

This was in an absolutely no bullshit tone of voice. I said I wasn't in the market, just interested. He continued: 'Gdansk is the centre of the car business in Poland, with Szczecin and Warsaw. But in Warsaw there are Russian gangs too. There have been killings in the last weeks.'

'Is there a Godfather in Gdansk?'

'Of course. But I cannot talk about it.'

Miroslaw touched my arm. Mr Swiatecki was a busy man. So was Miroslaw for that matter. Couldn't stand around in jewellery boutiques all day. As we left, the pop promoter said: 'Remember, I would be grateful for serious contacts. Not . . . not Turkish people, you know.'

Back in the car park the air was fresh, just cleaned by the rain. Miroslaw was pleased with the way things were going.

'You see, I know many people. All the important people, they know Miroslaw. But Mr Swiatecki is a good man. He is clever, too clever to be in the mafia.'

We headed north, parallel to the shore. Between us and the sea, on the right hand side, there was an area of woodland, and beyond it another hotel, more solid than the Poseidon but equally dull.

'The Marina,' said Miroslaw. 'If they are not at the Poseidon, maybe the Marina.' It was a squat block of light-brown stone with tinted brown windows. Mercedes clucked around its entrance ramp.

Miroslaw stopped while we were still in the wood and pointed across the road at a modern white house behind metal railings. A red Opel Kadett and a metallic blue Mercedes jeep were parked outside the railings under trees. There was also a closed garage.

'You asked Swiatecki about the Godfather,' said Miroslaw. 'This is where he lives.'

'How do you know?'

'I believe he killed his first wife. I asked her mother for information but she was afraid to speak to me.'

'Do you think I can take a picture?'

'Take it.'

Miroslaw was being very calm; no hurry, no melodrama. It was infectious. I walked back into the wood a bit, photographed the house and cars, and wrote a few notes in my book for the benefit of watching heavies.

We strode fearlessly on to the Marina, which Miroslaw said was good for high-class whores. He'd known one as a friend, having sided with her against racketeers who had banned her from the Marina for not paying them their cut. The racketeers included the police. Miroslaw had written to a police chief in Warsaw. Warsaw had done nothing. Miroslaw and his mother kept getting threatening phone calls from the local police. The woman had left town.

Miroslaw seemed to live on championing lost causes, including perhaps his own. He was a brave and natural stirrer.

There was no doubt that he 'knew people'. Within seconds of our scruffy entrance into the Marina's principle lounge a body-built man in a swirly silk shirt had crunched our hands and was answering Miroslaw's question, grinning. This man ran the Marina's nightclub. No, no one of interest was here right now . . . but the Godfather was definitely in town.

They excused themselves and went off to talk further without attracting attention. When Miroslaw came back his deep-set eyes were wide with excitement.

'We go downstairs. What my friend tells me is very interesting. Yes, I am shocked.'

The Marina was busy compared with the Poseidon. Poles in West German clothes in the colours of expensive mustards had been swaggering around the reception. Downstairs, rich youth sprawled flirtatiously over sofas and two commercial-looking women dressed in vinyl sat at the bar by the gym. Miroslaw said he knew the barman but the barman didn't want to talk, so we found an empty sofa.

'He is my friend, the barman. You know why he didn't talk? You saw those men who came to the bar?' I had seen them arrive just after us, and had assumed they had a predilection for vinyl.

'They were policemen. Secret policemen. They want to know what we are doing.'

I wasn't sure myself what we were doing. 'What did your friend upstairs say that shocked you?' I asked.

Miroslaw hooked his elbow over the back of the sofa and instead of answering gazed in a worldly way at the rich young things – not because of secret policemen or mafia stooges but because it was part of his style to choose his own moment for the release of information.

'Down here you can see a lot of young people who spend a lot of money. One question I have: Where they got it?' (This was an opener; casual talk, fact of life. In the Poland of the Balcerowicz austerity plan, rich meant crooked.)

Eventually he told me what he had learned from Silk Shirt. The

Godfather had had to leave Poland in a hurry to get a new identity and passport – a West German one. But he was already back, driving a Corvette Stingray, with a Polish visa in a West German passport.

'One question I have: Who gave it to him?'

Miroslaw was referring to the visa. This was a story about a hefty bribe of a Polish consular official. Of *nomenklatura*, in other words.

'Phew,' I said.

'We go,' said Miroslaw. And as we went, a blue Corvette Stingray swept up the ramp into a reserved space by the door.

'That's him. Take it easy. I recognize him.'

We walked to the balustrade on the edge of the ramp and looked out at nothing in particular for a few long seconds. The driver's door opened and then clicked shut behind us.

'Act naturally,' said Miroslaw.

Slowly and extremely unnaturally we turned round. The driver had walked to the balustrade and was eyeballing us from behind dark glasses. Then he turned and walked inside, his pleated grey baggies billowing in the air-conditioner breeze.

We headed down the ramp towards the wood opposite the white house.

'HH PY 1486,' I said, pleased with myself. Miroslaw wrote down the number in his diary and began mumbling.

'Why did he come, at this moment? He was checking something. He knew we were there, I am sure.'

We turned left down a path to get off the road. The path led to a café where Miroslaw had been before, and we had a beer each, then tea, then Miroslaw had vodka. I was getting scared. Till a few minutes ago there had been the idea of fear, as seen on faces in films, and a trace of real anxiety. It had been difficult to separate the two. Now a series of just supposings trooped through my head. Just supposing Mr Swiatecki ran a comfy sideline finding customers for the man in the white house. Just supposing the closed garage beside the white house had contained a Corvette Stingray. Just supposing the arrival of the Stingray on the ramp had not been a coincidence.

At this point four dark young men in expensive leather jackets arrived at the table next to ours. Just supposing this was not coincidence either.

Miroslaw did not seem bothered by the dark young men, but he had read my mind.

'You know, life is sometimes like a play. Like one big show. It is a film and we are the actors.'

'Yes, but in fact this isn't a film,' I said.

'An old man, who is dead now, once came to my house. He was a fortune-teller and he said to me, "you have a special ghost: Security". Often I am in dangerous situation – like now, I am in danger, but . . . no problem.'

'Miroslaw,' I said, 'you may have that ghost but I haven't. What about these four people behind us, for instance?'

'I know the owner of this café. He is my friend.'

My fear was passing back from real to ideal. I said: 'You're right, this *is* like a film. English cyclist meets Polish journalist in Gdansk. They spend an afternoon looking for the mafia and next day the cyclist sets off for Warsaw but is unfortunately totalled by a truck. The journalist . . . what happens to the journalist?'

Miroslaw went to the bar for another vodka. When he came back he said, 'In life there are two ways, break or spirit. I never break.'

I was looking forward to the dark anonymity of a youth hostel after lights out, so when Miroslaw invited me back to his flat for the evening I declined, giving the hostel's curfew as an excuse. In fact most of my fellow hostellers were up late to watch England beat Cameroon in the World Cup quarter-final (England 3, Cameroon 2, two penalties by Lineker). It was a welcome change of atmosphere after the conspiracies and confusions of the afternoon, and all Miroslaw's real or imagined encounters with the forces of darkness.

On our way to the shipyard on Monday morning we made an unscheduled visit to Solidarity's national headquarters. Miroslaw could tell by the dark blue Lancia Thema parked outside that Walesa was in there somewhere. A quartet of his entourage, including his driver in check bermudas, talked quietly and exclusively on the first floor landing. A yellow corridor led away from here. The oxygenated blood of Solidarity's logo dripped off every office door. We stopped and loitered outside the Solidarity Sports Commission, where one of Miroslaw's former bosses was now in charge. He was busy with a French delegation, trying to wheel them in to see Walesa, and was clearly a little dismayed to see Miroslaw.

Miroslaw talked fast, extravagantly dropping the name of the venerable British newspaper whose name featured on my T-shirt. He earned us the promise of a second hearing. There was a shadow of a chance that we might slide in to see Walesa with the French delegation. We continued loitering, and busy men and women opened and closed doors and did the gait of the employed up and down the echoing corridor.

Walesa's old driver from the pre-Lancia days was greeted by Miroslaw as a buddy and indeed had time for a few pleasantries. With a hard-edged laugh Miroslaw tried to suggest that the two of them were in the same boat – the one marked 'discards' – but the ex-driver would have nothing of it and was soon off down the corridor.

'These people,' Miroslaw hissed. 'They know me from the year eighty, eighty-one, but now they pretend I am nothing. Excuse me. Yes? We wait a little longer. It's a little play by me.' He was using me, or my T-shirt, to show this corridor of power that Miroslaw Sarnecki still counted for something. He admitted this on the spot. I felt my shorts must be letting him down.

The second hearing never came, so we stalked off before the brush-off was formally delivered. Miroslaw was upset. I bought a Solidarity badge and sticker on the way out and he said, 'It means nothing now.' Walking past Alexandra's building to the shipyard entrance he talked in harsh spurts about his future. It was bleak . . . and it would have nothing to do with Solidarity.

Miroslaw had to get clearance from the director himself to get us into the shipyard, and in the process he got us a formal interview. I was still in shorts. Passing a billboard-full of massive tonnages sold to the world since the war, and walking up the dark wood staircase of the administration building, past silent, framed black-and-white photographs of megalithic new ships splashing into the Baltic, I tried to think of questions.

There was no need. Hans Bernard Syze is too smart to let

anyone feel inadequate in his presence. At the varnished door of his vast office we looked each other quickly up and down. His silver beard and weathered smoker's face made compulsive viewing. He wore a cream-coloured blazer, black trousers and slip-on shoes with tassels. He took in my travelling garb but never commented on it. He sat down in front of a model of a container ship in a glass box. Miroslaw sat in front of a conference table on which stood a tidy row of Pepsi Cola bottles, of which he requested one. I sat in front of a supertanker.

Mr Syze spent thirty years in the design office before his impeccably non-Communist credentials qualified him for a swift shift into Poland's most political industrial job.

'I was never in the party and fight always with the Communists. I am, in the year eighty, eighty-one, close to Solidarity, and now also.'

I asked him if the government subsidized the shipyard and he replied patiently that it was more a case of the shipyard subsidizing the government.

He explained how business is conducted with his biggest client, Russia.

When the Kremlin or one of its tentacles places an order, the ships are handed over not to the Russians but to the Polish government, which barters them for commodities like oil and grain. The shipyard's payment comes mostly from Warsaw in non-convertible zlotys (for wages), plus a nominal amount of special convertible roubles to cover cabin trimmings bought in the West. So the shipyard gets what it needs, not what it earns, and the State gets the difference.

'Subsidies? What subsidies?' asked Mr Syze. His fine silver eyebrows flicked up, crinkling his forehead and apparently saying 'Yes, I know it's crazy'.

In my dimness I never asked the most obvious question, which would have been: Mr Syze, is the Solidarity government going to force job losses in the very shipyard where ten years ago Solidarity was formed to protect and improve workers' livelihoods?

Mr Syze answered the question anyhow. He volunteered a spiel on his hunt for a thousand extra workers to make a full-strength one-shift workforce which would produce twenty ships a year.

The yard had gone into liquidation in 1989 and welders had sought work as taxi-drivers; labourers had joined the trainloads queuing up outside the pawn shops of West Berlin.

But it's a boom time internationally for shipbuilding, said Mr Syze. Most of Poland's economy may be in crisis but Polish ships are world class – and competitively priced because the shipyard workers earn a twentieth of average Western wages.

'No wonder they prefer to work as taxi-drivers,' I said.

'That's the next problem. About payment. What I do in the shipyards last month? I increase the payment about 60 per cent. Not for everyone; for some 80, for some 20.' Foremen now earned more than workers and Mr Syze, who had been earning less than his driver, got three and a half times the average wage.

Was he popular?

He lit a cigarette, disappearing briefly behind the smoke, and compared himself to Lech Walesa. People who move on and up on the strength of local popularity risk losing it, he explained. 'Very many in the shipyard say "Why Walesa go to the national organization? He must stay here, only in the shipyard", and that is the mentality. If I was only a designer maybe I have a good opinion. But I think General Director never have good opinion.'

Miroslaw had sipped his Pepsi to the bottom.

Mr Syze summoned a guide with whom we headed for the clamour of dry dock three, where the hull of a timber-carrier for Russia was smothered in scaffolding. It would be plying the Red Sea to Africa or Southern Asia. You could tell by the hole in the prow for a special Suez Canal light – an old British regulation.

The cranes, which you can see from almost anywhere in Gdansk, rolled along overgrown rails, casually swinging monstrous asymmetric chunks of steel marked with yellow paint and chalk. After the war the Russians had marked steel to go east as reparations, on the grounds that Gdansk had been a German port. But the Polish marked it back, said the guide. 'To take steel marked "Gdansk Shipyard" is to take part of Poland.'

We called on Darius, who repairs electric trolleys and used to have Lech Walesa as a workmate. We boarded the *Pagoria,* a three-masted square-rigger once used exclusively by Party General Secretary Gierek but now a sail-training ship for international youth and a regular at Tall Ships' races. We ran our fingers along the baize-topped tables in the conference hall where Solidarity presented its Twenty-One Wishes to the Communists in 1980. Upstairs in the museum, behind a scale model of the innards of a factory ship built, like the ship itself, by shipyard workers, we saw a bronze tablet to V.I. Lenin, removed from the main gate on 27 January 1990.

Miroslaw was beat. He had stopped talking. He was tired of my questions and I was tired of asking them. We thanked our guide and went for a late lunch at Michal's, Miroslaw's favourite restaurant in Gdansk. To be uncharitable, it was where he took visitors who would be paying.

Among many citations to Miroslaw in the restaurant's visitors' book was one from Riotaro Takawa of Japan:

'3 March. The day of fiesta for girls in Japan. It is my great pleasure to come and eat at this kitchen or restaurant. Dishes are very nice and good atmosphere. It is only one day in Gdansk but I feel very nice to come to Gdansk. Surely I want to stay here longer. I am fully satisfied with everything at Gdansk. I would like to say "Thankyou very much for everything, Miroslaw."'

Miroslaw remembered Riotaro fondly.

We ate roll-mops in sour cream for starters. Then we had meat in breadcrumbs, with boiled potatoes, coleslaw, and grated carrot. After two beers and two vodkas Miroslaw said he had been close to nervous exhaustion, but that with food and drink his energy was returning.

He wrote his name in full in my notebook and annotated it. 'Miroslaw' – 'peace'. 'Piotr' – 'Apostle of truth'.

'And I am another,' he said, meaning he was another apostle of truth.

'You pay now,' he announced after a long and absorbed silence. 'We visit Spirit Father of Solidarity.'

Miroslaw wanted to net the big one; the man on whom Bush, Thatcher, and the Pope had all called when in Gdansk, the man with the bronze figure of Father Popieluszko lying in his church, the wielder of the Catholic block vote, Father Henryk Jankowski. I was still in shorts.

We loitered on the front steps of the expensively-restored period house in which Father Jankowski had his office. At about

eight he appeared, walking home. Jankowski, like Walesa, looked
overweight on power. Miroslaw fell into step alongside him. He
made an efficient, ingratiating pitch and was answered with a nod
and a word or two. We had an interview at eight the next
morning.

There was just one hitch. Miroslaw did not appear next morning and Father Jankowski spoke no English. An assistant translated the gist of his remarks, but the interview was still a
wash-out.

An American called Douglas sat beside me at Father Jankowski's round oak table. He looked like Chevy Chase and had been
travelling for fifteen months having put his legal practice in
storage in southern California. Miroslaw and I had met him the
previous evening when, looking back, Miroslaw must have had
an eye out for new clients for his guiding services, in view of my
imminent departure. Miroslaw had invited Douglas along to this
interview as a no-obligation taster.

After the interview Douglas and I went and stuffed ourselves
with a kind of take-away rhubarb crumble.

'I thought any moment we were going to be ejected from the
premises as frauds,' said Douglas. I confessed I was getting used
to feeling like a fraud.

We arranged to meet a week hence in Warsaw – which we failed
to do – and I left town, heading east, wondering what had
happened to Miroslaw.

I passed a sign saying 974 kilometres to Budapest and turned left
to follow the coast.

Beyond the Vistula, which had to be crossed on a ferry, the
coast road warmed to its task. It passed bucket-and-spade shops,
doughnut shops and the ends of sand tracks leading to beaches. It
passed boys in bermudas and girls with their mums. To the left,
the horizon was always low, being at sea level. In the middle of
the afternoon I rode down there for a swim. The sea was warm
and there was no one else on the beach, which led directly to the
Soviet Union. I balanced my camera on one piece of driftwood to
take a picture of me and my shoes on another.

Mazuria

Nowhere is faraway any more when you get there. The fact of being in a place erases impressions you may have formed of it from a distance. So it was with Mazuria, hard by Russia, under Lithuania.

I had imagined Mazuria as a forgotten corner of Europe. Remote, lonely and beautiful. The only thing I knew about it was from an old school dates sheet. 1916 – Battle of the Mazurian Lakes. They were going to be a find.

Certainly, this part of Europe is not oppressively populated. The land is beginning to stretch out and change scale; to spread itself under vast flat skies. After all, it must eventually become Asia. But it is neither lonely nor forgotten. Half of Warsaw takes its holidays in Mazuria.

From the lonely Baltic beach I rode to Morag (pronounced Moron). For much of the way the roads were lined with tall grass or nettles which swayed away in a single endless wave when tractors passed. If a tractor was going my way along the flat I would sit in its slipstream. Half an hour like that could mean twenty effortless miles. Beyond the grass and nettles were endless flat fields, and usually woods somewhere in the distance.

In the town of Morag I looked around desperately for a television. England was playing Germany in the semi-final of the World Cup. Two boys and a girl in the otherwise deserted town centre took pity on me. The boys were admirers on holiday but the girl actually lived there, and we went and joined her big brothers in front of the family television.

It was nil-all at full time and nil-all after extra time. The teams shook hands. From here on it was a question of luck. In the shoot-out, Chris Waddle hoisted his penalty over the goal and into the crowd. Germany won. Gazza's tears at being booked turned to tears of grief in defeat.

There was no commiseration in the sitting room in Morag; my hosts supported Germany. I thanked them and pedalled into the night towards Lake Narie.

Not just Mazuria but the entire North European Plain from Schwerin to Vilnius is awash with lakes. After the ice age, retreating glaciers left puddles instead of valleys. But the puddles have almost infinitely complicated shapes, like molasses trickled over a pan of snow.

I woke up on a grassy bank overlooking Lake Narie. Forest flowed over shallow undulations to its shores. A smart breeze whipped off its surface. Behind me were three rows of cabins made of breeze blocks. Their occupants presently emerged and went to breakfast in a communal dining room, one of them pausing to ask if I was from Polish Railways. The cabins and the grassy bank, as it turned out, were Polish Railways' property, but a little way along the shore there was a public campsite: a conurbation of tents, caravans, and bungalows occupying a whole peninsula. There were two discos, a kiosk selling shampoo and cigarettes, a food shop, pedalos, and an acre or two of lake was enclosed by a catwalk for swimming.

Back on my slope a group of railway children had decorated my bike with red roses. We used my rolled-up bivvi bag as an American football and played badminton without a net.

That evening I visited the larger of the two discos. I was impressed by the sophistication of its other patrons, whose aver-age age looked to be about sixteen. They smoked. They drank Pepsi. If male, they wore jeans and shirts with button-down collars. If female they wore tight tubular skirts which stopped at the top of the thigh. They exuded disco cool. They had rhythm. Dancing-wise, they were comfortable with rap and acid but they knew some real rock and roll as well. Bar mine there was not an unhip haircut in the house.

'Why don't you dance?' asked a waitress, and I took the question as rhetorical.

Next morning the same waitress served me an ogre's breakfast in the same place – which served as a restaurant during daylight hours. Through the glass wall which last night had been reflecting pumping bodies and crazy lights, lay the lake, mysterious again.

If you flew over it, low, in a propeller plane, and continued east over Rivers Pasleka, Lyna and Dajna, and over the town of Ketrzyn, and landed on a secret strip in the forest near Gierloz, you would be doing what Hitler did innumerable times between 1939 and 1945. In German the forest's name is Gorlitz, and in those years it hid the Wolf's Lair. Hitler ran the war from a group of concrete bunkers between Ketrzyn and Lake Dargin, twenty miles south of the modern Soviet border.

On the way to Gorlitz, the road swung into a lazy series of chicanes through a village consisting mostly of barns. I eyed them as potential places to sleep. Hay was the thing to look for; warm, dry, comfortable hay. It was late afternoon and drizzling.

In the doorway of the biggest barn some men were drinking their way through a crate of apple wine and eating tinned meat on bread. There was no bar in the village. The barn did instead. No one left it sober. A short and mildly deranged fellow in dungarees pretended to be mending a motorbike but pulled off the exhaust pipe and fell back into the hay. A little slapstick goes a long way on apple wine. It had to be curbed, however, when the owner of the barn arrived looking relatively suave in a clean blue T-shirt, to share a glass and make sure we weren't smoking in the hay.

One of the drinkers invited me to sleep at his house (in '*eleganz*'; it was unthinkable to sleep in a barn). Another (the owner of the barn-owner?) must have reported me to the police. Two plain-clothes officers arrived in a Lada around midnight and asked to see my passport. Jerzy, the one who was providing the '*eleganz*', looked on with a grave but still half-drunk expression. Perhaps he was thinking his trust had been betrayed. By a spy? Or a smuggler? More likely he wasn't thinking anything.

All was well with my passport.

'*Turist?*'

'Tourist.'

'Wo?'

'Ganz Ost-Europa.'

I showed the policemen my bicycle. One of them smiled and touched my arm, then they both left. Jerzy and I looked bewildered at each other and went back to sleep.

Mazuria is much more peaceful now than it was when the Red Army swept across it towards Danzig in 1945, destroying or confiscating everything the retreating *Wehrmacht* had not already destroyed, and gang-raping German women left behind.

Poland was wrecked by the war. Six million Polish citizens died. The casualty rate for the whole population was 18 per cent, compared with 0.2 per cent for the USA and 0.9 per cent for Britain. The Germans razed Warsaw. The Russians razed Danzig. In the words of Norman Davies, 'Poland became the killing ground of Europe, the new Golgotha.'

Ketrzyn (in German: Rastenburg) is the nearest town to Gorlitz Forest. Upstairs in its museum there is a map showing how the armies moved in 1945, and another of the concentration camps. Each major extermination camp was fed by a cluster of nearby forced-labour camps, but there were none near Rastenburg. Was it that Hitler could not have the stench from the gas oven chimneys drifting over the lakes and forests of East Prussia, the land once administered from Malbork by the Teutonic Knights themselves?

A great black steam engine emitted black smoke and gunshot bangs as it pulled away from the the remains of Hitler's hideout. This place is a major local asset. Twenty buses were parked on a square of tarmac from which a path led innocently away past two cafés and under the trees to the bunkers. I had not been there two minutes when a man with a moustache homed in.

'Was wollen Sie? Welche Sprache sprechen Sie?'

'Englisch.'

'English. OK. You wanna guided tour? You wan' liderachur? You come to my van.'

He was holding a kind of seminar with some West Germans in a West German camper van. I gave him two dollars for some photocopied sheets; an essay, published in an American Forces military history journal, which he said he had written himself. The essay was mostly about the July Plot.

On the morning of 20 July 1944, in a briefcase under a map table in a temporary conference room in the compound in Gorlitz Forest, a bomb exploded a few yards from Hitler and failed to kill him. That night Colonel Claus von Stauffenberg, who planted the bomb, was shot along with several accomplices.

Mussolini paid a flying visit the next day and Hitler boasted to him of his immortality. The war dragged on. As many lives were lost and as much property was destroyed in its last year as in its first four combined. Conventional wisdom says Hitler survived the blast because an open window and the map table deprived it of its full impact. The man in the camper van believed that Stauffenberg, in his bedroom, had been arming a second bomb which he intended to put in the same briefcase, when he heard footsteps in the corridor and snapped the briefcase shut. The meeting was due to start and he could not be late. The second bomb, which would have made an irrelevance of map tables and open windows, was left behind.

The Wolf's Lair was dynamited as it was evacuated. Lumps of concrete the size of double-decker buses remain among the trees, covered in lichen and sprouting tangles of reinforcing rods. These were the bunkers' walls. It is very difficult, leaning against one and watching the squirrels, to picture the last moments of the July Plot, but you can't help trying.

It would have been jollier to see Mazuria by boat like everybody else. There are many more acres of water than miles of road. Canals link the lakes where natural channels don't, and – this is the jolly part – you have to lower your mast to pass under the bridges. I took endless pictures of white sails against distant forested shores but they all came out as tiny dots, seeking out the secret places other forms of transport cannot reach.

Avenues of ash and lime shaded the roads and geese ruled the farmyards. It was a Sunday afternoon. The farmers were drinking – on benches, in ditches, along lakefronts, in bars.

I came to a proud old inn set back from the road. A cart was loading up with drunkards. The driver flicked the reins, the horse began pulling, and I took a picture. This was a mistake. Two young men jumped down and demanded my film. One of them imitated a Westerner laughing at a picture of a drunken Pole. I apologized. He said apologies were all very well. Give me the film or I smash your camera. He was not steady on his feet, but he was bale-heaving, bullock-shoving muscular. I tried not understanding and grinned like an imbecile. Eventually the punitive resolve of the second man broke and he held the other back while I escaped. I rode very fast to the town of Mikolajki and hid in the Taverna Lady Mary.

Through the taverna's window, out on a long arm of Lake Sniardwy, scores of dinghies heeled over, went about and ran before the wind. Along the jetties the bronzed shoulders of sailing bums kept a crowd of hire boats in order, and couples strolled the lakefront licking soft ice-creams.

A black earth track leads out of Mikolajki to the east towards another lake; small, round, shallow, shrinking, fringed with reeds and scarcely visited. It is home to Europe's largest community of wild swans. Wild swans! What grace and power, what awesome presence on the wing!

I never saw one. The light was fading by the time I reached the lake. The black earth had turned to sand, the sand to a mere path, and the path to duckboards leading to a hide. Not a swan in sight. Just the low orange sun and its reflection.

The real discovery that evening was a house at the beginning of the path. To say it was a field station belonging to Warsaw University's Department of Biology does not quite convey the romance of the place. It was a large house of exquisite proportions, miles from anywhere and covered in ivy. The garden was an oasis of lawns and lilies surrounded by woods and ragged meadowland. In the middle of the front lawn, under an enormous beech tree, a small group of students were taking tea on a rug. One of them wore a spotted neckerchief and was playing the guitar.

He and a friend called Lukasz (Polish for Lucas, pronounced Wukash) overtook me in a Polski Fiat on the way back to Mikolajki and invited me to stay the night. I continued to Mikolajki to watch the World Cup Final. Germany beat Argentina 1-0 with a penalty, and as Franz Beckenbauer and his boys dipped their heads in Rome the camera looked out of the stadium into the night and zoomed in on an aeroplane flying across a yellow moon. The same yellow moon hung over the Mazurian Lakes as I returned to the ivy-covered house by swan lake. Lukasz and friends were waiting up with canapés and vodka.

Warsaw

Mlawa is about half-way from Mazuria to Warsaw. It had been a flat day's ride getting there, most of it through logging country. In a restaurant in the town square I ordered *bigos*, which consists of shredded cabbage, sometimes verging on sauerkraut, with bits of meat and often mashed potato. *Bigos* is the biz. I got a smile out of the sullen waitress by asking for seconds, then I went for a walk round the square. There was a graffiti message on the church – 'RAP IS KING' – and there was a late night shop. Mlawans could buy chocolate, biscuits, pink plastic shoes, and vodka till eight at night.

It was nearly dark in Mlawa. The great northern sky was inky over the restaurant and dappled gold by the sunken sun over the late night shop.

Writ large in the back of my notebook was the following: CZY MOGE PRZENOCOWAC W STODOLE? which means roughly, PLEASE MAY I SLEEP IN YOUR BARN? It was time to try speaking Polish.

I rode out of town and down a farm track. Four drunk men tumbled out of a farmhouse.

'*Czy moge przenocowac w stodole?*'

Bingo. They understood. There were three barns, and a lean blond man with bleached eyebrows and bare feet showed them all off. No mountains of hay, just livestock; big pigs, small pigs, pink pigs, black and white pigs. There was shit and straw on the floor and an acrid smell of shit and piss heavy in the air. Mr

92

Barefoot waded through it all unconcerned. There was also a dovecot and a rabbit hutch. Barefoot kept stabbing his chest with a finger, to mean 'Mine, all mine'.

After the tour we rejoined the other three men and the wife of one of them in the kitchen. The kitchen was a yellow-lit cube with one door in from the passage and another out to a bedroom. There was room for a small square table, three stools and a sink. On the table were an empty vodka bottle and glasses and the remains of an onion sandwich.

Mr Barefoot seemed to be doing stretching exercises. He was reaching backwards into the corners of the room with both arms. First one corner, then another. Everyone had to duck. All the time his eyes were fixed hopefully on me, and he seemed to think a huge laugh was coming up. I twigged.

'Goalie?'

'Goalie goalie goalie!'

'Shilton, yes?'

'SHILTON!'

We established that 'goalie', 'Shilton', 'Lineker', 'penalty' and 'corner' were the words we had in common and that Mr Barefoot was a bit of a goalie himself. Then he asked me for money for more vodka, which started a row by embarrassing the others. One of them seemed to fear for the very honour of Poland if it took money from a stranger for vodka. Mr Barefoot apologized and announced to the wife (it was still unclear whose she was) that I would be sleeping in the house.

It was good to know I wouldn't be with the pigs, but next day I wrote earnestly in my notebook: 'the typical Polish farming family seems to consist of a hospitable alcoholic husband and a haggard, sober, overworked wife. In taking advantage of the hospitality I am abusing the wife.'

I did not know at the time that lice had crawled out of Mr Barefoot's sheets and into various hair follicles about my person, where they were to itch on and off for five months.

As I crossed the Vistula just inside Warsaw's city limits at about eight in the evening, the sun was arc-welding a band of grey cloud to the horizon. Broad rays of grey and gold fanned down over the river like a cardinal's Whitsun vestment. From the bridge, central

Warsaw looked like an American downtown, with the difference that the second tallest skyscraper was the palace of culture, built in the oppressively symmetrical neo-classical style of Stalin's era. Every side-wing and pillar is designed to draw the eye up, up, up the central phallus to the red star at the top.

Opposite the palace of culture I could see the Marriott Hotel, Poland's biggest, modernest, bravest hard cash syphon. It is a symbol for all that is brash in the New Poland, for all that is optimistic about the long term and shady in the short. I caught a whiff of high life there before my stay in Warsaw ended, but I started modestly, on the sixth floor of a solid grey monolith directly opposite the former headquarters of the Polish Communist Party; the youth hostel.

Most of the hostel's inmates were Polish and quiet. They padded between the dormitories and the washrooms with fixed, serious expressions, or lay motionless on their narrow beds, reading books or staring at the ceiling. A small group of young American Euro-railers, however, talked.

'America *is* the land of opportunity,' concluded a Californian male, majoring in English and Business at UCLA, after describing to an Anglophone Pole how the $22 for his Polish visa, which might take a Pole ten days to earn, could be earned in the United States in two hours.

I could not decently eavesdrop all night, so I went to wash, and met another American with one foot in a basin. There were no showers. He saw my English toothpaste.

'This is pretty miserable, huh? I'm beginning to hate myself already. We deserve better than this.' I found myself agreeing, especially with the notion that grim conditions can make you hate *yourself*. It had been a hot ninety-mile day, and my infested crotch could have done with a bidet.

The wide pavements outside the department stores on the east side of Ulica Marszalkowska and the north side of Aleje Jerozolimskie seethe with desperate, make-ends-meet black market trade. Bread, fruit, chocolate, liquor, sandals, skateboards, cigarettes, pornography, water-heating elements . . . *anything* from West Germany will sell eventually. The Ladas, Polski Fiats and tarpaulined pick-ups that brought the stuff are bumped up off the

streets and often house the vendors' sleeping families. There is
latent anarchy, crisis, chaos. The rows of zeros on the bundles of
notes everywhere being nervously thumbed recall the crazy inflation which may return any day. For the visitor with hard cash
there is excitement in the exhaust-laden air. For most Poles there
is only worry. For a slick-suited, smooth-talking few, shaking
hands and talking in shorthand outside the international hotels,
there is fast money to be made. But not all of Warsaw is so hectic.

After one night in the youth hostel I moved in with Slawomir
Ponichtera. Slawomir, or Slawek, was married to one of the
students I had met by Lake Mikolajki. He lived with his parents in
a suburb of great grey blocks in the north of the city. The flat
consisted of five small, orderly rooms. There was no craving here for
electronic consumer goods, and everyone wore identical pyjamas.

Slawek was serious and devout. He had a thick black beard on a
thin white face and was at first very nervous about his English. He
had never met an Englishman, nor any Westerner for that matter.
But he soon forgot his nervousness. One evening he invited some
friends round for an evening of Anglo-Polish cultural exchange.
We told each other jokes. Slawek's contributions included a
minimalist gag which said much about the esteem in which
policemen were held in Poland by the end of Communist rule: 'A
policeman was thinking . . .' (End of joke.)

I offered 'why did the chicken cross the road?' and the follow-
up, 'why did the baby cross the road?' (answer: because it was
stapled to the chicken), which won delirious applause and was in
due course widely repeated by Slawek.

Taking this as a licence to talk about more or less anything, I
raised the subject of contraception and decided afterwards that
this may have been a mistake. There were gulps round the table,
and downcast eyes, and a rush of blood to the cheeks of one
fiancée present.

'I think this question is different in your country,' Slawek said.
'For us . . . for us there is no question. When we are married we
follow the instructions of the Pope. We go with the months of the
woman –'

'The rhythm method?'

'The rhythm method . . . And before we are married, like I say,
it is not a question.'

'But isn't the rhythm method difficult, unreliable?'

People exchanged glances. No, said Slawek. He was confident that he and Ewa (still in Mazuria on her field trip) would be using it to have two children and no more.

On another occasion, after Ewa had returned, Slawek showed her a copy of *Newsweek* I had bought in the Forum Hotel, opened at a table of data on rape in America. She handed it back after a few seconds, wincing.

'In Poland people don't really talk about that. Anything about man and woman together makes them go red. It is taboo.'

On balance Slawek was a serious person. In Warsaw it may even be difficult not to be a serious person if you are a thinking person too. The city has had a very tough twentieth century, including being flattened, street by street, by the occupying Germans in 1944.

By the summer of 1944 the Red Army had built up a certain vengeful momentum in the thousand miles and eighteen months which had brought it from Stalingrad to the east bank of the Vistula. It was only a matter of time before the *Wehrmacht* withdrew from Warsaw, but when it did, Stalin knew it might prove difficult to install the right sort of Polish administration – a Russophile one – in its place. He had one ready, arriving with his troops: the Polish Committee of National Liberation (PKWN).

However, few Poles in Warsaw wanted a Communist government answering to Moscow any more than they had enjoyed the Nazi Occupation. Hidden within the city were 150,000 men of the Polish Home Army, under General Bor-Komorowski. It fell to him to choose the moment for the Poles to re-take their city; the moment of least German resistance before the arrival of the Russians. Bor-Komorowski heard of von Stauffenberg's attempt on Hitler's life on 20 July and took it as a sign that the *Wehrmacht* was cracking. On the 31st a patrol of T-34 tanks was sighted just east of the city and Bor-Komorowski gave the order for Operation Tempest to start at five the next afternoon.

A quarter of a million civilians died in the sixty-three days of the Warsaw Uprising and when the remains of the Home Army capitulated on 2 October Hitler ordered that the city be razed without trace. The Russians then trundled into the rubble with the PKWN. The rump of the Home Army fled to Hammersmith, where it has been ever since. And the re-building of Warsaw began, with a little help on points of detail from Canaletto's paintings.

The 'Old' Town Square, none of which is more than forty-five years old, is formed on all sides of tall, thin townhouses with triangular tops to their façades, reminiscent of Amsterdam. The surfaces are brick or painted plaster. The square itself is made of flagstones.

Homeless people sat in the narrow streets leading to the square holding pieces of cardboard saying, in English, that they had AIDS and were hungry. Slawek said the bit about AIDS was not always to be believed, but it elicited shocked sympathy from Western tourists. In the square there were long queues for ice-cream. A procession of white golf buggies tootled in from the Marriott Hotel, bearing a jazz band and advertising the hotel's new casino.

We walked north to the Barbican, the re-built 'remains' of the city wall. Following the wall west a little way, Slawek stopped at a modern café outside the wall.

'What do you see?'

I saw a café. Slawek pointed to the right of it, to a bed of red and yellow tulips. Beside it there was a small plaque with this sign: $\mathcal{W}$ (P.W. – for *Polska Walczeca* – Fighting Poland.) You see the sign wherever Poles lost their lives in significant numbers during the war. Slawek said that 500 had been gunned down at this spot during the Rising of 1944.

'There are many, many such places,' he said. 'Old people pause and pray when they pass these places, but young people don't feel anything.'

He went on to say, quite casually, that he had distributed *samizdat* newspapers at school when he was sixteen. He would pick them up from a friend and leave them tucked under the hinged flaps of their old-fashioned desks, and also in the teachers' desks.

'We used the old Fighting Poland symbol,' Slawek remembered. I said he must be proud. He said, 'it's history', but he said it in a tone which simply meant 'it's over'.

The students at the field station by swan lake had given me some other names to look up when I got to Warsaw, and one of these was Jolanta.

Jolanta worked for a foreign trade organization on the top floor of an office building off Warsaw's only ritzy shopping street, Nowy Swiat. She updated a contacts book of eco-caring Poles in her spare time. She was tall, sallow, un-made-up, and smoked. She rippled with gobsmacking stories, evenly delivered, about threatened bats and the misuse of environmental aid money.

High-grade concrete intended for the reactor-lining at the Zarnowiec nuclear power station had found its way into the beach houses of local bureaucrats. Untold millions of Swedish crowns intended to clean up industrial Silesia had been turned into chalets in the foothills of the Tatra mountains. The Minister of Environmental Protection was not protecting the environment. He was learning English in the country residence of his English counterpart. The Rockefeller and Ford dynasties were backing the export to Poland of insecticides too lethal to be allowed anywhere else in the world.

Jolanta sat with one long leg over the other and exhaled. I took a moment to think of my question.

'Do you know Radek Gawlik?'

'Yes, of Freedom and Peace.'

Gawlik was an anti-Zarnowiec MP. Freedom and Peace was an environmental organization based in Wroclaw whose members called themselves eco-commandos. The Zarnowiec nuclear power station was the current *cause célèbre* for Polish Greens. In 1989 the decision had been taken to scrap the power station altogether as the site straddled a tectonic faultline, the disposal of nuclear waste would be problematic, and Poland did not need another nuclear power station. Unfortunately, the (Solidarity-backed) Industry Minister prevaricated – to save jobs and perhaps as a result of pressure from civil servants of the old regime.

'Try the Parliament Hotel,' Jolanta said. 'And if Radek isn't there, ask for Jacek. Jacek Szymanderski.' Radek, Jacek, Slawek. Heroic names.

I walked down Nowy Swiat past a Benetton boutique and an 'American Reading Room' full of Poles reading Polish newspapers. The Parliament Hotel is across Jerozolimskie and then some way beyond it; a discreet, expensive building faced in white marble. It is where MPs stay when in Warsaw; not signposted and not open to the public. I told a policeman I was looking for Mr Gawlik, and he let me in.

'Mr Gawlik is in Wroclaw,' they said at reception.

'And Mr Szymanderski?'

'He may be in the *Sejm*. You can ask in the lobby there.'

The receptionist pointed through a glass wall at the back of the foyer to the Parliament building itself, then to an indoor ramp leading out of the hotel. I walked down it, under the street, and up into Parliament. It seemed rather easy. I might as well have been a terrorist.

'*Djin dobre . . .*'

A guard appeared from nowhere and continued talking in Polish until I said:

'Um. English. Jacek Szymanderski?'

Szymanderski was hauled out of a parliamentary debate on higher education, for which he said he was grateful. But he seemed rapidly to decide that he was not my man, or that I was not his.

He whizzed me along a semi-circular corridor behind the debating chamber – *the* corridor of power, this, full of craggy public faces and whispering cabals in alcoves. We stepped round television lights and cameramen pointing their equipment through oak-panelled doors over the delegates' tiered seating to the podium. I must admit I felt pretty much at the centre of things in this corridor. Poland was between eras. Everything, from the constitution down, was up for grabs, and this is where the grabbing happened. No wonder Szymanderski had better things to do than speculate about building sites with me.

We were heading for the parliamentary restaurant to find someone who could help me, really help me. (Szymanderski oozed politesse.) Now, where the devil was he? At a corner table. We walked over red carpet towards it. Szymanderski introduced me to an MP in a forester's uniform. Then he oozed some thanks and left.

The forester talked dismissively about Zarnowiec:

'It is a case of new versus old thinking. It is a remnant of the whole Communist approach, which was based on grand-scale investment in heavy industry while development in the West went in the direction of effectiveness and productivity. Now the West has won. Zarnowiec will die.'

On my last day in Warsaw I rode my bike into town because the trams weren't working, and got a puncture. I hauled the bike across the marble forecourt of the Marriott and one of the doormen, in a dazzling white suit with a red hat and plume, stepped forward.

'May I park your vehicle for you, sir?'

I thanked him for the thought, mended the puncture in the hotel garage, and took the oportunity to visit the casino.

I knew the manager was English. They'd told me at the Forum, where I'd known the manager was also English because they'd told me in Gdansk. (All over Poland there are casinos managed by Englishmen; Poles have decided since Communism that they like gambling and the English seem to have cornered the international casino job market.)

Suggestions on entering the Marriott: Notice the air-conditioning begin to act like a tranquillizer. Admire yourself in the polished lift doors. Ride the moving staircase up the side of the four-storey atrium. Trail your finger up the marble balustrade. Savour the calm. Stroll round to the casino.

'Sorry sir, no shorts.'

'That's fine,' I said. 'I'll come back later.'

The Liverpudlian assistant manager watched me.

'Are you the manager?' I asked.

'That's Mr Maclean, sir. Kevin Maclean.'

'Is he . . . is he talkative? Excuse my asking. I was hoping to interview him.'

'That a fact? Kev's your man then. Talk the hind leg . . . yep definitely. Kev's your man.'

I returned at midnight in grey flannel trousers and a herringbone jacket borrowed from Slawek.

Kevin Maclean was indeed a talker. He had a piping voice and chipmunk cheeks which made him look as if he was sucking toffees. He sat me at a bar with a view of someone he was watching, and told his story.

At seventeen he took up mock auctioneering on the Blackpool

Golden Mile. 'Mock auctioneer' is what he called the person who sells kitchen rejects off the back of a lorry and takes the price down instead of up.

'It was all about talk, and I didn't just kiss the Blarney, I swallowed it. I earned a lot of money in those days, and lost it in casinos.' He paused and looked up across the casino. 'I did have one good win.' He paused again. 'See the gentleman in front of us, on blackjack? He's twenty thousand up tonight.'

'Twenty thousand?'

'Dollars. He's been playing half an hour. Doing very well.'

'Will you let him . . . Is there a problem?'

'Best advert we could have is somebody winning like that. It encourages everybody else. Yes, I did have one good win. A thousand pounds in Leeds, when a thousand pounds could buy you something. I went crazy for about a week. I hired a minibus – took the family to see Shirley Bassey at the Batley Variety Club.'

Someone in a tuxedo dropped a quiet word in Kevin's ear. He excused himself to sign out a new tray of five hundred-dollar chips for the man on blackjack, and to assign a senior dealer to the table. The man in question was a pro, on his first night at the Marriott. He had a heavy gold watch and smoked Camels.

Kevin returned. 'I've already said good evening to him and he won't pay for any drinks tonight. We'll send drinks over to his room as well. Compliments of the house. Keep him happy. Keep them happy and they'll always come back.' He pointed out the man's assistant, standing at his shoulder and periodically removing stacks of chips to cash them in. Among Poles, this pair was exceptional.

'Poles are very shrewd,' said Kevin. 'If they want to gamble, usually they'll sit down with perhaps a hundred dollars. If they win fifty on that they'll go home. They've just turned over a month's salary in a matter of minutes.'

Kevin had worked in the Baghdad Sheraton under missile bombardment from Iran. He had worked at the Nairobi Safari Park and Country Club and ridden at Adnan Kashoggi's ranch under Mount Kenya. Most recently, he had married one of his quinqualingual Polish croupiers. It was all very different from the Blackpool Golden Mile. When we finished talking the man with the Camels was forty thousand up.

'Try your luck,' said Kevin.

A little extra cash would bave been useful. I bought 28 dollars' worth of chips with a 50 D-mark note and lost them all in three cautious goes on roulette.

The professional had moved to roulette too, taking with him a small crowd of spectators. For a while I watched him slide his red and black stacks across the baize and smile thinly when admonished for exceeding maximums. As I was leaving to catch a night bus to Slawek's flat for the last time Kevin touched me on the shoulder.

'Thought you might like to know he's lost it all,' he said.

The Vistula

Over some of its length, as it nears the Baltic Sea, the Vistula flows down a gradient of 0.002 per cent. At this rate it would have to flow for 50,000 miles to lose one vertical mile in height. Even over its central section between Cracow and Warsaw the slope is a relaxed 0.02 per cent, or one mile down for every five thousand along.

The Vistula is no torrent, yet neither is it stagnant. Over its 630 miles from the Beskidy Mountains to Gdansk it moves at an average speed of 2.6 feet per second, which can seem surprisingly fast when swum in.

It was night when I swam in it. The current was fearsome and the water oily black. I had over-eaten, as usual, and feared a cramp attack at any second. With me was a young man named Wojciech from the nearby town of Annopol. He knew the river, and said comfortingly that the biggest fish caught in these parts in recent years had been a mere two and a half metres long.

I was trying to impress a girl. Her name was Margareta and she stood on the bank with her sister, Wojciech's girlfriend. Margareta had watched the teen pelvo-thrust movie *Dirty Dancing* twenty times and she seemed, gratifyingly, to be projecting onto me her fantasies about its star, the rump-steak buttocked, sirloin-chested Patrick Swayze.

'I am Jennifer Gray,' said Margareta.

'And you can call me Patrick Swayze,' said I.

We danced the mambo in her sister's bedroom, and Wojciech,

looking on, had then informed me she was only twelve years old.
It must have been my brand new lycra shorts that did it.

The lycra shorts were the result of an emergency trip to West
Berlin. I had dashed back to the Western world for two days, on
the night train from Warsaw, to sort out the problem of my
itching. But on the big day the lice had gone to ground. The scene
in the genito-urinary department of the Polyklinik Charlotten-
burg went roughly as follows:

I was standing. The consultant kneeled and peered through his
tortoise-shell spectacles.

'Mm. I see nussing. I must examine your prostate. Please lean
over the couch, your legs apart a little.'

Prostate? Where, exactly . . .?

Rubber gloves were smacked on behind me and cold grease
daubed where I am accustomed to wiping.

Wham.

'Unnng.'

'Does zat hurt?'

'No. No. Just . . . a little odd.'

'Good. No gonorrhoea. You may re-dress. Perhaps you are a
lot sweating on your bicycle? Try washing and some powder.'

In addition, a bike shop recommended lycra shorts, lined with
leather and worn next to the skin, with Vaseline. No friction, less
sweat. I bought some and returned to Warsaw.

Regretfully, I packed away the knee-length khaki empire garb
from the Fulham Road which stood accused of incubating sweat
rash. I pulled off the road once out of Warsaw to Vaseline my balls
behind a tree and pull on the lycra. At that moment two middle-
aged Frenchwomen, also on bicycles, passed on my side of the
tree. (They were using a cycle lane.)

'*Mais regard ça!*'

'*Très sportif, m'sieur.*'

Sportif indeed. The leather made the new shorts unbelievably
comfortable. And apart from the leather I might as well have been
naked; lycra is if anything more revealing than bare skin. I sped
after the Frenchwomen, accepted their further compliments, had
a picnic with them in a wood, and continued narcissistically along
the Vistula.

About half-way to Annopol there is an old market town called Kazimierz. It hangs over the mouth of a minor tributary of the Vistula between a ruined castle on one promontory and an extant church on another.

The market square is a block up from the river. The sides of the square are formed by whitewashed houses of wholesome, rustic proportions. There is also a café and a trinket shop.

By eight in the morning the square was full of traders' vans and horse-drawn carts. The vans brought meat. The flies were at it already and the punters thought it too expensive.

The carts brought sacks of flour which their drivers made no effort to sell. They smoked and laughed in the morning sun, slapping their horses to make room for new arrivals.

'Rrrrrr.'

'Rrr. Rrr.'

'Rrrrrrrrrrrrrrrrrrr.'

The Polish for 'gee-up' and 'woa' seemed to be 'rrrrrr', and frequently there came the sound and steam of horses defecating on the cobbles. A piglet snorted in a wooden cage and a woman tried on a bra back to front round her middle over an overcoat. When it was clear the meat wouldn't sell, salami and tripe came out of the vans by the armful into blue plastic basins, and the mamas shoved in, baying for it.

In a wood on the far side of the church there is a stone memorial the size of a large bill-board. Kazimierz used to be a Jewish town, but its entire population died in concentration camps during the war. Their names, in Hebrew, cover both sides of the memorial.

Annopol, like Kazimierz, was predominantly Jewish till the war. Like Kazimierz, it remembers its dead on a site just out of town. But most of the gravestones have been taken for sharpening knives, and potatoes grow in their place. Potatoes, strawberries, plums, cabbages (for sauerkraut), sugar beet . . .

Annopol lies on a junction near the Vistula, equidistant from Warsaw and Cracow. The road from Lublin to Ostrowiec crosses the river on a box-girder bridge. I stayed in one of a row of holiday huts overlooking the river. The man in charge ran a disco down there on Tuesday nights and told a dreamy youth called Wojciech about me, which was how I found out about the gravestones being used to sharpen knives, and how I met Margareta.

Wojciech dragged me into the disco and next day we took a short cut back to Annopol for lunch with Agneska, his girlfriend. He had written '*Sexualnosc*' on his leather satchel and he gathered berries and wild mushrooms like a latter-day Pyramus. He had finished school in June. The idea was to enrol in the university in Kielce for the autumn – but they might not take him and he didn't mind much anyway. In Annopol he had Agneska, he had discos, he had his father's home-made wine. This was Wojciech's long, hot summer of *sexualnosc*.

It was after lunch that Agneska's sister, Margareta, danced the mambo as she'd copied it from *Dirty Dancing*. She had every gyration, every swivel, every lowered eyelid to a tee. She snapped her fingers for me to join her, and I did my best. Left foot forward, swing, grind. Left foot backward, grind, swing. Hand on buttock . . . I caught Margareta's eye. It was a despairing look she was giving me, and she was about to burst out laughing. She didn't rate my rhythm. Margareta didn't rate my rhythm, but it's true I rated hers. So Wojciech and I continued to his father's house to drink *kompot* of blackberries.

Harvesting was under way. At Annopol the Vistula turns southwest from south, if you are going up it. This meant riding into the sun in the afternoons. The view on either side, for mile after mile, was of wheatsheaves. They looked like the half-way stage of a radical hairstyle.

Rare, thundering combine harvesters provided breaks from wheatsheaves, but most of the toiling seemed to be done by horses, scythes, and extended families.

I crossed the River San near where it joins the Vistula. The San rises in the extreme south-eastern corner of Poland where the sickle of the Carpathian range turns down towards Romania. It gives its name to Sandomierz, a natural citadel on the west bank of the Vistula which had a useful view of the approaching eastern plain and its invading armies. Sandomierz is a tourist town nowadays.

SKIN FUCK OFF
EAT SHIT POLICE!!!

Thus spake a spray can, in English, on a high wall on the approach to the cathedral in Sandomierz. Inside, there was an anti-abortionists' display of photographs of mangled human foetuses.

Darkness fell another thirty miles up river. I had eaten only two pizzas and three apples since noon, and my system was screaming for protein. I found a restaurant two painful miles up from the west bank, in a village called Pacanow. I got down pork *kotelet* and potatoes, twice, before closing time, and bought a large bag of doughnuts to take away.

A man with a bonfire going in his field wouldn't let me sleep there – he seemed to fear for his family – but a lone woman walking home suggested I go with her.

She was a widow, living off 380 fruit trees and the rent from a hairdresser's and a flat below her own. She ran me a bath in a long iron tub and while I was in it she put out on the kitchen table tea and cake, plums and greengages, and vodka. After supper she asked me to pray with her, kneeling on my bed in the parlour under a Black Madonna. Before she went to bed herself she baked another cake for me to take in the morning. And in the morning she wrote, in Polish, a lengthy invitation to my mother, asking her to visit the following July.

In an English bookshop in Berlin the previous week I had bought *Schindler's Ark* by Thomas Keneally. There cannot be a more appropriate book to read while bicycling up the Vistula towards Cracow.

Schindler saved the lives of hundreds of Jews who would otherwise have been worked to death in Plaschow or gassed in Auschwitz, by employing them during the war in his enamelware factory in Cracow. The story is true and the book is beyond praise – beyond mine, anyway.

I got two punctures on the last day of the ride to Cracow and sat in the shade of apple trees while the vulcanizing fluid set, finishing *Schindler's Ark*. Its last sentence – 'He was mourned on every continent' – choked me up. It played through my head up to the edge of Cracow, and often returned.

The eastern edge of Cracow is a powerful sight. Long before

you get there, approaching along a low ridge which is the north side of the valley of the Vistula, you see the chimneys and cooling towers of Nowa Huta.

Nowa Huta is an industrial mega-complex whose heart is a steelworks producing vast amounts of steel with extreme inefficiency and dirt. It was put there by Poland's Stalinists not just to produce steel, but to bring a true proletariat to Cracow to dilute its bourgeois intelligentsia.

Priceless old Cracow sits in a basin, in a bend in the river. Nowa Huta is on the edge of the basin. Lenin Avenue – a triumphant dual carriageway lined with workers' living quarters – sweeps up to its main entrance. Meanwhile, near-lethal quantities of sulphur dioxide, nitrous oxide, carbon monoxide and fluorine drift down and hang over the city and eat its crenellations and get drawn into people's lungs. My black T-shirt turned a filthy yellow as I took pictures of the steelworks through barbed wire.

Then I raced a tram down Lenin Avenue to the old town. When Ulica Florianska suddenly gave forth into Europe's largest medieval market square I took my hands off the handlebars like a stage-winner in the Tour de France.

It was early August; peak season for tourism and unbearably hot.

Most tourists congregate along the Royal Way which bisects the Old Town and ends below the castle from where the Gestapo ran Poland during the war. One Sunday afternoon, using *Schindler's Ark* as a guidebook, I walked beyond the castle, through the old Jewish quarter and over the river. Here, during the middle years of the war, the city's Jews were herded into an oblong of narrow steets which became the Jewish ghetto. There are no reminders, no plaques.

A mile or so to the east, Schindler's factory still stands, but now it is called Unitra Telpod and turns out electronics. The silent Sunday afternoon streets were strewn with dead yellow leaves which crackled underfoot. I tried asking two security guards at the factory if they knew what it had once been, and pressed the book cover with its Star of David to the glass wall of their booth. No response.

Plaschow, where the monster of Keneally's book ran a concentration camp, is a few tram-stops south of the old ghetto. The camp commander's house is easily identified from the map in the front of the book, and is inhabited. Nearby there is a quarry, now disused and fenced-off, where labourers were summarily shot for not working fast enough, or for no reason at all. Behind it, slightly higher lumpy ground stretches back to the site of an old Austrian hill fort where bodies were burned on open pyres, and here there is a memorial overlooking the ring road.

The lumpy ground is where the inmates' dormitories and workshops stood. Now there is nothing but grass, a few cows and a wooden cross with a ring of barbed wire where Jesus's torso would have been.

An old man had lit a candle and was praying aloud behind the memorial. He was kneeling and had taken off his shoes, and his pink socks had been darned again and again at the heels. There was no one else up there and no other sound except that of a warm breeze. The old man finished praying and became interested in my book, which I tried to explain was set where we were standing. He spoke a tricky mixture of Polish, Hebrew and German, but he seemed to be saying that he had once been a baker in Leipzig, and had spent four years in a concentration camp.

Beaming and gesticulating, the old man set off for the tram-stop, walking backwards without his shoes. I found the shoes on the other side of the memorial under a single word of graffiti – 'Jude' – and ran after him with them.

'Gott mit uns, und mit dein Mutter!' he exclaimed, shaking my whole arm. He then began a discourse on the bandits with whom Jesus was crucified.

As we walked down beside the quarry three young bloods roared up from the ring road on motocross machines, and we looked back to see them practising their skid turns round the memorial.

Most visitors to Cracow go to nearby Oswiecim. Oswiecim is Auschwitz. Roughly two-thirds of the Holocaust took place in the neighbouring camps of Auschwitz and Birkenau. The camps have been left more or less as they were found. Auschwitz itself has been turned into a museum, and it deals with the problem of visitors being numbed by the scale of the slaughter by filling whole floors of the prison blocks with the suitcases, shoes, spectacles, and hair of those who died.

The famous and harrowing documentary film made by the Russian troops who liberated Auschwitz is shown in four languages and the English version ends with an extraordinary misprint of Churchill's declaration of intent concerning Nazi war criminals: 'We will pursue them oven to the ends of the earth.'

Auschwitz must be a grisly place to live beside, and Oswiecim is a sizeable town. The camps are not extravagantly signposted and the photograph on the front of the official street map is not of Auschwitz but of children swimming in the Sola River. Nevertheless, two million people find their way there each year. They are bussed in, they sometimes feel sick in the museum, they wilt on the long walk through Birkenau to the site of the two main gas chambers, and they are bussed away again.

They call Cracow a melting city. That is, the noxious gases in its air are corroding its ancient stonework. You have to look carefully to see the 'melting'. One of the stone heads along the top of the Cloth Hall in the Town Square has lost an ear, and most have flat noses.

The Western world has decided the city deserves special attention. The Pope comes from Cracow and has got the Vatican to fund special satellite transmission to it of RAI, the Italian television network. And when George Bush visited Poland to congratulate it on the end of Communism he announced a gift of $15 million to clean up Cracow. Congress voted another $20 million at the end of 1989.

To find out how this money was being spent I went deep into Cracow's vast city hall, to its heart of obfuscation, to a Mr Wertz.

Mr Wertz, director of the Department of the Protection of the Environment, was an appointee of the old days staying on in his job because he was competent. He was a big man with a little hair still growing above his ears, from where it was pulled over his pate. He had a large fifth-floor office with armchairs and a coffee table and a view through two windows of nineteenth-century Austro-Hungarian Cracow. His first line of defence was two secretaries in an ante-room. They typed, brewed coffee, painted their nails and answered the telephone. They fended me off. Mr Wertz – he have a meeting with a minister. I returned the next day and was seen.

I felt that Mr Wertz was evasive about the money from the US Congress because he had to be seen to be grateful for it. Yet ten of the original fifteen million dollars would actually be going to an American company – whichever company won the contract to install de-sulphurizing equipment in a local coal-fired power station called Skawina. $10 million is what it would cost to install the equipment in *one* of Skawina's ten furnaces. Polish companies would then copy the American design to de-sulphurize emissions from the other nine furnaces and from hundreds more across the country. American help would continue to be available, at Polish expense. The contract for the prototype would be awarded in Pittsburgh, Pennsylvania, in October.

And Nowa Huta?

Nowa Huta was a different scale of problem. The only environmentally acceptable solution was to close down the steelworks and its 700 ancillary plants. But Nowa Huta was a bastion of Solidarity and its workers' jobs were sacred.

Poor Mr Wertz, Mr Civil Servant Sandwich Filling. If it wasn't Warsaw and the Party it was Solidarity and Washington.

'Hi,' he said rather sadly as I left. 'Hi' is Polish for 'bye'.

Cars are barred from most of the old town and the size of the market square dissipates what sound remains, so that just as nothing too rectilinear assaults the eye, nothing too percussive jars the ear. The place has the effect of a gentle massage.

In amber light by the west side of the Cloth Hall bohemian types sat cross-legged selling ear-rings and chess sets. Round the corner, facing south so that they were half in sun and half in shade, a belly dancer and her bongo drummer very gradually picked up speed. On the hour, every hour, a solo trumpet at the top of the tower of the Church of Our Lady warned Poland of an impending Tartar invasion, or a Mongol one, depending which guidebook you read.

It is worth going to Cracow just for this trumpet call, which cuts through daydreams and is then itself cut off by the ghost of an Asian arrow.

My destination after seeing Mr Wertz was a den of revolutionaries on the east side of the square. Down a few steps, in a

self-consciously black cavern belonging to the university, one of
two rival leaders of the Polish Green Party sat with Jean-Pierre, a
bug-eyed Trotskyite from Paris. They, like me, were waiting for
Staszek Zubek of the Green Brigades; eco-commando and general
bruiser. After a few minutes he swept in with a retinue of
mountain climbers.

Down here it was all still happening. Down here new fights
were being picked, old Stalinists uncovered, cigarettes chain-
smoked and voices strained because polemic was the standard
mode of conversation.

Down here they knew society as a rotten artichoke with only
the geriatric frontmen so far peeled away. Therefore to be anti-
social was the only honest course. Down here they could not bear
to let the revolution end, or, in their own words, it was only just
beginning.

The leader of the Greens had to purge his party of Communist
spies, then save the planet.

Jean-Pierre, the Trotskyite, was canvassing support for his new
pan-European workers' movement, founded October 1989.
Now was the time! Now, more than ever! In the wake of 1989, as
a *result* of 1989, Europe's workers faced the most concerted
challenge of the century to their livelihoods and rights; the
challenge from the triumphant, told-you-so free-marketeers.
Now was the time for *true* Communism!

Mr Zubek, meanwhile, was for action, direct action. He had
just finished a 525-day sit-in against a hotel planned for land partly
owned by his father. PanAm had been a potential financier, so
Zubek had made a banner: 'Panamerican gangsters go home.'
They did and he won. Hence his belief in direct action.

His next target, a dam in the Pieniny Mountains on the
Slovakian border, was altogether tougher, being already four-
fifths built. Still, Zubek had started moving people in to lie down
in front of diggers.

He was thirty-seven, which is old for an eco-commando. He
was lean and hard-faced, with a scab on the side of his nose and
hair shaved almost to his scalp. When he talked, which he did
without humour and with the occasional respectful prompt from
a mountain climber, veins stood up on his temples and neck.

They would continue the Pieniny action till they won. Then there would be a ball in the lake bed.

Next morning I set off in the direction of the Pieniny Mountains.

The Spine of Europe

Cracow's south circular was one giant choking diesel engine, jammed up at every set of lights and throbbing into the hot air. It carried endless hundreds of unlabelled vans and trucks to their sticky black turn-offs to Tarnow, Novy Targ and Katowice. It passed the bleak stanchions of the Plaschow concentration camp memorial and swooped across an urban valley over tiered platoons of housing blocks. Eventually it let me off on a south-easterly tangent.

The ground reared up and the road doubled immediately back on itself. These were the first hills since the Sudeten Mountains south of Wroclaw. Suddenly the northern plains were done, crossed, and I was in Central Europe again. It was good to have the third dimension back, and to yank down on the left-hand gear lever and feel pain along the tops of the thighs. Fields in stripes of green and gold were draped over the rollicking topography instead of sretching away into invisible infinity. This was the spine of Europe. The land would not be flat again till after Budapest, and the relief of relief made me warble like a migratory bird celebrating landfall.

A smart tour bus from Orbis stood in the centre of the town of Wieliczka. Its passengers were probably down the local salt mine, or visiting an underground cathedral built there under the influence of a Byzantine princess. I visited neither, partly because I was in a hurry, partly because I was unaware of their existence.

(Nowadays travel is possible in which the waylaying is all and the transport is pre-paid, air-conditioned, high-speed and forget-table. Bicycling is different. The process of movement is necess-arily as intoxicating or soul-destroying as what you move through. And the means of transport largely determines the nature of the waylaying. You get hailed by potato-pickers. You take tea with the farmer who lends you a bucket to find a puncture. You pedal up a side road because you are going slowly enough to notice it. The stopping and the going are of a piece; a very satisfying one. But it is also a balance. If you want to speed up from an average of five to fifteen miles an hour you have to cut down on the gawping. You have to summon up directional momentum.)

In every farmyard along the road, pine saplings had been stripped and dried and their thin trunks sharpened into stakes. These would become the skeletons of obelisks of drying hay.

A horse-drawn wheat-flattening device was working along the edge of a field. As the device rolled forward a wooden board fell backwards and a man sat silhouetted over it wielding a wide wooden rake as if he were paddling a kayak, separating each new row of flattened stalks from the falling board.

Further on, a man with biceps like rugby balls and pectorals the size of self-governing regions stood facing the sunset in the doorway of a loft, pulling up buckets of meal on a rope.

Further still, amid strangely little fuss, a barn burned to the ground and a pleasant pall of woodsmoke hung in the valley.

The Pieniny Mountains, not far from their bigger cousins the High Tatras, are gentle tectonic ripples, well top-soiled except along the middle of the range. Rock strata do stick through here, rising in orderly fashion from the centre of the earth. But they break off rather timidly as soon as they encounter air and light. Even these outcrops are modestly concealed by pine trees, except to users of the only road which passes through them. From this road there is an almost aerial view of the mess made by the Pieniny-dam builders.

The Dunajec River approaches the mountains from the north-west and cuts through them at their western end along an S-shaped valley. This valley, guarded by castles on steep hills on the inside of each bend, is the one earmarked for flooding. The dam is directly below one of the castles. It looked finished but the flooding had not yet begun. There was no sign of any direct action being taken by Staszek Zubek's eco-commandos.

The water flowed along a broad concrete groove and down a side-sluice in the bottom of the dam. When the sluice was closed the water would start to rise quickly.

Below the dam the Dunajec follows the southern edge of the mountains before turning north again and eventually joining the Vistula. Here the landscape really has been hacked to pieces – by works traffic and its access roads and pontoon bridges, by coffer dams and diversions and rediversions of the river. It is all gravel and silt.

I rode through it and up onto a giant earthwork beside the dam wall. The sun beat down. Two teenage girls in jeans and bikini tops walked along the downstream side of the wall past concrete reinforcing rods and graffiti which included BRIXTON SUPPORTS THE FIGHT. They had left their boyfriends and two overloaded frame rucksacks on baking pebbles on the far side of the canalized river.

A bulldozer, a crane and a man in work trousers stood on top of the earthwork, looking like a still from an advertisement for some thirst-busting lager. I took a picture of them. The man walked slowly over and stopped a foot away, looking at my camera.

'*Japanische?*'

'*Ja.*'

His face was set absolutely and his voice was dry.

'You an ecologist?' he asked.

'Not really. I'm a tourist first of all.'

'Tourists go to the castle. They are not allowed here.'

'OK. I'm an ecologist, and a tourist. Do you work here?'

'I live here, and I work here.'

'You live . . . in the valley?'

'In Niedzica. New Niedzica. It is a new town, not far. The old church has been moved, stone by stone. Old Niedzica will soon be under water.' He touched his hands together over his head and smiled a little.

'Is the dam finished?'

'Ninety per cent finished.'

'And will they fill the lake?'

'Of course. Why build a dam and not fill the lake? This is not for tourists. It will be a beautiful lake. Very, very beautiful.'

'Then will it be for tourists?'

'Tourism, drinkwater, hydro-power. You ecologists, from Germany, from England. The vipers from Cracow. Everybody thinks Pieniny is only their holiday park.'

I told him I'd met a viper in Cracow, Staszek Zubek of Freedom and Peace (VIP), and the dour man in work trousers nodded.

As I got back on my bike, he said: 'A moment. I'll make a picture. Go over by the dam and I'll make a picture with your camera.' I did as he said and before handing back the camera he savoured its weight, and the feel of the wind-on.

'Pentax!' He kissed the tips of his fingers but his face was still set. 'Pentax, Yashica, Nikon . . . Pentax is magic. And now you have a picture for your ecologist friends.'

From old Niedzica a track led into watermeadows where a second crop of hay was being cut. The river flowed by twenty feet below. I walked over to an old man who was watching the haymakers from the shade of a cedar tree. I mimed rising water and asked whether he thought it was a good thing:

'*Dobra?*'

He pointed to the river and copied my miming.

'*Da, da,*' he said. Yes indeed, the water would rise.

But did he want it to? Did the prospect make him happy? Was he looking forward to a very, very beautiful lake?

'*Dobra?*' I asked again.

'*NIE dobra! NIE DOBRA!. Nie, nie . . .*' There followed a torrent of anti-dam invective.

I should doubtless have been saddened on his behalf. But the flood hadn't happened yet and I had seen the place before it did. The heat of the day was past and the sun, from an angle, was turning everything a slushy gold. The village shop had re-opened to sell me two bottles of pop. And I knew that over the next horizon the Tatra Mountains were waiting.

Rolling west down the hill out of old Niedzica was the single most blissful moment in the entire six bicycling months. The road was narrow, with no verges but an even surface. It slalomed through unburnt stubble and occasional clumps of trees. The contours were like the back of a giant sleeping dromedary, and half-way down it the High Tatras slid suddenly into view to the south; the whole lot of them at once, slicing up through the haze against a dizzying spectrum of green, gold, and blue. Real, jagged mountains. I nearly gagged on the excitement. I thought of friends behind desks in Egham, friends selling uniforms in Croydon, cursing traffic on the Isle of Dogs, manning checkouts in Welwyn Garden City. Check *this* out, I thought.

For about twenty miles the High Tatras form Poland's frontier with Czechoslovakia. I spent a bracing week in the valleys on the Polish side, tramping through unseasonable sleet on their upper slopes and failing to spot the bears which are said to inhabit the forests lower down. Then I crossed into Slovakia. At this point, 300 miles east of Prague, Slovakia is only 60 miles wide, a mountainous panhandle between Poland and Hungary. It seemed more prosperous than Poland, and more visited by Westerners. I skirted the eastern end of the range (which is entirely in Slovakia). Beautiful, beckoning paths led into the mountains from the road. They were torture to resist, but the need to keep moving was acute by now. It was mid-August and I wasn't even half-way to the Black Sea. I didn't look back till I was down through the forest and dodging lorries on main roads again.

The Foodies

If you possibly can, avoid cottage cheese pancakes in Slovakia, especially cottage cheese and strawberry ones from the Hotel Start in Kezmarok. Just thinking about them makes me want to be sick again. They had tinned strawberries inside and chocolate sauce on top. Never a promising combination. And for cottage cheese, read bacteria bonanza.

In Levoca I met Eric and Rimkje from Amsterdam. They had been attacked by ice-cream in Poprad; laid out there for two days in a hotel. You would need that sort of reason to stay in Poprad. It is due south of the Tatras. I'd freewheeled there from the mountains, and my only memory of it was seeing a child run over by a Skoda. Miraculously, there was a clinic at the very junction where it happened and the white-faced driver scooped the limp child off the road and dashed inside pursued by a screaming mother.

Anyway, Eric and Rimkje were relieved to be out of Poprad, but above all they were relieved to be back on food. They were graduate students riding from Amsterdam to Athens in a hundred days from monastery to monastery; 75 kilometres a day. The ice-cream assault had put them behind schedule but before they rode anywhere they were responding to an overwhelming physiological clamour for food. They were stuffing themselves with pizza and chips.

'Our friends said we should write about our travels,' said Rimkje, 'but all we can think about is food.'

That made me feel good. A lot of the time all I could think about was food. In Poland I had regularly inhaled half a dozen doughnuts at a sitting . . . as a starter, a snack. Whenever I saw doughnuts I would buy a large bag of them. I was ashamed of my eating habits – the cottage-cheese pancake had followed a large lunch and two cream slices. My belly, my bun gut, my long-range fuel tank, had become an embarrassment. I had taken to covering it up to ride through towns.

Eric and Rimkje were actually fatter than I was. They could be my friends any day.

The Fiddler

Kosice is the capital of Eastern Slovakia and one of the few really pleasant cities close to the Soviet Union. The main road from the north cuts through the city and on summer evenings becomes its principal strollodrome (heavy traffic having been diverted). The music of a gypsy trio schmaltzed succulently out of an ancient first-floor window hung with wine-red curtains.

Upstairs, the table in that window was free. The joint felt reasonably authentic. The wine had no rough edges. The table would have served for shove ha'penny, it was so worn. Beside it the youngest of the trio played a double bass. One of the things about this music is that the bass is bowed, not plucked. It makes every number haunting; it is the Night. And when the player really levers down on the strings so they catch on the horse-hair and then jump away, well that means passion. This player was the pin-up of the three, with black hair pulled back by a leather lace to give a clear view of his smooth-skinned mustang face. He was also bored, utterly bored.

If the bass is the night, the zymbal is the fire in the night and the zymbal man the bringer of fire, bringing it with felt-tipped tongs which shimmer in his hands over the zymbal strings. The zymbal man sat at the mustang's elbow. His gaze shifted constantly between his zymbal and the dancer.

The dancer is the solo violin, circling the fire in the night. This dancing was as light and fast, as slow, voluptuous and perfect as the dancing of Scheherazade herself. The violinist was huge. He was like a great toad. But he piloted the supertanker of himself with epic grandeur. His black trousers and white shirt were carefully tailored, meeting not under some apologetic overhang but at the frontal apex of his body. And even way out there in front of him, he retained full muscular control, so it could not be called a gut or belly. He was by far the oldest of the three. He had no hair. His face and neck were like a scoop of butterscotch ice-cream.

Mazurkas, polkas, gypsy ballads, marches, love songs and cadenzas on an orgiastic scale . . . for Great Toad and his fiddle all this and more was in an evening's work. Those who globe-trot after Perlman and Anne-Sophie Mutter and listen to their compact discs in Saabs and scrubbed pine studios should call in on the Great Toad of Kosice for a listen to the real thing.

I stayed until the chairs were being upturned on the table, then lay awake in a hotel room while the music ducked and dived around, and gradually faded, in my head.

Budapest

In Poland and Czechoslovakia I had got the hang of jump-starting conversations with a spiel of pidgin Slavic and German meaning roughly 'Er. Ahem. English. I do not speak Polish/Czech/Slovak, sorry. Is there any food?'

In Hungary this was not going to work. Hungarian is the fiend of East European languages. There is nothing Slavonic in it, nothing Romantic, nothing Saxon. It is said to be related to Finnish, but my Finnish was not good enough for this to make a difference. Besides, Hungarians often do not like to be reminded of the link, resulting as it does from similar migration patterns across Asia fourteen centuries ago: when they got to what became European Russia, the Finns turned north while the Magyars continued into Central Europe. The Magyars settled round the Danube Bend and Lake Balaton, but some of them subsequently moved to Transylvania where they now regard themselves as an oppressed minority. The cruellest insult a Romanian can throw at a Magyar is to call him a descendant of 'an Asian tribe'.

Predictably enough, Hungarians have a stock of insults to throw back at Romanians. This was demonstrated on my first evening in Hungary by a big, red-faced man called Erno, who resorted to Latin to overcome the language barrier.

'Plebs!' he shouted. 'Moldavia! Plebs!'

His point was that in Romania the Moldavians would steal my stuff, while the Hungarians would not. Hardly a Magyar whom I spoke to could resist a cautionary tale about Romanians.

I met Erno in a bar in Meszes, not far south of the Slovakian border in the valley of the Rakaca River. He ordered me one shot of vodka and one of Hubertus (a plum liqueur), and sat watching while I drank them. I was eating from a tin of Soviet mackerel in tomato sauce. Erno decided I lacked bread and dispatched an old man with a watery glass eye to fetch some more. The man returned with bread, a block of pork fat and some apples.

Erno spoke no English, which infuriated him. On the way up to his summer house, where I spent the night, he exploded with frustration, hitting himself on the forehead and yelling guttural curses across the valley.

The summer house was still being built – by Erno himself and a wizened hired hand who needed six or seven cognacs every morning to control his shakes. He was half gypsy, half Jew. Erno and his wife Katarin thought him hilarious. I joined him next morning in his liquid breakfast and felt very sleepy for the first two hours in the saddle.

That day I became profoundly lost in the Bukk Mountains National Park. I was aiming for the town of Eger and some civilized inebriation. It is the wine capital of Hungary, famous internationally for Bull's Blood. But the roads in the Bukk Mountains are relentlessly serpentine. I lost my sense of direction and when the turn-off came I went the wrong way. Instead of tumbling off the mountains into a wine cellar the road petered out at a hunting lodge owned by the Nimrod Corporation of Miskolc. Two families had rented it for the weekend.

Georg and Bela consulted briefly with wives Edith and Marta, and with brother Tibor and grandfather Julius. They invited me to stay.

They were still pinching themselves about the end of the dark age:

'No Communists in Hungary,' said Bela that evening from across the dining table. Georg, Edith, Marta, Tibor, and Julius pushed back the benches and stood up, cheering.

'No more Communism in Hungary,' said Tibor over breakfast the next morning. Spontaneous laughter and applause followed from Georg, Edith, Marta, Julius, and Bela.

Bela was the most passionately relieved. He was a young father with an Adidas tracksuit and an English vocabulary consisting, perhaps as a result of Hungary's arrival on the Grand Prix circuit, of the phrase 'pole position'. Pole position was where he wanted the Alliance of Free Democrats to be in parliament. He was desperate to convey how it felt to have no experience of democracy (which made me wonder rather blankly how I felt having had that experience). But there were tears of pleasure in his eyes as he gestured at me over the table. His message seemed to be: 'Experience of democracy will come. The important part is having ditched the Communists. Now we can walk tall with Westerners like you.'

Georg had some blunter opinions to air. He called Romanians barbarians and made me promise when in Romania to stay only with Magyars or in campsites. He did a Fascist salute for Saddam Hussein, who had been in Kuwait a fortnight, then explained angrily: Hitler, Stalin, Ceauşescu, Saddam Hussein. (Would they ever stop?) And he recommended the local Médoc as more thirst-quenching than Bull's Blood.

Eger's wine cellars are arranged in a horseshoe round a public garden dug out of the side of the Valley of Beautiful Women. There are about forty cellars, and the west side of the valley rises off their doors, covered with vines and a few houses.

On the evening I had put aside for drinking the action was in Cellar 23. German was the language being spoken, mostly by East Germans. When I arrived there was a space between a wine barrel and a girl dressed in brown leather reading Günter Grass, but soon there was no space and too much noise even to contemplate reading. I asked for a glass of Médoc.

'A *glass*? No, my friend: half a litre or a litre. From which country are you . . .?' The proprietor, with a litre of red over his shoulder in a glass bladder with a urethra as long as his arm, ordered four young men on a neighbouring table to make room for me. He believed they spoke some English. He took his finger off the end of the urethra and the wine gushed into a jug.

My drinking partners were engineering hippies from Rostock. In fact everyone in the cellar except me was from Rostock. They all knew each other. They had hitched here from the Baltic every year for years. Tonight was the night, the night of the rendezvous in Cellar 23. With each new arrival a roar went up and a song began. The Germans bellowed outrageous welcomes at each other and clambered around over the tables, stooping under the arched brick ceiling, wrestling, hugging, kissing. Hair was shoulder length. Denim was tight and often torn off into shorts. Torsos were bare or clad only in string vests. Médoc was a hundred forints a litre and these Rostockians were six times richer than the year before, trading Deutschmarks instead of East German *alu-chips*. The landlord loved it. He was all over the place with his bladder of Médoc.

A messiah joined our table ('He's a philosopher,' someone said) and a Mary Magdalene sat on his knee. He was built like a climbing frame and had an extremely long, intense white face. Mary took a toy guitar from his ham-sized hand and sang some Status Quo. But the general din overwhelmed her and she turned to plaiting the messiah's hair.

A hippy engineer across the table said: 'I don't know why I come a thousand kilometres to have a good time when now we can all meet in Rostock and do this . . . but anyway I come and I love it. Hungary was always the only place where we could be free – where we could sleep in a park and not have the police asking for our passports.'

This truly was a happy hippy, but one of his *Kameraden* was turning maudlin. I had asked some vapid question about life before the revolution, and he said:

'Please don't use that word. It's not a revolution, it's a rush for money. Maybe the people who started it were revolutionaries but they were very few – and no one is talking to them now.'

Next day I rode very carefully – because some cartilage in my left knee seemed about to tear apart – through fifty kilometres of vines and sunflowers on the southern slopes of the Matra mountains, with a hazy view to the left of the Hungarian Great Plain. In the afternoon I continued to the Danube Bend.

This is where the Danube realizes the Caspian is out of reach and heads for the Black Sea; having flowed roughly east from long before Vienna it suddenly turns south. It divides at the tip of a long island called Szentendre Island, and thirty miles later it meets the northern suburbs of Budapest.

I was seduced by a ritzy restaurant on the island. You could sit outside under red lanterns and gaze at the river. You could even listen to a gypsy ensemble like the Great Toad's in Kosice, only this was a quintet, and talentless. I ordered Wild Meat From The Island and a half bottle of Pinot Noir. Then midges swarmed in, so I bought some Kent King Size and smoked them away. Then the quintet sidled round in red tuxedos and played 'I Could Have Danced All Night', abysmally. The oily violinist beamed at me whenever I could bear to meet his eye. Afterwards he growled in my ear that his boys drank beer. A waiter materialized.

'Will that be one bottle of beer, sir, or five?'

'Um . . . what do you . . .?'

'I think . . . five, sir.'

They all chose Pilsner Urquell, the Plzen export brand, the most expensive available. By the end of the meal I felt ill and broke. I consoled myself with the thought of having covered a thousand kilometres since Gdansk. I preferred not to think of the thousand still to go to Istanbul.

A rainstorm broke as I rode in the dark across the island looking for a place to sleep. Visibility wound down to zero. (In the rain, unless you have wipers on your glasses, you have to take them off.) What life existed on the island must have been tucked up in bed. Except . . . except. Down towards Budapest beside a ferry terminal in an otherwise comatose village called Pocsmeyer a sound leaked out into the storm from a bar. It came from a woman in white singing querulously to a group of die-hard liquor-takers. Another group played cards at a table: there was a ferryman in a heavy blue blazer and brocaded cap, an angry retard who hit the table with a fist every time he played a card, and a third player who was silent. I asked at the bar about a bed, and the liquor-pourer had a word with the silent one, whose name was Jozsef. When the cards were over, he motioned for me to follow him. We rode back up the island across country to a pair of heavy gates.

He told me to wait outside, then went through himself to be met by three large, black dogs to whom he murmured soothingly for some minutes. Then he returned to the gates.

'Please come in. I think they will be quiet now, but one of them is very wild – wild enough to kill you.'

He lived in a spartan room at the far end of a long, white bungalow in which he bred horses. He bred them and the dogs guarded them. He owned them and rode them too, in the Olympics if everything came right at once. They had the best rooms in the house. They stepped around restlessly over the straw, their black outlines larger than life in the night. Occasionally they clanged the metal grilles which kept them in, and whinnied, and Jozsef would calm them down. Their tickover breathing was as loud and regular as a mechanical bellows.

There were six horses altogether, two of them champion show-jumpers worth 300,000 forints each. And one of the colts was the grandson of the legendary Imperial. ('*The* Imperial,' I said never having heard of him. 'Wow'.)

Jozsef said goodnight to them and made us spritzers which we drank while looking at photographs of tournaments. He steeple-chased, evented, jumped, and sprinted. He even trotted and could drive a four-in-hand. He rated Prince Philip with a four-in-hand, having ridden against him and lost.

I slept on a low, hard bed which smelled of sweat and leather, and dreamed of the three black dogs.

Imperial's grandson went sick overnight and lay down. In the morning I found Jozsef ashen-faced and pulling the horse's tail with all his strength to get it to stand up. Once or twice it did stand up, and stumbled dangerously round the stable. Jozsef tut-tutted. It was a case for the vet, who lived an hour's walk away. The storm of the previous night had settled down into continuous heavy rain. Jozsef put on a jacket and a cap, said goodbye, and set off down the island for the vet.

'I am a billboard. I sell your products,' said a billboard which would soon be selling products. Samsung and Goldstar had smothered Budapest's trams with adverts. The Foreign Trade bank had ECU on its exchange rate board. The *Herald Tribune*, the *Guardian*, the *Financial Times*, *Le Monde*, *Die Zeit* and *Corriere della Sera* were all on sale by eleven every morning. There was international direct dialling from all red public payphones, indivi-dual Durexes at the checkouts in ABC supermarkets, and an

almighty crush from eleven to eleven at McDonalds. Budapest
was almost there, cloned, Westernized.

It is true that things went wrong later in the year. Petrol ran out,
transport men went on strike. The city ground to a halt. But
Budapest has momentum in the direction of mod cons. It is to
Vienna what East Berlin is to West; the brave new market. The
gridlock cleared and the neon surged on in.

I met an engineer called Janos who was riding the wave. He was
delighted by the new Minolta and Philishave signs along the top
of the Hotel Forum. He was tickled by his busy letterbox. 'You
know, we get *free* newspapers now,' he said. 'Advertisers pay for
them.' And he was blasé about Levis: 'Four years ago, if you had
Levis you were king. Now everybody has them.'

Janos was a graduate of Karl Marx University, Budapest's most
prestigious. He worked for a private firm set up with Austrian
capital. Money was no problem for Janos, not even real, Western
money. But to make absolutely sure he sold lace to tourists at
weekends in a car park near the Danube Bend.

He lived with his wife and baby daughter in a small flat in the
Beverly Hills of Buda, with sixteen-channel satellite TV, Tech-
nics hi-fi, Siemens coffee machine, Braun toothbrush, Miele
kitchen and a drawerful of maps and brochures of places he'd
been, including, most recently, the Plaza Athenée hotel in Manhattan, with a dollar millionaire friend who rented a helicopter for
an hour to get on top of things. Also Kaprun in Austria, to
summer-ski. I must say I thoroughly enjoyed staying at Janos'
place. Particularly after Mrs Herceg.

Mrs Herceg was no doubt more representative than Janos of the
average quality of life in Budapest. She was a widow and music
teacher who rented out her spare room through Ibusz, the former
state travel company, now privatized. She lived on the eighth
floor of a privately-managed block in Szigoyni Street, west Pest.
(Graffiti: OH BABY I LOVE YOU SO. FUCK OF
KOMMUNISM.)

She had rules: shoes off immediately inside the front door; use
bedside light only; in case of single occupancy, place nothing on
spare bed counterpane; showers maximum ten minutes per day;
no washing of clothes except underwear; no entry into kitchen or

living room. The rules were written out in German, French, Spanish, English, and Japanese.

All perfectly reasonable, you might think, for an elderly woman taking in strangers. Very well. It was the enforcement that irked. If Mrs Herceg saw the main bedroom light go on even for a few seconds she was in at once for a harangue about the price of electricity. She said it doubled after 10 p.m. in this block, but not in the state-run block across the road. '*So! Mein Gott! –*' she could become distinctly guttural, '– if you see lights burning over zair all night, you vill know *vai!*' She inspected the bathroom floor for puddles every time her 'guest' had used it. She wrote a note reminding him that *shoes stay in the hall* when he forgot to use the slippers late one night. And she called him Poopi.

She called me Poopi. So I took to spinning out the evenings in McDonalds over chocolate sundaes. Anything to avoid meeting Mrs Herceg in the hall.

McDonalds deserves a special mention. I patronized it not by default, nor with too much shame. Budapest is overrun by restaurants and cafés, but McDonalds beats them all in one important respect: it is by far the most popular. It is where young Budapest foregathers, and where, if lucky, it works. The entrance is just off Vaci Utca, Budapest's pedestrianized retail artery. City Burger, McDonalds' Magyar rival, is across the street and is always full of sly queues that miss the till you thought you were aiming at and drag on forever round the L-shaped counter. But McDonalds inhales the human herd through a front door half-a-block wide. McDonalds is ready for you. You may still be ten yards from the till, staring into space, when you realize a bright-eyed boy is waving his red McDonalds tennis vizor at you from way down by the deep fat fryers, shouting '*next please!* Can I take you order, *sir?*' The kids with the jobs at McDonalds *run* from the fryers and burger-chutes and soda-fountains to the tills. They twang each other's dungaree straps and wear their hi-achievement stars with something that could actually be pride. They yell, laugh, earn their money and then swagger off down Vaci Utca in the fancy clothes they've bought with it. You should see them.

Back up the Danube, beyond Szentendre Island, there was a civil engineering abortion which for reasons of contemporary history required to be seen.

The Danube Bend is in fact an S-bend. The water, which has had a lazy, island-cruising time of it since Vienna, is forced into a fast-flowing channel by two great interlocking promontories. On the second of these stand the remains of the citadel of Visegrad, built by Hungarian kings in the thirteenth century to fend off Mongol invaders.

The first promontory is longer and lower. Near the other tip of this promontory, which some say is the most beautiful place in Hungary, there is a village called Nagymaros. Before the revolutions, the Hungarian, Czech and Austrian governments planned to build a hydro-electric dam here. It was not a popular plan. The unofficial but tolerated opposition seized it as a test case. Opposition to the dam would be difficult to outlaw as subversive, and would be sure to win mass support.

Shortly before the annual conference of the Hungarian Socialist Workers' Party (The Communist Party) in May 1989, Mikhail Gorbachev informed its General Secretary, Janos Kadar, that as far as the Kremlin was concerned his services were no longer required. A spate of high-level personnel changes followed, including the replacement or removal of a third of the Party Central Committee and most of the politburo. A new Prime Minister emerged in the person of Miklos Nemeth and he scrapped the dam. This enraged the Austrian and Czech governments, which had put up much of the money for it, but was a triumph for Hungary's nascent opposition parties.

Meanwhile building had already started. They got as far as filling in half the river with sand. A vast D-shaped wasteland now protrudes from the end of the promontory. When I arrived there were no people on it, just machines: a yellow digger filling red lorries with sand.

Then a lorry driver jumped down and laughed at me emptying sand from my shoes.

'*Kommunismus kaput*,' I said.

'Yup. Sure is. And now they're paying us to take the sand back where it came from.'

'Where's that?'

'Austria.'

The Danube Bend is a favourite locale for weekend retreats for the middle classes, and I borrowed the garden of one such retreat to photograph the D-shaped infill. The owner of the garden drove a BMW and had devised a solar-heated shower with a black plastic tank in a glass box in the garden. He explained that barges travelling upstream now had to be towed through the strait created by the D because the downstream current was so strong.

He passed me some binoculars through which a dozy freight leviathan could be seen succumbing to the current. A tug pushed out from the north bank and linked up with it like an in-flight re-fueller.

'Ridiculous, no?' said the BMW driver. 'It should never have been started, but having been started it should have been finished. Now what do we have? We have an abortion. A gigantic abortion at the bottom of the garden.'

It was whilst I was trying to hitch back to Budapest that I met Janos of the Braun electric toothbrush. He whirred to the rescue in a Trabant station wagon. He had just packed up his lace kiosk for the day in the car park below Visegrad, and he chauffered me right back to Mrs Herceg's door.

He had nothing better to do – except watch a video (his wife and daughter were staying at his summer house by Lake Balaton). Having said that, he wasn't bored, not ever. He actually loved videos. Videos, freedom and democracy, but above all . . . well, above all freedom. He'd voted FIDESZ – the student party – and they'd been impressive. They held the moral high ground because many of the other so-called democrats had been in public life. One way or another they'd collaborated. But in his opinion that didn't mean as much in Hungary as . . . You see, he said, Hungarians weren't out for vengeance against former Communists, not like the Poles and Czechs. That would be looking backwards, and Hungarians look forwards.

Did this car belong to him? No WAY! He'd never buy a tomato crate like this. It was a friend's. His Fiesta was at Balaton and the Fiat was being serviced. No *thankyou*. Trabants, frankly, were humiliating to drive.

Janos was twenty-eight, fluent in four languages, and doing

fine. He was the first person I'd met in so-called Eastern Europe for whom life had been sufficiently amenable since birth to set him up for the big years, 1989 and 1990, without bitterness, ill-health or even worldly pessimism.

As he dropped me off he gave me his home number.

'If – when – you have it up to your neck with Mrs Herceg, call. Our sofa is a sofa-bed and you can use it till my wife returns from Balaton.'

I did phone Janos, and spent two or three nights on the sofa-bed. We ate out. We bought beer and Danish pastries from his local ABC. We sank three pints each in the new John Bull pub near parliament. We watched *Emmanuelle III* on satellite TV. I washed my clothes in his machine, borrowed his word processor. Janos prided himself on his Magyar hospitality.

Legend had it, he said, that King Matthias was given to travelling incognito among his people to see how well or ill they lived. So every lonely traveller was taken in and fed and even fêted, lest he prove a king.

I also lost the key to my bike lock. At a bike shop at the foot of Castle Hill they sawed through my old padlock and sold me a new one. I could have bought new tyres, new tubes, new brake-blocks. You can *get* things in Budapest.

From the bike shop I rode down the river on the right bank, past the Chain Bridge, towards the cliff on which stands a statue of a brave and now merely historic Bolshevik lady. I crossed the river using Elizabeth Bridge – it is a grand sight, Budapest and the Danube from Elizabeth Bridge – and caved in to one final McDonalds' chocolate sundae before taking the main road to Romania.

The Tailor of Arad

I left Budapest re-fuelled with carbohydrates, sleep, blood-sugar, film, notebooks, and tubigrip. Ahead lay the Hungarian Great Plain and the Balkans. My left knee had quietened down. The bicycle purred along, well rested, full of beans. The sun was on my right shoulder, clip-on shades were on my spectacles, and the evening rush-hour traffic was trying to squeeze me off the road.

The plain, the Puszta, is a hundred and fifty miles by a hundred and fifty miles – dwarfing Salisbury Plain but not in the same league as pampas and prairies. It is Europe's biggest landlocked paddock, bounded on three sides by mountains and on the fourth by the Danube. It once hosted the only cowboy culture in European history, but the cows – a creamy longhorn breed – and the boys, who if the brochures are to be believed wore white skirts and red waistcoats, exist nowadays only on tourist reserves. The rest of the Puszta is under plough. State farming has created single fields the size of three small Western farms. You can often ride for an hour with no change in the view. In mid-August that view might be of parched black earth, for the wheat has been harvested, or of dead or decapitated sunflowers, the sun having frazzled what still stands.

The people of the Puszta – some of them at least – still live in homesteads set back off the road. Within shouting distance there is usually a tethered cart or tractor, and geese, dogs, and a tree or two. Each house has a well, sipped by a bucket on a cantilevered arm. The well-heads are the Puszta's windmills; what you tilt at.

In the middle of the plain, dead centre, there is a village called Lakitelek. In a farm near here on 27 September 1987 a group of intellectuals held a meeting at which Imre Pozsgay, guest of honour and senior Communist Party member, called for a new constitution guaranteeing freedom of expression. At the end of the day the Hungarian Democratic Forum was founded. Janos, my host in Budapest, had told me there would be nothing to see in Lakitelek. He was right. Two bashful sets of spray-painted initials, MDF, hid in the shade of vine leaves on bungalow walls. The village supermarket was open and a smirking woman behind the deli counter sold me the necessary for a picnic. Otherwise there was evidence of nothing but siesta time.

I spent two nights on the plain, both with a clear view of the Big Dipper. The daytime I used to cover ground and to eat. If the rumours about Romania were even half true there would be little food there. In the town of Oroshaza I bought a whole salami and two packs of Kent cigarettes (for use as currency). For the record, I could also have bought apples, plums, peppers, lettuce, chicken, noodles, chocolate, car spares, preserving jars . . .

I mention all this because it was soon to be soft-filtered in my mind into a kaleidoscope of unimaginable bounty.

From Oroshaza it was a straightforward two-hour ride due south to the border crossing.

A rap hit from 1987 called 'Fight For The Right To Party' was jerking out of a kiosk selling cigarettes and green fizzy pop. This was the last outpost of Hungary. Two Turkish truck drivers aired their bellies outside it under an awning and wished me luck in Romania.

I was anxious to like Romania, but aware that this might be difficult. Once upon a time, Romania had apparently been lonely and beautiful. But since that time Ceauşescu had been raping it; working through a list of seven thousand ancient towns and villages to be bulldozed.

However, you always hear about the bad news, not the good. *Some* of this country must have survived. Some of it must still be the magic, secret land which Patrick Leigh Fermor walked through in the 1930s.

Modern Romania has three main regions: Moldavia, down the country's eastern side and amputated by the edge of the Soviet Empire; Wallachia, along its southern side, bounded by the Danube; and Transylvania, separated from the other two by the reverse L of the Carpathians.

One administrative area which fits into none of these is Banat. Geographically, Banat is an eastward extension of Vojvodina in Yugoslavia. It is flat and cut off from the rest of Romania by mountains. Politically, it used to be ignored but now it commands some respect as the crucible of the revolution. Its most important city is Timişoara, where the shooting started on 15 December 1989.

The second city of Banat is Arad, and from the border this was the only place to go.

The road chicaned through the frontier town of Nadlac, then went due east for seventy kilometres under a continuous avenue of eucalyptus trees and a very hot sun.

Nadlac was barely breathing. It was a one-storey town. The only metalled road was the one to Arad, and beside it an Electro-Technica store offered in its window two wood-burning stoves and a bidet.

A platoon of National Service conscripts stood silhouetted on a rail freight wagon, shovelling gravel out of it. I photographed them and they climbed down to ask for cigarettes.

'How do you find Romania?' one asked.

'I've only been here half an hour,' I said. 'How do you find it? How is Iliescu?' I offered a thumbs up and a thumbs down on the leader of the National Salvation Front.

'Iliescu: Ceauşescu number two.' Thumbs down.

A furry green crop was being grown in oceanic quantities on either side of the road, and harvested a strip at a time. Children lay on their fronts in the shade of the eucalyptus trees, propped up on their elbows and armed with sickles.

I drew level with an old man on a bicycle who was also bound for Arad. We agreed it was thirsty weather. I said I'd be stopping at the first opportunity for a drink and he said ride on pal, the first opportunity is the Hotel Astoria in Arad. But in a village on the way there, the offspring of an extended Magyar family sat me down with a soda siphon and let it be known they would rather be living in Hungary.

Arad was guarded by concentric rings of eleven-storey housing blocks which looked pink and poetic from a distance in the evening light. Closer to, the poetry vanished. The blocks stood on crudely-poured concrete stilts which created open dungeons of builders' waste. A plague of squealing starlings filled the trees here, and covered the buckled pavements with guano. A suburban cow was being grazed on dry grass and unmixed cement. I stopped at some traffic lights. To the left, a shambling tram on protesting tramlines, and in its windows a hundred expressions of terrifying boredom. To the right, a 'crystal shop' selling nothing but brown glass vases, all of one shape, and brown plastic cups.

I followed signs to 'Centru'. Language, at least was going to be easier than in Hungary. Romanian is the closest modern descendant of Latin, a fact of which Romanians are intensely proud although it is a result of the Emperor Trajan's subjugation of their own ancestors, the Dacians, in the second century AD.

The centre of Arad is the Boulevard of the Republic, whose Palladian façades and tree-lined central promenade were a relief after the city's Stalinist outer fortifications. In the fading light I didn't see the bullet holes.

I consulted the street map in my guide book. A short, slim man stepped forward out of the lazy river of strollers.

'I wonder if I can help you,' he said. The accent was studied but impeccable. I said yes indeed, he could help me. He could have a drink with me. They warn you not to drink with strangers in Romania, but I wanted very badly to talk. I hadn't had a real conversation since leaving Janos in Budapest.

Of course, by all means, said the man . . . and would I be so very kind and change some money?

His name was Traian, after the conqueror Trajan. Traian was a tailor, now retired. He limped, very neatly; his left leg didn't bend and swung along instead like a piece of prosthesis. He had tidy grey hair and wide cheekbones but no spare flesh at all. We found a café on the boulevard. Everyone was drinking brandy with a red synthetic chaser. It was that or nothing, so I had that and Traian had nothing.

When the waiter had come and gone, Traian leaned across the table. In a low, beseeching voice he firmed up the money-changing deal. How much? A hundred Deutschmarks. No more? He would change more; a hundred fifty, two, three hundred. As many as I wanted. I could never know how much it meant to him to get the Western money.

'I know. I understand,' I said. 'I *will* change, but a hundred Deutschmarks' worth is all I need.'

'Do you know why I have to have this money?'

'Because . . .'

'I'll tell you. For Vienna.'

He sighed. He neighed softly. He rocked backwards and stroked the edge of the table with his tailor's fingers.

'You see, I *have* to go. Now that we are able . . . I never thought I would, but now, I can allow myself to think of it.'

He came back to earth, tears in his eyes.

'I have promised my wife. I will take her to Vienna.'

'It's very beautiful. The Ringstrasse, the . . .'

'You've been there? To Vienna?'

I nodded, not meeting his eye.

It was for the music. By Vienna, Traian meant the city of maestros in powdered wigs. Now that he could travel if he had the money, Traian had set his heart on treading the cobbles round St Stephen's Dom that Mozart, Schubert, Haydn and the others had once trod. Before he died he meant to breathe the air they breathed. Because music was his thing, his fix. It had seen him through the dark years.

I asked him, 'Do you have a record player?,' and he exclaimed, 'Of course not! No! It was the BBC, *your* BBC!'

The World Service can have few more ardent fans than Traian. For thirty years he had siphoned his music clandestinely from the ether. Every Sunday at six o'clock: *The Pleasure is Yours*, with Gordon Clyde. And at Christmas, *Carols From King's* and *The Messiah. The Messiah,* oh! . . . it is so wonderful, so *wonderful!*

Under Ceauşescu Traian had worked a six-day week including sixteen hours every Saturday. He had always worked through

Christmas Day – there had been no Christmas. He had only ever eaten stale bread because it was ordained that fresh bread should be stored a day or two, then sold, or else the populace would eat too much.

'He had a very good head, Ceauşescu,' said Traian, meaning he was devilish clever. 'We didn't enjoy our lives. But we have two eyes, two ears, a nose – like Western people. We are normal people, aren't we?'

Later, he said: 'We lived like dogs.'

'We didn't enjoy our lives.' 'We lived like dogs.' Traian was passing on facts in case they were of interest. His self-respect was miraculously intact, his tone that of a Bush House continuity announcer. But it was stunningly clear that Romania had been through a nightmare of a different order from the various traumas endured by the rest of Eastern Europe.

We knew that all too well already, in a sense, from *Panorama* Specials and four-page 'Downfall Of A Tyrant' pull-outs. But here was Mr Average walking out of a crowd and voluntarily matching his own experience to the media's grisly highlights.

We met up again next morning. Traian wanted to show me Arad in daylight. First, I pleaded for breakfast, and he led the way to a coffee house, saying he would stay outside with my bicycle. I persuaded him in, but he would have neither coffee nor the pungent cheese pastries being sold with them. He waited with a smile on his face while I ate and drank, saying he was pleased there was at least something.

It was a cool, clear morning. High summer was past and we were sliding down into early autumn. The Balkans have a disarming whiff of Asia in their weather. There are no baking Mediterranean sureties here. Still, it was not too late in the year for the streets to hot up after ten.

There were queues for salami and cigarettes in Bulevardul Republicii. He confirmed what they'd said in Hungary; that there was even less food in the shops than before the revolution, because the West had stopped sending relief convoys. That was to show displeasure at the use of miners, bussed in from mining towns in the Western Carpathians, to beat up students in Bucharest in June. The students claimed that President Iliescu and his

National Salvation Front were old-style Communists by another name. The Western press went along with the students.

'They think we are Communists again,' Traian said.

'*Are* you?' I asked.

'I can travel. I met you. You helped me. That was never possible before. We have opposition parties and a new election in two years. If the people think Iliescu is trying to bring back Communism there will be another revolution.'

Outside the local offices of those opposition parties half a dozen different newspapers were being sold from a trestle table.

'We really like our papers now,' Traian said. 'We have so many, and they tell the truth. They say what really happens.' He bought a copy of *Adevarul*, The Truth.

Daubed on the opposition parties' building were three English words: FUCK THE FRONT. Traian protested mildly as I photographed them.

A little further on, the boulevard opened out. The town hall was set back on the right-hand side. On the left was the local branch of the state bank. Both were impressive buildings, nothing different from Haussmann's Paris. Both were riddled with six-month-old bullet holes, windows smashed, front doors boarded up. In front of the town hall there was a small ornamental garden and in front of the garden, on a modest wooden board, twenty-one names were painted, 'in memory of the heroes who died in the revolution of 22 December 1989'. (22 December is now Romania's National day.)

Traian explained that the Securitate had been holed up in the bank, besieged there by the regular army and a huge civilian crowd. 'The whole of Arad was here,' Traian said.

After Hungary there was a noticeable increase in the level of mutilation on the streets – related probably to a dearth of health care rather than to shootings. A quivering stump of gypsy woman's leg, raised from the pavement on which its owner sat, was pulling in some useful change. Another woman, walking slowly towards me, couldn't play her part in the usual give and take of urban pedestrian movement, the constant unconscious swaying to avoid collisions, because her feet pointed straight at each other. I began to recoil at every glimpse of an oddly-folded limb.

Back down the boulevard some orthodox priests and army veterans gathered at midday in the unimpeded sun to remember gravely the dismemberment of Moldavia in 1940.

Romania sided with the Axis powers at the beginning of the war, unaware that in a secret protocol to the Nazi-Soviet pact of August 1939, Hitler had ceded control of parts of Bessarabia and Bukovina to Stalin. The Red Army moved in the following year and has stayed there ever since.

This was the fiftieth anniversary of the invasion, and the first which the Romanians had been allowed to mark with a ceremony. The veterans sang hauntingly and sweated buckets. A basket of woven loaves was consecrated and anointed with a golden wine, then distributed to the veterans and members of the crowd.

'You want some?' Traian asked. 'In fact I think we should leave it for the poor people.'

We went to his house, where his wife was preparing lunch. She had wanted to attend the ceremony, but if there was to be company for lunch, lunch was to be special. We started with clear soup in which balls of semolina floated. Then we had pieces of fried chicken with mashed potato and a salad made of green beans and tomatoes. Then peaches, then coffee. None of these things was available in shops. All had to be home-grown or somehow wangled.

The house in which Traian and his wife had lived their forty married years was a delightful russet-coloured cottage, one storey high, in the shaped of an L. It had a walled yard, in one corner of which stood a shed, the whole compound being roughly the size of two large caravans side by side. The difficulty was that two other families shared it. Traian and his wife had the use of three rooms and a lavatory. Lacking a shower or bath, they washed dishes, clothes, and themselves in the small triangular kitchen sink. They had done so for forty years. Forty years of sixteen-hour Saturdays, to retire to this. They weren't complaining. Material hardship is only relative. They had grown used to this. It hadn't starved them. The idea of a lusher life had never come close enough to taunt them – until now. Now acquaintances were travelling, foreigners were visiting. For example, here was someone who had *seen* Vienna, sitting at their table. Ah well, you had to laugh, and hold the lid down tightly on your hopes, and treat a bonus as a bonus, not demand it as a right – not when you were old. That would hurt too much, looking back.

'You know, the worst thing with Ceauşescu was not how we lived. I mean, not the house, the food, the work. It was lying all the time. Everyone, to everyone. No one told the truth. So there was no respect . . . between people. There could be no respect.'

Some Western analysts reckon one in four Romanians acted as informers for the Securitate. Traian put it at two in three. Whatever the truth there had been 'no respect'. In its quiet way, this was the most horrific thing he'd said. It implied a population set against itself not along tribal or class lines, but individually; millions of people unable, because of endemic mutual suspicion, to like each other. 'We did not enjoy our lives.' 'We lived like dogs.'

I said I very much hoped they made it to Vienna, and promised to send a tape of the *Messiah* in time for Christmas. As I wheeled my bike out of the yard, Traian was on the point of tears again.

Timişoara

'. . . numbingly poor . . . the kind of bleak town you want to forget as soon as you have passed through it.'

Observer

This is harsh. It may be that one is more easily impressed by places when approaching them slowly, out of a peasant world, than when arriving on a media roller-coaster which stops only at international headline flashpoints. Or it may be that the roller-coaster had created a reputation for this place, a reputation which now preceded it. Either way, I found Timişoara worth remembering. It seemed to have sophistication, chutzpah, depth.

It was nine in the evening and dark as I rode into town. The signs to *Centru* stopped at a taxi rank by an expanse of marble in front of the opera house. On the far side a bored crowd of eighteen-to-thirties queued for pizza from a pizza wagon with Pepsi machines but no Pepsi. On the near side a swathe of marble was taken up by café tables, at one of which I sat, to be joined in no time by a tall youth with a red rose. He was good-looking, well turned-out, killing time before going to meet his girlfriend off a train. He spoke French and English.

Yes, he said, there could be another revolution, because Gorbachev and Iliescu had been fellow students and Iliescu had brought a pro-Soviet team to power. But it would not be bloody like the last one.

'People have had enough of death,' he said. 'And if a peasant has a full stomach, he is happy.'

My companion was a student, in computers, with sure-fire job prospects. So sure-fire, in fact, that graduating didn't matter. Next year he meant to move to his girlfriend's town and marry her. For now he lived alone in Timişoara where he had not had hot water for a month. He looked at his watch. He had to go.

'Enjoy your stay in Timişoara, if that is possible,' he said, and legged it to the station.

I stayed at a campsite where the balding night receptionist, Dalemian, turned out to be a passionate advocate of colonizing outer space. My fellow guests included four Lebanese hoping to find work in Italy, a Kurdish refugee from Iraq who spoke out against Saddam Hussein's genocidal nerve gas attacks on his people, and a Palestinian student from the West Bank who supported Saddam Hussein's invasion of Kuwait because Kuwait was rich but had not been helping poorer Arab nations. Timişoara was on the road to the Levant.

The tram screeched slowly to a stop. This seemed to be a market square, though only news and Loto stalls were trading. The streets were cobbled but cobblestones had been torn up to let the tramlines in. In the shopfronts and townhouses there was a latent, beat-up beauty; plaster painted red and pink had been exquisitely arranged round doors and windows, scores of years ago – since when it had been left to crumble. Timişoarans queued, talked, filled the narrow pavements. Five products were on sale in the food shop: peas in jars, beans in jars, flour, unwrapped brown soap, and ship's biscuits in packs of ten. In the butcher there were hunks of wizened pork. The greengrocer had eggs and tomatoes.

To be honest, the absence of any discernible fun or point in life in downtown daytime Timişoara weighed instantly and heavily on the soul.

But the shopping scene perked up a short walk away over a dirty canal into which fearless whippersnappers in tatty swimming trunks were diving from the top of a flight of steps (which they approached at a run). Over this canal was the market proper; heaps of produce, unadorned but fresh and real. Grapes, aubergines, paprika, garlic, tomatoes, carrots, potatoes, melons, cucumbers. And across the road, in a private car-boot import kiosk: hazelnut chocolate spread, black jeans, bubble gum, filter cigarettes, a radio, electric bulb sockets, one pair of pink high-heeled shoes, Elton John LPs in Russian sleeves, Queen's *Greatest Hits*.

It was time for a sit-down. My last haircut had been in Prague, two and a half months ago. For some time it had been in the back of my mind that if I saw a barbershop . . . *et voilà*. Back over the canal, in desirable corner premises: a *Frizerie Categoria Lux*. I took a seat beside the manicure lady, and made eye contact with three other men waiting for haircuts, so they knew I knew I was number four.

There were ten chairs in operation and three groups of aspiring customers, waiting.

I waited for an hour beside the manicure lady. Her clients were always women. They would arrive with perfect nails and have them stripped, washed, cut, washed, trimmed, washed, filed, washed, shaped, washed, varnished, dried and painted. They would chatter throughout, and the manicure lady would listen with a long face.

The barber in my sights spent fifty minutes patting the blonde curls of a man built like a stick insect. To his right an apprentice who was wearing almost nothing under her white work coat fondled the black locks of an admirer. My man took one more from his queue, a tramp in galoshes. He ran an electric shearer over the tramp's wrinkled skull, turning him in three minutes into a skinhead. Then he packed away his tools and disappeared.

I moved to another cluster of would-be clients and waited

another hour, at the end of which three adjacent chairs became available at once. No one filled them. The barbers waited. Then the room darkened as two men appeared silhouetted in the doorway. A car door slammed outside. A third man swaggered in, between the other two, and led them in an arrowhead to the vacant chairs. They all sat down, the barbers standing ready with pristine neck towels. The man on the right gave the leader a Camel cigarette and lit it. The man on the left, I realized, was fixing me with a cordite stare in the mirror. I dropped my gaze. He had snakeskin slip-ons, white socks, baggy trousers, designer short-sleeved shirt, a dark brown face, and dark brown executioners' arms.

I made my exit then, without a haircut.

U.S.L.A.

Emerging from the barbershop I wandered aimlessly for a while, became lost, and asked a tall man with one or two surface capillaries burst on his cheeks, which way to the centre. He looked around quickly and hissed in German:

'Where are you from?'

'England.'

'Good, very good.' (Switching to English.) 'Now, what are you doing here?'

'Sightseeing, I suppose.'

'It's not possible! There is nothing to see, nothing touristical in Timişoara. So. You are interested in our so-called revolution?'

'Yes.'

'So. I knew it. Now, if you are *really* interested in our so-called revolution you must go to Radio Timişoara and ask . . .' He broke off and looked around again. A small boy was approaching with a crate of empty soft drinks bottles. 'And ask about oosla.'

'Oosla?'

'Sssh!'

'Can you write it down for me?'

'Of course. No. You write it. U.S.L.A. Usla.' (Whispering now.) 'That is *Unitate Speciale de Lupte Anti-Terrorist,* the new

Securitate. It is worse than with Ceauşescu. Ask at Radio Timişoara. Now we have *neo-Communismus,* so for what was our
so-called revolution?'

Radio Timişoara was situated in a large house in a southern
suburb of the city. It seemed a cosmopolitan place, broadcasting
in German, Hungarian, Serbian, and Bulgarian as well as Romanian, to cater for Banat's minorities. When the shooting started in
December 1989 the foreign press descended on it to use its
telephones to send their copy home. Inquisitive Westerners raise
no eyebrows here.

A young man came downstairs and said he would be translating
for one of the news editors, who would be along shortly.

'But I must tell you,' the young man said, 'this station is run by
the state, so the editor may not be able to answer all your
questions . . . candidly?'

'Candidly, yes. I see.'

'He knows a lot, but perhaps he will not say a lot.'

The editor waddled down. He had a double chin and a fine
selection of warts on his face. He suggested we go round the
corner to a café. Once there, seated under a pavement umbrella, I
asked about censorship.

'We have an absolutely independent editorial policy despite
being financed by the state. Ceauşescu closed us down in 1985,
along with all regional radio stations, because he wanted to be the
only man in the country behind a microphone. But we were the
first to re-open, on 22 December. If the government issues a new
censorship law I will put down the microphone and go back to
selling potatoes.'

As a journalist unfettered by censorship, then, did he regard
what had happened in December as a revolution? (Our translator
was doing only fairly well at translating Romanian into German.
It turned out that the editor had fluent German after all and he
took over.)

'What happened in Timişoara from 15th to 20th December was
real revolution. What happened in Bucharest was completely
different. We say in Timişoara they have stolen our revolution.
They want everything. They want to work like socialists and live

like capitalists. But in Timişoara we are much closer to the West, geographically, mentally.'

But for the country as a whole, had the so-called revolution done the job? One system out, a new one in?

'Romania's was the first revolution in Eastern Europe which said categorically, "no more Communism". In Czechoslovakia it was a revolution in *Hausschuhe* – in slippers. We had to struggle. We won our freedom, and that freedom is safe. Now the rest of Ceauşescu's people must go.'

Could there be another revolution?

'Yes, it's possible. If there must be, there will be. But we hope there won't be. We have wives and children.'

'And what is the role of USLA in Romania at the moment?'

'USLA?'

'Yes.'

'It's nothing. It used to be a sort of commando unit, but it's gone now.'

He said we should be winding up. He had a bulletin to prepare. I asked his name.

'No. I prefer not to say. This was informal, with a cup of coffee, yes?'

Finally, I asked: 'What should I have asked that I haven't?' and he thought for a moment.

'You might have asked why I didn't speak German at first.'

'Why didn't you speak German at first?'

'I thought maybe I would have to be careful. I didn't know what kind of questions you would ask.'

Dalemian, the night receptionist at the campsite, was still on duty as I prepared to leave the next morning. As I strapped on the panniers he leaned in the doorway, smoking, and looking generally knowing.

'It has been demonstrated,' he said after a while, 'that if you are moving along, say on a bicycle, past people who are standing or just walking slowly, you feel some kind of superiority. Don't you feel that? On your bicycle, don't you want to whistle or sing?'

'Yes, I often sing – badly, to myself. But that doesn't mean I feel . . .'

'I know, I know. That doesn't mean you feel superior. But bear it in mind. You Westerners, you underestimate Romanians.'

He grinned. I think I took it in the spirit he intended, and grinned back. But as I rode away I kept my mouth shut.

The Magyar Groove

A young man, a hairdresser by the name of Marcia, had fallen in love with my bicycle in the campsite in Timişoara. It was a becoming love, which he knew would be unrequited, and he was content simply to admire its object from a respectable distance – from a partially shredded car seat under a tree.

We got talking. He said he would rather have a bicycle like mine than a million dollars or a Western car or a fancy woman. I said he could have a ride round the car park if he liked. Marcia gulped at first in disbelief, then went over and stood touching the brake levers and gear levers, murmuring with delight. He felt the tyres and flicked the spokes to hear the ping. He swung a leg over and got used to the saddle, and put his toes in the toe-clips and tightened the straps. Then he pushed off and changed down several gears, and began to describe slow, swooning figures of eight over the tarmac. After a while he changed to loops. He would turn by the reception, turn by the shower block, and accelerate, tensed, between them.

Soon, brimming with expressions of pure pleasure, he returned to where I stood. He pointed to his own bicycle, a red shopper with a baby seat and a saddlebag. I hadn't noticed it. From the saddlebag he produced a piece of nougat sandwiched between layers of honeycomb and gave it to me.

Marcia lived a few kilometres outside Timişoara on the road to Lugoj. I was bound for Lugoj, so we left town together, side by side. He would often look across and talk about *ritmo*.

'*Ritmo, ritmo,* ah *ritmo!*'

'Ritmo?'

'*Ritmo,* yes. *Ritmo* so good. *Ritmo* . . . so important! On your bicycle I could be in Lugoj in one hour.'

Marcia was bragging, naturally. It was sixty kilometres to Lugoj and I had found the maximum sustainable speed by a normal person on a laden bike to be about twenty kilometres an hour.

We reached Marcia's village in the heat of the day and I was quick to accept his invitation to lunch. We sat on a bench outside his house flicking grain at chickens while his wife fried eggs and chopped tomatoes upstairs.

The music which accompanied lunch was, for the first time in months, not Europop. It was Balkan siren music with a voice and something like a balalaika going at full stretch without pause for breath or beat. I said how good it sounded and Marcia waved me down – no need to be polite, just wait for the next track. The next track was the Lambada.

'For my wife, it is the favourite,' said Marcia, and sure enough, his wife seemed to have withdrawn into some imaginary pleasure dome, behind the shuttered eyes and private smile of the sated junkie.

Since Marcia cut people's hair, I told him about my abortive wait to have mine cut the day before. He knew the kind of thing. Oh yes, he could just imagine it happening to someone like me. 'Gypsy *mafiosi*', he said. Timişoara was a big Mafia town, first stop inside Romania on the smuggling route from Yugoslavia. Some of Romania's richest 'businessmen' (*bisnitsar*) operated from Timişoara, and most of them were gypsies, Marcia said. He showed me his packet of Port cigarettes, Product of Yugoslavia, '*mafiosi cigaretti*'.

Lugoj was not remarkable for anything. Outside a sports hall there was a bronze statue of a girl doing modern rhythmic gymnastics with a ball. Hoping to find latter-day Nadia Comanecj doing tumbling tricks, I stopped and nosed around but the place was locked and silent. Lugoj could not even offer anything to drink. Once through the town I stopped to pee, and the pee was thick and orange. A familiar and unwelcome pounding began in my head, distant at first, but heading purposefully for that tender spot between the eyes. The sun burned on down. It had got a new job as migraine-bringer. I now craved water. Water, please, anyone.

At Lugoj I left the main road, and the Banat Plain. This time there was no pleasure in leaving flatness behind. The slight uphill gradient was intensely hard work. The pounding had arrived in my forehead like a thrash metal band. What saliva was left in my mouth was viscous and salty.

Then I came upon a watermelon stall. It consisted of a heap of melons at the bottom of a melon field, and an old man sitting behind a table with a knife. One of the great things about a heap of watermelons is that it cannot be faked by a mirage. The man cut up a whole melon and nodded approvingly as I gorged myself on it. He goaded me to eat the whole thing, which I did, the eating of watermelons being merely drinking by other means. Then I sat down under a tree and let the liquid begin its progress towards my bladder. This was perfect – the timing, the melon itself, the shade, the westward view over the plain. Now, I thought, let Transylvania commence.

Beyond the melon stall it was a short, hot grind to the first horizon. Then the road settled into a lolloping rhythm, over hummocks, into dips, round the ends of wooded noses, through collective vineyards. The road was virtually unused. It passed through Traian Vuia, a village on a bare hill without a single car or tractor. It had a well, though, twenty metres deep, and a man levered himself off a bench to lower the bucket for me. Along the high street three old women were sweeping gravel from between vegetable patches in front of their houses and a man was pulling grass out of the storm drain.

A big crescent moon rose long before the sun went down, so nightfall was extremely gradual. Higher hills to the south rolled towards the road in four descending stages and four different shades of blue. As the road approached a crest, two desiccated farm labourers appeared against the sky, acting as their own pack-horses, pulling wooden tubs full of grapes on handcarts.

At the crest there was a sharp left turn and a sign welcoming travellers to Dumbrava. I attracted some attention at the bar in

Dumbrava by locking my bike outside it, collecting some beer and cigarettes, and sitting down to write. After about quarter of an hour a displaced Moldavian peasant dared to talk to me. He carried a baby.

'*Aimego, aimego.*'

'Nice baby,' I said.

'*Aimego, aimego.*'

'Yes, yes.'

He wanted me to go back to his place and drink vodka. He was insistent, and foolishly I gave in. A third party who wanted to change Yugoslav dinars for dollars tagged along saying the man with the baby was drunk and uncultured. I asked what '*aimego*' meant.

'*Amigo*. Friend.'

So I was the friend of the man with the baby. This did not fill me with joy. In fact, when he surrounded me with brothers and tried to lock my bike with his own lock, it filled me with alarm. I said that my own lock would do fine. We all repaired from the kitchen, which the bike was sharing with a rooster, to the only other room in the house. The Moldavian's wife was pregnant again. They were both very young and their only possessions seemed to be their clothes, a few blankets and a single shot-glass. Flies were everywhere. The shot-glass was passed round and I tried not to drink but the din of protest this raised was irresistible.

The brothers seemed to be determined that I spend the night here. I was convinced I had been stupid to get myself into this. On my first night in Romania I had been separated from my penknife by half a pint of whisky. With my bike in the kitchen the stakes were a little higher. I observed, by opening and shutting my mouth silently, that we couldn't understand each other, and the peasant sent for yet another brother.

'*Francia, Francia.*'

A French-speaking brother would be along in no time at all. The moment he arrived a wave of guilty relief hit me. Guilty, because here, recognizable at once, was a member of my tribe, the middle class, and I knew things were going to be OK. Meanwhile, because of his crushing poverty, I had failed to trust the man with the baby.

The man who spoke French was tall, alert, polite, and wearing only red football shorts. He did not in fact speak French. That was his wife, who followed him into the room. But both spoke a little English, and, as their mother tongue, Hungarian. There was a sense among the others that someone of importance had arrived. They fell silent, and offered stools and vodka.

The new arrivals' names were Marton and Cilla. Our conversation was exclusive from the start, and, in case I was in any doubt, Cilla said at once: 'We are Hungarian, you know.'

At first the man whose *aimego* I was supposed to be looked on smiling, pleased at having brought together these speakers of foreign tongues. Then he barked a question at Marton, who relayed it to me:

'Where will you be sleeping tonight?'

'Here, I think. They want me to,' I said.

Marton invited me to his house; it was big and comfortable, he said, with a spare room and Yugoslavian television. I said I didn't want to cause offence by getting up and leaving, unless he thought it would be foolish to stay. Marton misunderstood, thinking I was worried about the old ban on contact with foreigners, which had gone out with the revolution.

A bit later, he volunteered: 'I do not trust these people,' at which point I opted to escape.

As I stood to go the Moldavian put down the baby and tugged at my arm. He started haranguing Marton, and darted in front of us into the kitchen to lean against my bike. Marton lifted him bodily aside and threatened to call the police. To me he said: 'Take the bicycle and follow my wife.' I stumbled out, unable to look the shouting Moldavian in the eye. I walked fast with Cilla back along a dirt road towards the bar, apologizing for barging into her community and bringing only strife. She steered me up her garden path, locked my bike in the garage, sat me down in the kitchen with her father and a cup of tea, and said not to worry – the strife was there already. Marton appeared, out of breath. The Moldavian was at the garden gate, he said, and wanted my assurance that I wouldn't go to the police about him. Also, if possible, some cigarettes. I dug a packet of Kent out of a pannier and went and gave the Moldavian my assurance. Relief spread visibly into his face under the moon, and we parted, if not as friends, then as *aimegos*.

Marton could afford to behave as he had with the Moldavian because Magyars were in a majority in Dumbrava. The village was founded in 1892 by Hungarian protestants from near Bekescsaba in western Hungary, where the land was too poor to support the growing population.

Next morning, the first Sunday morning in September, Cilla and her parents went to church – to the simple white church her great-grandfather had founded with the other pioneers in 1900. They wore their Sunday best, and so did their neighbours, whom they greeted quietly along the footpath through the churchyard. All the principal people of the village were there, and the congregation numbered about forty-five.

Churchgoers had been fewer under Ceauşescu, Cilla said, but weekly services had still been held. The older people had attended; those with less to lose. My Moldavian *aimego* was not, of course, at church. If he had religious inclinations they would probably be Orthodox, but Cilla suspected he was sleeping off the previous night.

Over breakfast I remarked that in Hungary itself all I heard about Romania was tales of oppressed ethnic Hungarians, but in Dumbrava there was little sign of that. Cilla answered:

'If you want a better life and you work, then you can get it. Maybe all that the Moldavians *want* is to drink.'

Marton was altogether more relaxed than his wife. He watched the television in his football shorts instead of going to church, and he took a mellower line on the inter-ethnic question. He avowed that stealing had become a way of life for some Moldavians and gypsies, but he blamed it on Ceauşescu. By spiriting away for export everything of value they produced, the dictator had driven them to crime. And as for those Hungarians campaigning for the return of Transylvania to Hungary – they were chasing a red herring.

'If I have a passport, and if I may change lei into forints, what does the border matter?'

He drew a map of how to find his parents' house in Cluj-Napoca and said he'd phone ahead to warn them I was coming. I was going to be expected somewhere. That was a novel and very welcome feeling.

The river which drains most of Transylvania is the Mureş. It mimics the layout of the Carpathians, but flows to the north and west of them, collecting all the water from the shorter, straighter mountain rivers.

The Mureş valley has been a vital transport corridor since Roman times, scything through countryside where easy engineering terrain is scarce. Over most of its length the river is flanked by a railway line and two paved highways, one of them a thundering truck alley. This is one of the grimy guts of Romania, and a hundred and fifty miles of it lay between Dumbrava and Cluj-Napoca.

In the town of Faget, half an hour beyond Dumbrava, my tyre went soft and my pump stopped working. An English-speaking Hungarian fixed the pump for me and on the way back to the bike he pointed to an empty plot in a line of old houses on the main street. 'That used to be the bank. It was a fine building of two storeys, in the same style as the houses. They destroyed it.'

In other words, Faget's name had come to the top of the list. Ceauşescu's engineers had begun the job of making Faget a town fit for Romanians to live in. A spaceship-like restaurant complex in white marble was one result. Forlorn blocks of flats visible through the space vacated by the old bank were another.

A moisturizing mist was settling on the hills between Faget and the valley of the Mureş. The parched grass needed it. The trees glistened under it – there was no wind. The mist fell softly out of a thick duvet of cloud, dampening colours and the infrequent sound of hooves or engines.

It was a Sunday afternoon, the first of the autumn. De-dum. Pause. De-dum. Pause. De-dum. Change down again. De-dum. The road was made of rough concrete slabs and the wheels noticed every join between them.

A dog barked, higher up. About a dozen wooden houses lined the road at the top of the hill. They were long and low, arranged side by side like a fishbone, and bore traces of the olden days. Boxes of sturdy red flowers lit up the windows facing the road and beside each house there was a carved wood gateway high enough to take a haywain. A few women in dark shawls talked over their proverbial garden fences but it was still a lonely, muted place, now overshadowed by a radio transmission tower.

It took a day and a half, with blinkers on, to get to Cluj-Napoca. The first moments on the main road up the Mureş valley were exhilarating; there was the luxury of real tarmac and the fuel injection of a following wind. But on the wind came the malevolent black outpourings of smokestacks tucked into every geo-alcove along the river. On the far side, the contents of several giant open-cast mines were on display in miles of terraced slag-heaps. Dumper trucks shuttled between the mines and the road, unloading onto juggernauts which pushed bow-waves of diesel-heated air. These hit you with an unsettling time delay of about a second and a half.

Approaching Cluj-Napoca after dark, I crashed into some unmarked roadworks at the bottom of an awesome sequence of hairpins which takes traffic off the surrounding hills into the city. The bike seemed OK, however, and Marton's map to his parents' house was accurate in every detail.

Cluj-Napoca has a population of 320,000 of which only 5 per cent is Hungarian, because of settlement in accordance with Ceauşescu's Romanianization programme. However, I hardly spoke to a single Romanian there; I was in the Magyar groove.

Marton's father, a retired lawyer, had not seen an *Englander* in all his sixty-one years. He was waiting up with schnapps even though he seldom drank it, surgeons having removed most of his gut. Marton's mother was up too, waiting to cook. Marton's cousin, Jozsef Kocsis, and the cousin's girlfriend were also there, waiting to eat. I realized they had been waiting for some time and apologized for being late.

'You are not late, you are *here*,' said the father. The cousin translated this into German, the girlfriend into English. The mother said she hoped I was hungry. I said food was my *benzin*, my petrol, and everyone seemed reasonably happy with that. The father poured the schnapps.

Marton's parents, Mr and Mrs Orban, lived on the ground floor of a three-storey building which, with the Botars on the second floor and the Kocsis family on the third, they had built themselves ten years before. The three families were one extended family. Everyone was everyone else's cousin, aunt, uncle, nephew, or niece.

The building had one entrance, an archway through the ground floor as in a coaching inn. Intentionally or not, it was a good defensive arrangement; shut the gate in the archway, and anti-Magyar rioters or the Securitate would have to shoot their way in.

Behind the house there were two garages, a pig-pen for four pigs and trellising for vines.

Mr Orban, whose first name was Attila, raised his glass and we drank to Anglo-Transylvanian relations.

Annamaria Ferenc, the cousin's girlfriend, asked what I planned to do in Koloszvar (which is what Hungarians call Cluj-Napoca). I mentioned MADISZ, an organization of Hungarian youth in Romania, and she looked sad and said that some of her friends, organizers of MADISZ among them, had had the courage to pack up and go west and get out of 'this *miseria*' – but not she. Escaping was too expensive.

Her *miseria* consisted of making paint brushes from eight to twelve each morning for 4 lei an hour ($0.30 at the official rate, $0.06 on the black market). In the afternoons and evenings she studied electronic engineering at the university.

Annamaria went to bed – she had to leave for the paintbrush factory at six. Soon I went upstairs too, to the Kocsis' sitting room where I was to sleep. It had been a 170-kilometre day, my longest yet.

Jozsef, known as Josi, weighed a hundred kilos and was proud of it. Next morning he cooked *Eierbraten* for breakfast using an onion, six inches of chopped salami, and six eggs. He too studied engineering. He had important exams looming, but would not think of revising for them when he could be showing me round. Besides, only one exam needed real preparation. He had already secured a pass in the other by the discreet deployment of a packet of coffee and a litre of brandy.

'Everyone does it,' he said. 'African students get entire degrees with Kent cigarettes. That professor has everything.'

We walked to the MADISZ office in the university through the city centre. In Cluj, as in Arad, the bloodiest day of the revolution was 22 December 1989. The venue: Piata Libertatii. It remained a gracious Hapsburg square, having escaped Ceauşescu's razing-and-rebuilding tendencies. But its south-west corner had been comprehensively shot up and not yet repaired. Fresh flowers were still being laid and candles lit where civilians had been gunned down: a wreath over a post box opposite the Hotel Continental, candles along the north wall of the university bookshop, where piles of Ceauşescu's books had been burned and where Securitate machine guns had exacted brief revenge. There were candles, also, under an old statue of a she-wolf suckling Romulus and Remus.

Josi said: 'Ceauşescu liked his years as president to be referred to as "the golden Era," or "the twenty years of light".'

We walked west, to the university and MADISZ.

Here, up a broad stone spiral staircase in rooms of effortless neo-classical proportions, a handful of students was trying to re-kindle Transylvania's traditional inter-ethnic harmony.

Historically, Hungarians and Romanians in Transylvania got on. They understood each other's languages and had enough to eat. It was Ceauşescu's forced resettlement to Transylvania of Moldavians and Ortanians (from Wallachia) that upset the balance. The newcomers resented Magyar foreignness. They blamed Magyars when things got tough – as things did under Ceauşescu – and they supported Ceauşescu's abolition of Hungarian in schools and universities.

Hungarians and Romanians forgot their differences during the revolution and for a brief honeymoon after it. Then Hungarians demanded the reopening of the Hungarian university in Cluj, closed in 1959. In response, Romanian nationalists propagated the idea that Transylvanian Hungarians wanted Transylvania to be returned to Hungary. On 19 March fighting broke out between Hungarians and Romanians in Tîrgu Mureş, east of Cluj. Six were killed.

A young and garrulous journalist by the name of Laszlo Torok came in from the neighbouring offices of a youth magazine and spoke on these matters – in American – for MADISZ.

The fighting in Tîrgu Mureş, he said, was a case of 'manipulation of the population by the government'.

The idea that Transylvania should be part of Hungary came from everyone but Transylvanians themselves.

'Even the Hungarians from Hungary can't understand our situation. We don't want Transylvania to return to Hungary because six million Romanians live here. We just want to study in our mother language. Romanians say if we are Hungarian we should go to Hungary, but we were born here and we want to stay here.'

At that point the MADISZ people ran out of things to say, so Josi and I left.

Naomi Ferenc wanted to be a concert pianist. She swivelled round on her piano stool.

'Which concerts have you been to in England? Do you know Michelangeli? Who is your favourite composer for the piano? Mine is César Franck –' she swivelled back and tore into Franck's *Praeludium Chorale and Fuge,* '– and I will play that piece in Budapest for the conservatoire.'

Naomi was Annamaria's younger sister. Her piano, a Jan Wirth boudoir grand, filled the sitting room in their flat across the city, half-way up the hill on which I'd crashed. She was tall, eighteen and easily flushed. She had been to a summer school in Budapest and the professor there had said she was good enough for the conservatoire. What a triumph that would be! To go west not as an economic refugee but as a bright young talent with an invitation.

So how good was she, really?

'Do you like Beethoven?' I asked. 'Can you play the sonata with the really fast left hand and the tune in the right hand?'

'You mean number ninety, I think,' said Naomi, and she played the entire first movement flawlessly, from memory.

Annamaria sat slumped in the sofa watching her sister play. Josi was in the kitchen doing electrical repairs for their mother. I more or less forgot I was in Romania. But after the Beethoven, Annamaria reminded me; we returned to the subject of her *miseria*. We agreed that in fact it was probably more courageous to stay in Romania than to flee it, but this did not console her for long.

'Many people say, "I only have one life",' she said. 'Two thousand Hungarian students are leaving the university this year to go to Hungary. They say they will come back, but they won't. After five years they'll be used to that other way of life.'

Josi's parents were in Hungary on a shopping trip, but were due back at any time. We had to go and tidy the flat before they arrived. Naomi said goodbye pink-faced and excited, Annamaria with a doleful smile.

We walked down the hill, the Ferenc home receding into a bank of a thousand stacked boxes. But at least they all had balconies, and from many of these, satellite dishes faced hopefully up into the western sky. Some were bought but most were home-made. One, more like a tin bra than a dish, was a signal thief. It was directed not at the stratosphere but at another dish off which, in principle, it could siphon the West in all its sensational, porno-graphic gaudiness into its ingenious designer's living room.

'I could make one of them,' Josi said. 'But not the decoder, and the decoder is too expensive to buy.'

Among the goodies which his parents brought back from Budapest that night were two books on TV aerials and dishes. There was also beer, wine, cream cheese, pork crackling, and a loaf of bread the size of a pillow.

'They know how to bake in Budapest. Not like here,' Josi's mother muttered. But she was not a mutterer by nature. She was a bustling incarnation of cheerfulness, given to brief intervals of despair. She wore yellow most of the time and was no taller than your average long-handled broom. Her final car-boot flourish was to produce for Josi an enormous printed Indian cotton shirt, price 900 forints, which made him look like Pavarotti. She stood on tiptoe to be kissed. Josi, whose hobby was potholing, thanked her 'from the heart'.

When I eventually left Cluj-Napoca/Koloszvar it was with the address of a potholing friend of Josi's in Tîrgu Mureş – Hungar-ian, of course. The friend would be expecting me; the Magyar groove continued.

Tîrgu Mureş or the Front Line

The population of Tîrgu Mureş is half Romanian and half Hungarian. It is not a comfortable place to sit on the fence when the halves are at loggerheads; in respect of this particular Balkan tension, Tîrgu Mureş is the front line. And Josi's friends, the Pechy family, were correspondingly virulent in their views, though none more so than Sandor Pechy's girlfriend, Juliet.

'Romanians don't want to work. No really. Balkan people – Romanians, Bulgarians, Turks – they *do not want to work*.

'I can tell a Romanian at a glance, at fifty paces. Most of them come from villages. They dress differently. They *smell* differently.'

I had arrived after dark. The ride from Cluj had not been pleasant. The road was made of concrete slabs again. The air was full of penetrating grey damp. My forks turned out to have been knocked loose by the crash on the hill into Cluj. And a screw had gone from the pannier rack so that it clicked between the slabs. De-click. De-click. De-click.

I arrived in time for supper with the Pechys (and Juliet and two card-playing associates of Mr Pechy's). It was an intense affair. They were reserved at first, but they became impassioned. The talk was bunker talk, the liquor neat Polish alcohol flavoured with cherry concentrate, the smoking non-stop. We ate tomatoes, ham and *pasztet* (chicken paste) off a white tablecloth under a strong white light, smoking all the time. Juliet sat on my left, Sandor on my right. They both had dark brown eyes and long, straight, dark brown hair. Both were short and lean. Sandor's face was dominated by a big, downturned moustache, and he lacked only a beaten helmet of leather and iron to look like a medieval warring Hun. Mr Pechy and the other men sat further down the table, talking, eating, constantly replenishing the cloud of blue tobacco smoke beneath the light, and hardly ever laughing. Mrs Pechy and her daughter, Marta, hovered round the table filling up the bowls of food when they ran low. It must be like this when terrorists get together to plot.

They were discussing the mass exodus of ethnic Germans from Transylvania. They may not have been Hungarians but at least they were not Balkan peoples, and as a non-Romanian minority they were fellow sufferers of Romanianization. Now they were going. With the borders open they were exercising their constitutional right to citizenship of the Fatherland. Twenty thousand had gone since the revolution and thousands more escaped each week.

'Why are the Saxons running away?' Juliet demanded, and the answer seemed to be 'because they can'.

For Hungarians in Tîrgu Mureş, who could not escape, relations with Romanians turned violent. Mr Pechy had been in the town centre on 19 March with his brother, and had seen the fighting.

'We were not frightened because we never thought there would be shooting,' he said. Then the army had opened fire into the crowd.

'Six people died,' said Juliet. 'Three Romanians, three Hungarians. Fifty-fifty.'

'Five Hungarians, one Romanian,' snapped Mr Pechy.

Whoever really started it, a spark was all that had been needed – and another spark now could set off something similar or worse. Their exposition of the Magyars' plight seemed as if it would never end. I had walked into a hive of fanatics. Perhaps they saw their visitor as a megaphone to the outside world.

'We are waiting for another revolution,' Sandor said. 'I am sure it will come.'

When it did, he wanted an independent Transylvania in which indigenous Hungarians and Romanians would live together in harmony, as they had for centuries. But to campaign for such a Transylvania was impossible, Sandor said. Even to talk about it was dangerous.

'When you talk to Romanians please do not talk politics. Especially do not say what we have talked about. It will only make things worse.'

Juliet offered to show me round. Sandor was chauffeur. We zoomed off up a hill in Mr Pechy's red Dacia and admired Tîrgu Mureş from a lookout point littered with broken bottles. The River Mureş passes Tîrgu Mureş to the north, in a grand sweep. On the near side of the river a factory which Juliet said produced furniture was belching thick brown smoke. But up here the air was clean and the view beyond the factory was of khaki hills and pine woods.

Ceauşescu himself had apparently enjoyed this view from a Securitate retreat near the lookout point.

'But he did not like to come to Tîrgu Mureş,' Juliet said. 'There are too many Hungarians here.'

The high point of the tour was Count Samuel Teleki's library. Among the 40,000 volumes collected by Teleki were priceless hand-coloured incunabula and important collections of ancient scientific and medical books, including the first book ever printed in Hungarian on medicine, a 1695 translation of Hippocrates. Occupying an entire display case was a giant history of astronomy open at a Ptolemaic map of the universe, with the world at the centre like a peach stone.

But the best shelves were of the French philosophers of Teleki's time. There were first editions of all the major works of Descartes, Rousseau, Montesquieu, Voltaire . . . *Candide* – a 1759 edition; a copper-cornered *Contrat Social* of 1795; a 1770 set of Diderot's *Encyclopédie*.

It had been here all the time. Tucked away in Tîrgu Mureş while Ceauşescu destroyed the country in his egomania, the entire intellectual arsenal of the Third Estate, the books which had brought rational thought to the Western world exactly two hundred years before, waiting to be read.

At four o'clock we sat down to a massive lunch and Juliet asked where I was headed next. I showed her on my map where I hoped eventually to cross the Carpathians.

'No. It is not possible,' she said. 'Sandor, tell him it is impossible to do Trans-Fagaraş by bicycle.'

Sandor obliged: 'Trans-Fagaraş – impossible.'

Juliet returned to the attack. 'There is no food, there are no people, there may be snow. On the other side you will be robbed. You must go the way I tell you.'

I had seen pictures of this forbidden road. It crosses the highest section of the Carpathians between the two highest mountains in Romania; a prestige project masterminded by Nicolae Ceauşescu himself. I left Tîrgu Mureş relishing more eagerly than ever the prospect of Trans-Fagaraş.

Trans-Fagaraş

I spent two nights and a day in the foothills of the Eastern Carpathians. It occurred to me that however other-worldly the way of life of those who lived here seemed, for them it was the very definition of normality. And anyway, life in these hills may not have been so other-worldly. School for children. Farming and carnal knowledge for grown-ups. Eat, drink, sleep for everyone. Is that so different from Dorset? True, they managed without telephones and microwaves. But that was no reason to gawp and scribble. So instead of anthropologizing, I went native, and slept in cowherds' huts wherever nightfall found me.

We, the bike and I, were always going up or down, never on a level. The scenery was not spectacular but it nourished the soul. Watching the hills and villages unfold and inexorably rearrange themselves around my slowly moving point of view had the mesmerizing feel of watching snow fall, or waves break, or a fire.

The season was over in the spa town of Sovata. There were several large bathing pools overlooked by steep forest and extra-vagant hotels, but all were sealed off with barbed wire. Visitors contented themselves with sliding into obscene drunkenness in the rationed highland sun, and I left Sovata tut-tutting to myself in favour of Hungarian Protestant workaholism.

When the foothills handed over to the real mountains, the Muntii Harghita, the real mountains turned out to be no more than swollen foothills. That is, there were no sharp edges, cliffs, outcrops, drop-offs, gullies, waterfalls, ravines; not even any obvious summits or ridges. Very gradually, the ground beneath the pedals simply rose, like baps in a proving oven. Forest, fields and unploughed grassland took their turns along the road, but away from it, covering the quiet undulations, the trees prevailed.

Braşov, pronounced Brashoff, is sold by tour operators as Dracula Town, but it has the sort of relationship with Dracula that Troy has with Hector. The character never existed as his chroniclers portray him, and the only real person on whom the legend is in part based did not come from Braşov, or anywhere near Braşov. Count Vladimir Tepes, Vlad the Impaler, lived in the Fagaraş Mountains in the fifteenth century where he displayed the heads of captured Turks on sharpened stakes along his castle wall. The rest is myth. Even Bran Castle, in a gorge south-west of Braşov, has nothing to do with black cloaks or white fangs. It started life as a German customs post and continues it as a victim of hype.

Braşov is not so much Dracula Town as tractor town. There is a giant tractor assembly plant on the outskirts of the city beside the road to Bucharest, and its workers were the only people who ever dared, before 1989, to tell Ceauşescu that enough was enough.

They had no Lech Walesa, no '21 Wishes'. This was a desperate down-tools by workers too tired and hungry to go on – and as such it was easily dealt with by the Securitate. While crowds ransacked the Party headquarters and hard currency shops on 15 November 1987, the Securitate stood back and let their video cameras roll from the safety of an armoured car. They moved in next day to make arrests. Ring-leaders and 'expecially deviant cases' were mostly imprisoned or expelled from Braşov. A few perished in road accidents in the following months. Tractor production resumed. But on 9 September 1990, a Sunday, a local politician was able to announce to a gathering in the medieval town square that Bulevardul Lenin had been re-named Strada 15 Novembre, in memory of the tractor workers.

I was round the corner at the time, phoning home. I only heard about the gathering because most of those involved then moved to the forecourt of the Hotel Carpati, craning their necks for a glimpse of a young, bearded man called Marin Munteanu.

Munteanu had nothing to do with tractors or with 15 November 1987. His visit to Braşov was merely the occasion of the Lenin Boulevard announcement. Munteanu was the living icon of the struggle, in his own words, against neo-Communism.

'*Zona Libera de Neo-Communism – Marin Munteanu.*' The declaration was still there in black paint on the wall of the Russian Library in Piata Universitatii (University Square) when I got to Bucharest. A charismatic philosophy student, Munteanu had led a continuous sit-down strike against the National Salvation Front in University Square until he was beaten up by miners-turned-state-vigilantes in June and imprisoned for three months (at which point another slogan went up on the Russian Library: Piata Tiananmen II.)

Today, 9 September, Munteanu had just been released. During his three months in prison the miners who had beaten him up had seen the light, or were claiming to have done so. They had invited Munteanu to the Hotel Carpati for three days of heart-on-sleeve reconciliation. The miners claimed to have been infiltrated by Securitate *agents provocateurs* and manipulated (that word again) into terrorizing Bucharest. They offered a formal apology, which Munteanu accepted on the students' behalf. They declared that in the light of their reassessment of the events of June 1990 there was reassessment also to be done of the events of December 1989. The violence of the revolution not been Ceauşescu's doing alone. The prime suspects as co-culprits, so the miners said, were his successor, Iliescu, and RTV (state television).

This was breathlessly relayed to me by a Romanian journalist in the lobby of the Hotel Carpati.

He continued: 'The miners *were* infiltrated. Do you think they knew anything about Marin Munteanu? Do you think they knew where to find the headquarters of the Liberal Party in Bucharest [looted in June]? Of course not. They had to be told – by the Securitate.'

The *Herald Tribune* had been reporting the theory that the execution of Ceauşescu had been a palace *putsch* for which the concurrent street battles all over Romania were a mere smokescreen. For this journalist, the coup theory was axiomatic. December 1989 had been a beginning; the beginning of the Romanian people's struggle to rid itself of an alien tyranny.

I acquired a self-appointed minder by the name of Mihai, who said of the revolution:

'Of course it was a coup. Anyone with any sense knows that.'

Mihai was amiable and intelligent, and a breath of fresh air after the fetid paranoia of Magyar nationalists and anti-Iliescu conspiracy theorists. He was an engineering student, a tall, easy-going, jeans 'n' trainers type. It was not that he had nothing to say on politics or ethnic problems. He did: until March he had been specializing in mining engineering in Petrosani, where the vigilantes were recruited. He had seen them pile into buses and head for Bucharest three times before the June outing which caught the attention of the international press. So he had ample grounds for cynicism about Romania's new 'democracy'. And on the ethnic question he gave a matter-of-fact riposte on behalf of Romanians: 'I don't like Magyars. It is what they say about Romanians that gives us a bad reputation abroad.'

The refreshing thing about Mihai was that none of these themes obsessed him. He seemed, relatively, to have taken the trauma of revolution in his stride. His preoccupations were earthbound:

'I admit, I am a materialist. I want to be a magnate, like in America.'

In Poland, so did virtually everyone, to a tedious and sometimes depressing extent. But in Romania such extravagant hopes were rare and uplifting.

'With a profitable business anything is possible, right?'

I responded in Victor Kiam rather than *New Statesman* vein. Things like 'Yeah, triple A', and 'Go for it'.

From the Hotel Carpati we had gone to a pizzeria he knew in the old town. When it came to paying for the pizza Mihai would not be treated.

'I pay mine, you pay yours. That's the capitalist way, right?'

After saying goodbye to Mihai I rolled north from Braşov to the beginning of the Pitesti road, then south-west along it as far as Risnov.

The dark green lower flanks of the mountains rose sheer off the plain to the left. Higher up, swirling clouds joined and parted over the summits like a stripper's chiffon.

Above Risnov a castle commands the entrance to the gorge

which carries traffic to Pitesti. Here I headed west along a minor road to investigate a mountain cul-de-sac.

I was in Dictator Damage Assessment mode. The idea was to find somewhere heartrendingly beautiful to spend the night, to be sure that not all of Romania had been despoiled. On the edge of Risnov a small factory under a skein of grey pipes and chimneys straddled a stream and turned it an opaque blue. The water stank of chemistry practicals.

The next smell came from a 'meat farm' set in meadows which sloped up to the craggy southern horizon. The 'crop' – presumably pigs – was being grown entirely indoors, in a windowless hangar from which the smell of meal and faeces wafted towards the road.

There followed a pleasant interval of poplars and fresh air, and clear views straight ahead to a looming massif reminiscent of the Dolomites. Then, in the town of Zarnesti, a rust-coloured assembly line drew up alongside and stayed on my right shoulder for about a mile. It claimed to be a bicycle factory but turned out to be a munitions factory, producing, according to the locals, 'bicycles which turn into guns'.

I took a gravel road beyond Zarnesti into the mountains. It was about half past seven and the light was fading. Cabana Plaiul Foii was twelve kilometres away. The road followed a river up the bottom of a gentle valley. For nearly an hour it curled round the northern edge of the massif, which revealed itself as if unwinding; a series of tremendous limestone cliffs, shored up by forested ramparts and spliced by dark green gullies. A haywain passed, pulled by two horses. A Dacia overtook. Another haywain. Otherwise I had the valley to myself. Cabana Plaiul Foii was going to be as lonely as you could wish. The track crossed the river on a raft of logs. The tops of the cliffs glowed pink in the last of the sun. Everything else was in deep shadow, fast becoming night. Sputtering orange camp fires came into view some way ahead beside the river and I knew it was going to be one of those perfect nights.

Then I heard the beat. A disco was in progress in front of the cabana. Shortly after hearing the disco I got a puncture. I dragged the bike the last hundred yards to the car park – there was a car park – and waded across a terrace of twisting schoolchildren to inquire about sleeping.

'No.'

'Camping?'

'No.'

I looked pained and nonplussed, because I was. It was a young man with impressive bare arms who was saying no. He was putting chairs on tables and sweeping the floor in the dining room.

'Sorry. Full,' he said. Then he stopped sweeping and looked at me. He rubbed his thumb and forefinger together.

'Lei?' I asked.

'Dollar.'

'Deutschmark?'

'Deutschmark. How many?'

'You tell me. How many?'

'Two.'

'Two?'

'Three.'

'Three. OK.' That was about a pound. He put down the broom and took me upstairs to a room with two beds, clean sheets, a stack of thick blankets and a view – when the shutters were opened – of the river and the valley.

'*Discoteca* no problem,' he said. '*Discoteca* kaput ten o'clock.'

In fact the *discoteca* was kaput by 9.30, when the current, which had been fading all evening and reducing ABBA and the Eurythmics to largo maestoso, gave out altogether.

There is a particular shade of blue characteristic of those Transylvanian farming villages which were not bulldozed by Ceauşescu. It is a pale, pastel blue, bluewash rather than paint, often applied to the walls of houses when these walls form the edge of a street.

In a village called Sercaita the foot of the northern slopes of the Fagaraş Mountains there was an excellent example of the bluewashed end wall, which I stopped to photograph.

Some locals stopped too. They seemed pleased that one of their end walls had attracted the attention of a tourist.

Our little gathering blocked the road, which didn't matter because very little traffic used it and most of what did consisted of humans or beasts of burden, walking. However, a Trabant chose that moment to appear from the western end of the village. It stopped.

'*Qu'est-ce que vous faites?*' asked the driver.

'I was photographing this house,' I said.

'I live in a house like this. Do you want to sleep there?'

That was how I met Dr Costiner Elmano, child psychiatrist, his wife Maria, a lecturer, and their friend Sorin Vieru, Professor of Logic at the University of Bucharest and founder member of the Group For Social Dialogue.

They had been half-way up the northern side of the Trans-Fagaraş (the Trabbi had suffered) and were coming home for tea.

Dr Elmano got out and walked with me. Maria and Sorin drove on. The Doctor explained that we were going to what had been his parents' house until they died. It was now the Elmano's country cottage; a retreat from suffocating Bucharest, where they all worked.

We turned up the hill, up a mud track. A wagon rattled down it pulled by a horse and the Doctor said that in Sercaita to have your wagon pulled by a horse instead of oxen was considered 'pretentious'.

'And you know, there are now sixty bicycles in Sercaita,' he said. 'Forty years ago there were only three, belonging to the three richest families. That's progress for you.'

He said I should not expect luxury. They had kept the house as he remembered it from this childhood.

It was white, not blue, and consisted of two bedrooms and a kitchen side by side, all facing up the mountain – though the mountain could not be seen for plum trees. The house was built of dovetailed logs pointed with mud, and only in the kitchen were the inside walls painted. The roof was of oblong tiles, for which the Doctor apologized.

'The oldest ones have rounded bottoms,' he said. 'The house you photographed has such tiles, but still, this one is at least a hundred years old.'

The Doctor and his wife collected *art naïf*. Glass icons in that style hung on the walls in the larger bedroom. There was St Nicholas, holding a book in a six-fingered hand; St George on a horse with human eyes, triumphant over a slain dragon; and

Jesus, bleeding holy wine straight from his spear-wound into a chalice. They had all been etched in a monastery not far from Sercaita where, the Doctor said, the monks would have found me a bed had I needed one.

Round the sides of the room there were benches carved by Transylvanian ethnic Germans, which could open into hard beds when the house was very full. And in one corner there was a wood stove and a single antler on which I hung my shorts when I had washed them.

The Elmanos had made one concession to modernity. They had installed a shower in a back corner of the kitchen, and walled it off with planks. The Doctor sat with his back to the shower box, enjoying several cigarettes with his tea. He smoked in that labial way which treats the smoke as a viscous liquid. I think he became bored the fastest of the three with the idea of an unexpected English guest. Or he felt the least obliged to make polite conversation. He played the conversational maverick, keeping silence for long periods and then exhaling, with a sculpted lungful of smoke, some terse factual correction of his wife's discourse on Romanian history, or a sarcastic dismissal of ecology, or an improper remark about peasants' IQs. He was nearing retirement and according to his wife was one of only 15,000 Jews left in Romania. His parents had been Polish, but had moved south to settle in Bukovina, in the north-east corner of modern Romania, at a time when Bukovina was still Hapsburg territory. His mother tongue, in so far as he had one, was German.

Sorin sat on the right side of the Doctor, and Maria sat next to me when she was not at the stove or re-filling teacups. She was the most energetic and passionate talker of the three, an agile sixty-year-old with short grey hair and a weasly face.

I said I was lucky to be having tea with them in this place, and Maria said they were lucky the place existed.

'We were on the list. Oh yes. Sercaita was one of the villages to be destroyed, but fortunately Ceauşescu was destroyed first.'

Villages nearer Bucharest had borne the brunt of the dictator's mania for bulldozing, she said. She described the technique which had been evolved for erasing houses like this one: dig a large hole in the garden, the size of a small bomb crater, and put the soil from it to one side. Then push the house into the hole and cover it with the soil.

Four-storey blocks had been built in place of the old houses. It was quite common for octogenarians to find themselves four floors up without running water, and with only a shared WC on the ground floor. Maria was nearly crying as she spoke.

As for Bucharest itself, the Paris of the East . . . '*Le Bucharest de mon enfance est disparu,*' she said, and changed the subject.

They had a son who had got out and made good, though the getting out had been an act of desperation. The son had a young family for whom life had been hard at the best of times. But in 1986, when the children were toddlers, the Chernobyl reactor had irradiated Romania's cows. Milk ceased to be available, the children more or less stopped growing, and their father sought a radical solution. His mother, Maria, wasn't Jewish, but his grandmother was. This proved enough to get the family to Israel, where the son was now an applied mathematician at the Weissman University.

Maria paused. Then she reminded me that this was the Ceauşescu whom the Queen of England had honoured with an invitation to her palace in 1977.

'I was furious,' Maria said. 'The people of Romania were furious.'

'Perhaps it was not known at that time how ordinary people lived here,' I said.

'It was known,' she snapped. 'Oh, it was known what we were suffering, but that counted for nothing. It was enough that Ceauşescu said "no" occasionally to the Kremlin and "yes" occasionally to America.'

The tea party then broke up so that we could watch a herd of rare Egyptian cattle pass the house on its way down from an afternoon on the high pastures. The animals were black and horned, of the buffalo ilk, and produced a very white, almost blue-white milk, so high in fat that the fat came to the surface almost as butter. We had some of it later on in coffee. The herd passed twice a day, going up in the mornings and coming down in the evenings. They had done so since antiquity, Maria said. For centuries, at any rate; their forbears featured on the Dacian coat of arms.

While Maria was preparing supper she returned to the subject of history; rival versions of Romanian history.

'But . . . but listen. *Jeune homme, écoute*. The fact is that the Dacian people have been here since *before the Romans*. In AD 101 or 102 there was a battle, at Sarmizegetusa on the south side of the mountains. At Sarmizegetusa Trajan's army defeated the Dacians – yes, the Dacians were defeated, *but there was a battle. So there must have been someone to fight*.'

On the more delicate and specific subject of Transylvania Maria was careful not to claim too much; simply that in the twelfth century a Wallachian prince called Radu Negru had come over the mountains and established a new principality two villages down the road from Sercaita, at Breaza.

'*C'était peut-être le fondation de la Transylvanie. Mais . . .*' – she gave up being careful – '*mais les Magyars, ils ne sont qu'un tribu Asiatique!*'

It rained the next day, and above about 2,000 metres it snowed. I left Sercaita after a lackadaisical morning of picking plums like purple testicles. They had been burning stubble along the road from Sercaita. The air smelled of wet ash. The bottoms of the Fagaraş Mountains, green and pyramidal, pushed out from under the cloud in a uniform line parallel to the road and about a mile south of it. I was riding west. Occasionally there were glimpses of fresh snow high up in the steep valleys behind the pyramids. It was a lonely place and a lonely, wind-blown time.

I passed a sign to Breaza and could actually see the village where Radu Negru could be said to have founded Transylvania. It stood at the very foot of the mountains, separated from the road by a giant field of maize, connected to it by a lane and a line of poplars. I paused in homage to Radu Negru and history in general, and at that very moment, with epic drama and symbolism (symbolism of something) a shaft of sunlight lasered through the cloud and struck Breaza's white church tower.

The Trans-Fagaraş road actually seems to be called the Trans-Fagaraş*an*, pronouced FogoroshAN, as fiercely as you can manage. It was finished around 1975 and built, like Ceauşescu's other civil engineering showpiece, the Danube Canal, partly by

Romania's conscript army. It is seventy miles long and incorp-
orates perhaps two hundred hairpin bends. It gains and loses a
vertical mile in height, links no important centres of population,
serves no conceivable strategic purpose, and is closed for half the
year by snow. It is a triumph of unreason and I was thrilled to be
on it at last. It started gently, crossing the band of fields in a
straight line to the bottom of the pyramids. Here, in a campsite,
three West German students were cooking risotto next to their
three bicycles. It was dinner time. I procured two bottles of
Bulgarian white wine and joined them. They were the first
Westerners I had met in Romania; two physicists – one from
Regensburg, one from Heidelberg – and an engineer from Karls-
ruhe (all male). Lennon specs, Goretex overgarments, hyper-
rugged bikes loaded for total self-sufficiency . . .

There was an unfamiliar aura of purpose about them. They
were going up and over towards Bucharest next morning. I
would go with them, yes? It is better so.

On balance I agreed, wistful none the less at the thought of my
heroic solo ascent that was not to be.

We started at 10.25 next morning. The cloud was down further
than ever. Soon we were in it, and in rain. Three hours followed
of continuous, viewless pedalling in the lowest of my eighteen
gears. We passed a flock of sheep, a bus, and three cars, all going
down. The ascent was effectively a solo after all; within half an
hour the other three were way ahead. The temperature fell
steadily. The rain turned to snow. I tried to stay in the Germans'
tracks but they were soon covered. I remembered leaving Timişoara in scorching sun with Marcia the hairdresser. 'Ritmo, ritmo,'
he had said. Rhythm was all there was left up here, to keep
moving and keep warm. I could not believe how long the road
went on climbing, but eventually the pressure eased, the cold
intensified, and the Germans came into view brewing tea in the
entrance to a tunnel.

This was the top of the climb. I decided to keep going, but the
tunnel was colder than the blizzard, and pitch black. Not wanting
to accelerate out of it like a bullet, I had to use the brakes, round
which my hands froze like chicken bones.

The tunnel ducked under the main Fagaraş ridge, which

marked off separate weather zones. The road flicked out of the southern end of the tunnel still way up in the gods, clinging to the headwall of the valley which takes it down into Wallachia. The first steep, desolate twists of this valley were on show from up here, and the road could be seen snaking down them in a virtuoso series of switchbacks. The theatre was empty, even of snow. This was loneliness at its best.

It took all afternoon to get down the valley. By the end some sun was angling in over the western skyline and picking out hints of autumn in the forest above the road. Sheep had scattered droppings over most of the descent. At first I thought they were slate chippings and dodged them, then I relaxed and let the partially-digested grass coat my wheels and shoes.

For twenty-seven kilometres the business of losing height was delayed while the road skirted a reservoir.

A piece of elastic had worked loose from a pannier and played high, eerie music in a minor key on the spokes.

I approached the dam which held back all this water in the state of morbid fascination in which one might approach the scene of a plane crash. There is something sacrificial about dams. They can be spectacular but you can never forget the price; the dead valley is always there under the water.

The dam lay in shadow in a deep rock defile. The water was low, blown in wavelets by a chill breeze against the north side of the wall. The road used the dam as a bridge. I looked over the empty side and gripped the railing. It would have taken a good four seconds to hit the bottom. The dam was concave, one of the dangerous, expensive ones which use physics rather than bulk to hold back the water. It felt deserted, but I looked around and shivered when I saw that I was being watched – by a giant steel figure high above the dam, guarding the defile from the top of a crag. He was half man, half pylon, terrifying and triumphant, celebrating the electrification of Romania and keeping the electrified in awe. (In South America they put Christ the Redeemer in places like this.)

From the dam the road plunged steeply again and I rode as fast as I dared back to the land of the living. At one point I noticed a ruined turret on top of another crag which, they told me later, is all that remains of the real castle of Vlad the Impaler.

Bucharest

Having heard so much about Piata Universitatii I rode straight there. Dead straight, in fact, along an eighty-kilometre line across the Danubian lowlands. The line started as a bald black strip across a flat brown steppe, then thickened and clogged up, and incorporated tramlines when it hit the suburbs. Eventually it became Bulevardul 1 Mai which ends near the centre of Bucharest at Piata Victoriei, opposite a half-built building eleven storeys high and thirty-five rooms wide.

Beyond Piata Victoriei, Calea Victoriei passes through Piata Gheorghe Gheorghiu-dej, the most scarred battlefield of the revolution. The façade of the Museum of Art was shot to pieces and nine months later repairs had not begun. A young man wandered up and said in English that the stone carvings on the front of the Univeristy Library had been melted by napalm. He said that two houses opposite, of which only shells remained, had been Securitate offices, and that gold and ivory had been found in the black safe which still stood in the bottom of one of them. The Party Headquarters from which Ceauşescu addressed his people for the last time on 21 December and from which he fled with his wife by helicopter the next day, was relatively unscathed.

Piata Universitatii is behind the Party Headquarters. Here the communal de-briefing on those unreal days nine months before was still in progress. About a hundred people sat on the edges of dry fountains, talking and reading newspapers. Others studied petitions and profiles of imprisoned students in the windows of the Russian Library. Others bought and lit candles to the dead. They burned continuously on the pavement by the Law Faculty and blackened the first few courses of its stonework. I photographed the words 'Piata Tiananmen II', and instantly a group formed round me. First they asked the questions – provenance, age, occupation – then I asked what most urgently needed to be changed in Bucharest. A man with half an eyebrow obliterated by a scar and covered with black make-up replied without hesitation:

'Free TV.'

'Why? Not food?'

'We must have free TV to establish political truth. We must have political truth for political stabilization. And we must have political stabilization for economic stabilization. Then we will have all the food we can eat.'

It was well-rehearsed. He acknowledged as much and pointed across Bulevardul Balcescu to the Hotel Intercontinental. Most of the foreign press corps hung out there and clearly they enjoyed a convenient symbiosis with Joe Public in Piata Universitatii. Here, a thirty-second walk away, there was a steady source of quotes and eyewitness accounts for colour pieces and vox-pops.

His name was Niculae Niculescu. He was thirty-two, he worked in a plastics factory and he said he was taking evening classes in construction engineering. At his right shoulder, also with some command of English, was Vasile Trofim, twenty-three, a worker from the Dacia car plant in Pitesti. About twenty others stood round listening.

'This is good, I think,' said Vasile. 'Until last year people talked in public only about football, in Cismigiu Park. Now we talk here, only about politics.'

He translated for the others and they gave a ripple of assent.

We returned to the question of political truth. Niculae Niculescu said the truth had yet to be told about the revolution, its aftermath, the elections in May, the beatings in June . . . about everything. It was exactly what Laszlo Torok had said in Cluj-Napoca.

The elections had been fair, inasmuch as the voters had been unmolested on the day. But the campaign had been 'dirty, very dirty, like in Lebanon'. After the June beatings forty-nine bodies

had been taken to Stranlesti Cemetery, their existence unac-
knowledged by State TV. On 22 August, a hundred demonstrators had been arrested in this square 'for interrupting traffic'.
They were still in jail, with a news blackout on why or how long
they would stay there.

Niculae reminded me of Miroslaw in Gdansk. One had the
feeling that if 'political truth', his Holy Grail, were ever found, he
would be mighty bored.

A third man, a different sort, had worked his way to the front
of the circle. He too was young, but doleful-looking where the
others were high on debate. He spoke beautiful English, learned
from the BBC, and a tremor sometimes entered his voice. His
name was Mihai.

'The decline of Romania,' he said, 'is like a big rock rolling
down a hill which must be slowed, stopped and reversed. It will
be ten years before we see some real progress, and there is going
to be more unrest, but maybe for the better. It could not be worse.
Romania with Ceauşescu was like a madman's dream.

'I am very sad because I spent the first thirty years – the most
beautiful years of my life – in such a bloody system.'

Mihai was doubly sad:

'You know, your special culture is based on one thing in
particular: the ability of English to say so much with so few
words.

'Now that I am able to, by law, I want to read your newspapers. But they do not reach here. Two copies to the British
Council, perhaps, two weeks out of date. What good is that?
Meanwhile France is sending films, newspapers, television pro-
grammes . . . France is gaining over England, and personally I am
very sad. We respect your tradition, your civilization. We are not
fools, after all.'

It turned out that Mihai, too, was a worker at the Dacia factory
in Pitesti. He and Vasile had come independently to Piata
Universitatii. When they discovered that they worked in the same
place they were both slightly embarrassed.

Sightseeing

It was a Sunday afternoon. The streets were empty and so was the vast Museum of History, almost. Downstairs in the treasury a few people were looking at treasure. And in the lapidarium a few more were inspecting plaster casts of Trajan's column (which celebrates that emperor's Dacian wars). But the fifty rooms which chart Romania's rise to greatness had not a single visitor bar me.

It might be possible, approaching this exhibition with a blank mind, not to notice anything forced about their depiction of Romania's past. But having been alerted by both Magyars and Romanians to the high stakes attached to the question of 'who got here first', it was clear at once that room after room had been hijacked by Romanian nationalism.

I was hounded along by a growing pack of security women, one more for each room visited (they had decided with no particular reference to the official closing time to shut up shop), so I experienced a breathless tour of sixteen centuries of Romanian history.

Room 11 showed that the Geto-Dacians (Romanians' ancestors) had occupied the Danube basin 'for millenaries' [sic], during which they had attained 'high material and spiritual development'. This development was evidenced by a scrap of chain mail, a sickle blade, a bracelet, and assorted bits of metal and ceramics.

Room 18 described the birth of the Romanian people between the fourth and sixth centuries, and stated that its 'material culture' provided 'proof of the continuity of life of the autochthonous people on the same territory where their ancestors had lived'.

Rooms 24 to 26 sought to illustrate 'the major contributions of the Romanian people to the enrichment of world civilization'. And Rooms 27 to 50 were closed pending the rewriting of history in the light of recent political developments.

Also closed was the Ceauşescu floor. The entire top floor was once given over to a celebration of the Presidential Couple: 'The greatest son of the Romanian people', the 'helmsman of national destiny', 'the genius of the Carpathians' – and his wife, Elena, 'the most eminent personality of everyday and international scientific life'.

So I went in search of other monuments to the Ceauşescus, far more difficult to remove . . .

The classic view of Casa Republicii (House of the Republic) is from Piata Unirii, which is the mid-point of the triumphal axis forced through the centre of old Bucharest by Ceauşescu. From here the building looks light and heavy at the same time. Light, because of its white marble façade, and because of the sloping grass in front of it which from a distance looks like a hovercraft's skirt; heavy, because of its blunt, sawn-off lines, and because it is so huge.

This is the building by which Ceauşescu intended chiefly to be remembered. It is all Mitterrand's *grands projets* rolled into one and multiplied and larded with insanity. From afar it looks like the bridge of a cancerously colossal inter-galactic cruise liner. Close up, it looks like its own mausoleum.

As you walk down the Boulevard of the Victory of Socialism (which is a hundred metres wide and lined with marble fountains, ornamental lamp posts, and brand new ministerial and apartment buildings), the House of the Republic comes gradually into view in all its girth. In front of it there is another piazza; parking space for a division or two of tanks. From here you need wide-angle vision to take in the whole building. Only a wrap-around screen and 70 mm film would get it into a cinema. Its size is hypnotic.

I stood in the middle of the piazza and counted 426 windows and 49 pillars on the façade alone. The occasional Dacia described a lonely arc across the piazza, missing me by light years. Two people, dots, began walking across the bottom of the picture and were still in it five minutes later. A lone sentry could be discerned behind them in the overgrown grass. I walked to the perimeter fence and he walked down to it from the other side. Nearby, an unfinished gateway was filled by a rusty steel plate and behind it there were a couple of skips of builders' debris.

'*Entrare?*' I asked.

'Cigarette?' said the sentry.

I gave him four Kent and he asked for the whole pack – as a gift for his parents.

'You can have the whole pack if I can get in,' I said, in English and sign language.

'Just give me the whole pack,' he said, in sign language, so I did. He said thank you, brother, and gestured for me to go to the side entrance.

At the side entrance there were two more sentries.

'*Entrare?*' I asked.

No way, officials only, they replied.

'But your amigo said I could get in round here,' I said.

'Cigarette?'

'Your amigo has cigarettes. A whole pack of Kent. Can I come in?'

'Monday morning. Nine o'clock.' The two sentries set off to get some cigarettes from their friend.

Monday morning. Nine o'clock. That left an evening to kill and a place to find to spend the night. I had been staying in a depressing urban campsite next to an airport in the north of the city for $23.50 a night and had been thankful, that morning, to check out.

Killing the evening was easy. I went to see *Crocodile Dundee* at the Patria, in English with Romanian subtitles. It was my first visit to a cinema in six months. The guilty pleasure in wasting two precious Bucharest hours on Hollywood junk was intense. Besides, *Crocodile Dundee* is not junk, it is a fine, fine movie. The Romanian audience thought so too. They gasped at the the Plaza Hotel in Manhattan. They loved the scene in which an aborigine tells the reporter 'You can't take my picture,' and she says 'Oh, do you believe it'll take away your spirit?' and he says 'No, you got your lens cap on.' And we all applauded when Croc and the reporter finally got it together over the heads of a subway-platform crowd somewhere near 5th and 42nd. A fine movie, like I say.

Finding a bed was not so easy. I rode out to University City, a phalanx of halls of residence whose corridors drip to the sound of leaking urinal cisterns. I asked two goddess-like Greek medical students if there were ever student rooms to rent. They said no. I asked a group of Iranians coming in from playing football. They also said no, but one of them made a phone call on my behalf.

'OK,' he said, putting the receiver down. 'I have a friend. His name is Petrica and he says you can sleep in his apartment. He's about thirty-five, a little *solide*, lives alone. He is OK, but he is

Romanian so I cannot swear your things will be safe, not as if he were my brother.'

Petrica lived back across the city, on the eastern side. He was waiting for me outside the cinema Aurora at ten o'clock.

'*Solide*' turned out to mean podgy and soft. He had a flat nose and a woman's voice. He liked to touch your arm, though this did not at first feel like touching up. We had to sleep in the same bed because he had four Turkish Kurds staying in the sitting room, friends whom he had met in Istanbul. We all sat for a while round a table, drinking Old Smuggler's scotch, chasing it with Pepsi, smoking Marlboro 100s and failing to converse. I excused myself and went to bed. Petrica followed. By the time he had stripped to Y-fronts and was climbing in, I was over against the wall trying to read about the General Strike. He pretended to read too, for a few minutes. Then he asked:

'How old are you?'

'Twenty-four.'

'A beautiful age. Are you married? Are you a father?'

He had rolled towards me and propped his head up on his arm. 'No.'

He sat up a bit. He made a hole with two fingers of one hand and pushed two fingers of the other throught it. He raised his eyebrows.

'No,' I said.

'OK,' he said. He switched off the light and seemed to go to sleep. Personally, I found going to sleep quite difficult. Bits of Petrica kept slithering over to me. I lay like a stone figure on a Norman tomb, wide awake till two in the morning.

At breakfast I gave Petrica 300 lei. He tried to get me to stay a day or two, and seemed to be promising some fancy hetero activity if I did, but I didn't.

It was a filthy, soaking, honking Monday morning. A million or so citizens were stumbling and splashing to work. The cobbles were shiny with grey rain. Taxi drivers abused me verbally for riding between the tramlines, but it was the only place smooth enough. Loto ticket and newspaper vendors were busy as usual, but crowded out of the rain under awnings.

I reached Piata Unirii at 8.55 a.m. and followed a Globus

Gateway coach with West German plates to the side entrance of
the House of the Republic. About thirty glowing individuals
descended from their air-conditioning in a catwalk display of
Burberrys and Rohan designer travel gear. Super-soft sneakers
were much in evidence under the rain gear, the kind that bouncy
female tennis stars wear with bobble socks, the kind they kill for
in Washington, the kind they weep over in Eastern Europe. The
camcorders and the compact autofocuses were Japanese. The
accents were American. I had forgotten people could look so well.

This lot must have been told Monday nine o'clock as well. I
tried to blend with them. I got friendly with a couple from
Philadelphia and another from Portland, Oregon.

'Wr rl please-meecha, Charles, gladdav ylong,' said the woman
from Philadelphia. But their German tour guide had me down for
a parasite. It turned out she had fixed the whole thing; bribed the
necessary guards and workers and an engineer who knew the
building. No other tourists got in. Her group was paying $8 extra
each for this, so I gave her $8 and she was happy.

The engineer led us into the main lobby and unleashed some
data.

Height: 86 metres. Storeys: Twelve. Underground storeys:
Four, including nuclear bunker with multiple water and electricity supplies. Rooms: 1,100. Offices: 450. Construction
workers: 27,000. Architects: 1,400. Chandeliers: 11,000, of which
4,500 so far installed. Square metres of marble: 13,000 (quarried),
5,000 (in place). Earthquake rating on the Richter scale: 9. Building started: 1982.

All the marble, all the crystal, all the architects and all the gold
(we would be seeing the gold in a few minutes) were pure
Romanian.

The engineer paused. I was not the only one who was scribbling. We entered the main lobby through one of four steel doors,
each about the height of the Parthenon and each worth 1.5 million
lei, compared to Romanian average monthly wage of 3,500 lei.

The main lobby was a hundred metres long and twelve metres
wide, floored in pink and white marble. It was too dark to see the
pink marble contrast with the white because the wiring wasn't in
yet. But we could gape at the dimensions and imagine roller-
hockey or a game of cricket in them.

We went upstairs – marble stairs of course, the width of about four elephants – and were ushered into a vast chamber. It was in this state room that Ceauşescu intended to overawe the leaders of other Warsaw Pact nations when it was his turn to host their meetings.

Floor size: 2,180 square metres (or a little over half an acre). Ceiling: 7-carat gold leaf and on vaulted pink marble.

A deep balcony ran the length of the room. We walked out to take the salute from poor old Bucharest, sunk in drizzle and smog and waiting for something better than Ceauşescu.

'Let's have a cigarette out here,' said the tour guide. 'Then we can say we smoked a cigarette on Ceauşescu's balcony.'

The tour guide was glitzier than any of her charges. She wore a full-length coat of fine black wool and two-tone pink angora headband. Her face was mercilessly reconditioned. This group was the fifth she'd managed to get in here. Earlier in the year the building had been open to the public but since then there had been a damp-down. Our guide had not been put off. ('I decided this is what people should be seeing in Bucharest in 1990, so I fixed it.') They were doing 4000 miles from Munich to the Balkans and back in 3 weeks, next stop Braşov. ('Dracula's castle,' she said. I started saying it wasn't Dracula's castle, but she was attending to a client.)

We straggled back across the Warsaw Pact room and through a few ante-rooms and vestibules and down a corridor or two. The ceilings looked stained, though in fact the marble had merely been oiled to prepare it for gilding.

We came to the meeting room of the Communist Party Central Committee and spread out round a ring-shaped oak table inlaid with rare white hardwood. The table seated sixty. In the middle were rostra for cacti and fountains and above that a one-and-a-half tonne chandelier, six metres across, incorporating 180 bulbs. Price: 2,500,000 lei, or fifty-eight years' earnings for a worker.

Ceauşescu's chair was on the north side of the circle, extravagantly carved and with a coat of arms in gold leaf on the back cushion.

'Please, go to the wall behind and push it,' said the engineer to the person nearest the chair. When pushed, the oak panelling

swung open. Behind it there was sitting space for four of Ceauşescu's orphan-bodyguards.

On our way back down we paused on another set of stairs, a
double set this time. It had been re-built three times because
Ceauşescu had not been satisfied with the first two styles – yet he
liked to see a design fully executed before dismissing it.

'He could not read a plan,' said the engineer. 'He was a cobbler.
He attended school for a total of four years.'

Partly because of Ceauşescu's whims the interior decoration
was far from finished. The National Salvation Front had under-
taken to finish it – at a further cost of seven billion lei. It had not
yet been decided to what use the building would be put.

Sofia

From Bucharest I rode south to the Danube. The opposite bank was Bulgaria, and the Bulgarian city of Ruse. The prestigious Riga Hotel stands on the riverfront at Ruse and from its twentieth floor there is a panoramic view of the poison park which some say started the Bulgarian revolution.

Ruse was the birthplace of Ecoglasnost. A Romanian metallurgical complex in the town of Giurgiu across the river emits chlorine-based gases which caused an increase in lung disease in the area from 965 cases per 100,000 in 1975 to 17,386 per 100,000 in 1990. Some cases of malformed babies were also attributed to the pollution, and the women of Ruse rioted. That was in 1987.

A group of film-makers from the Ecran studio in Sofia went to Ruse to make a documentary about the women. Together, the women and the film-makers formed the Ruse Defence Committee, the seed from which Ecoglasnost later grew. Starting at a CSCE Environment Conference in Sofia on 16 October 1989, Ecoglasnost organized the first legal opposition activity in Bulgaria for forty years, creating the climate for Foreign Secretary Peter Mladenov, with Gorbachev's backing, to denounce President Todor Zhivkov and resign. Zhivkov's thirty-five-year presidency ended two weeks later.

There are many other things to be said about Bulgaria's revolution. For example, it is doubtful whether it was a revolution at all. The Communist Party never lost power, either at the time or, as the Socialist Party, at the elections of June 1990. And in what upheaval did occur, human rights activists and the country's one million-strong Turkish minority probably played as important a part as environmentalists.

Still, the metallurgical complex across the river was undeniably significant – although to look at from the roof of the Riga Hotel it was an anticlimax. It looked harmless. The chimneys were having an off day.

I sat on the hotel terrace with a beer and a *croque monsieur*. A light breeze idled off the river and riffled the pages of my free copy of the *Sofia News*. Contented, complacent, sure here of the power of my traveller's cheques, I read the editorial.

> For the time being we can do nothing but hope our little hopes which we secretly wish to see fulfilled, somewhere in the dark of the economic, political and social crisis of the moral and material degradation that has reduced to nought basic human values like work and a normal existence.

So Bulgaria was in crisis. I saw no evidence of it yet. After three weeks in Romania this seemed to be a land of milk, honey and electricity. Ruse had streetlighting which came on at night. It had cafés and bars with something to sell. It had a sassy youth scene, with much black leather and pornographically short skirts.

I moved from the Riga Hotel to a café on Lenin Square where I smoked, drank coffee and cognac, and ate ice-cream. Then I rode to the municipal campsite.

There was another café here, on a hill above the river. The waitress said 'we are in crisis, you know,' and brought a bar of chocolate, a bottle of Riesling and a plate of gherkins. Chocolate! Wine! Gherkins! *Crisis?*

A hulk walked in and was seated at my table.

'This is Marek,' said the waitress. 'Marek is a friend of ours. ' Marek was a Pole and a smuggler, from somewhere between Lublin and Kazimierz on the east side of the Vistula. He had an easily astonished face but did not seem to be an easily astonished person. He bought jeans, jackets and fake Turkish visas in Istanbul and traded them for gold in western Russia. In Russia, gold was cheap. In Istanbul Marek got the going international rate. He used a blue Lada for work, but said he had an Opel at home. He wore a good deal of gold himself – a bracelet, a necklace, two fat rings – and he secured an evening's supply of liquor for the two of us by presenting the waitress with a fake Cartier watch, which she didn't realize was a fake.

Music-wise, we had the Lambada, we had Glenn Miller ('In The Mood'), and we had a rock 'n' roll compilation which touched the spot perfectly. We were doing a *slivova* each roughly every five minutes and in my case that was on top of a bottle of Riesling. Boy, could I drink that night.

Slivova is the Bulgarian national drink, made from plums. It sneaks up on you from behind. I woke up at about two in the morning with my head on the table. The waitress showed me to a cabin. Marek continued drinking till eight, then stumbled in and fell twice onto my bed before managing, incredibly, to swivel back to the door and open it before urinating and vomiting.

It was tomato time. As I left Ruse, millions of tomatoes were rumbling in in dumper-truck convoys. It was also walnut time, and the road was lined with walnut trees. Women filling plastic bags with walnuts would appear from thickets or greet oncoming traffic with their skirted bums as they rummaged through the fallen leaves. For every walnut team there would usually be a Lada, bumped up off the road under the trees.

North of the Danube, as it passes through the Balkans, the land appears completely flat. But to the south there is a sudden swell, and an unfamiliar softness. In the mountains of the Stara Planina, which transect Bulgaria from Yugoslavia to the Black Sea, limestone cliffs break through the swell. But there is still this softness, of colour and profile. Sooner or later you click. The difference, after Romania, is that the valleys here aren't filled with factories and the hillsides aren't shafted with mines.

Stalin had a vision for his two Balkan satellites: Romania was to be a wheat basket, Bulgaria a market garden. Romania rejected its role and industrialized, but Bulgaria toed the line and preserved at least some of its natural good looks. In fact, it looked how I had hoped Transylvania might look.

While Romania industrialized and paid off its national debt by living in slavery, Bulgaria stayed relatively agricultural and borrowed dollars to maintain the highest standard of living in the Balkans. Then the Soviet economy collapsed. Bulgaria lost her principal trading partner and her cash flow. She was unable to service her $11 billion foreign debt and unable to borrow more. This was her crisis – a crisis not compared with Romania, but with what Bulgarians were used to.

So far, the only Bulgaria I had seen was *tranzit* Bulgaria. Ruse is on an international *tranzit* freight route and I felt I'd got about as much of a feeling for the country as a piece of international freight might get.

What made Bulgaria Bulgaria? Was there such a thing as essence of Bulgaria?

Veliko Tarnovo is lodged in the heart of the Stara Planina eighty miles south of Ruse. It was the cradle of the Bulgarian National Revival, and capital of Bulgaria for the reigns of twenty kings. The whole place seems in danger of sliding into a gorge. Many houses, in order to have a front door at street level, have it on the top floor while the bottom floor clings patriotically to a cliff.

The gorge, cut from limestone by the River Yantra, winds through the town as tortuously as a duodenum. It creates two promontories, a low one and a high one. The low one is now occupied by a vulgar profusion of prancing metal horses. The high one has something much more real; the ruins of the royal palace from which Bulgaria was ruled from 1186 to 1393, and a jutting rock from which kings pushed traitors to their deaths.

On a narrow isthmus leading to the high promontory, a building which has served as town hall, prison and constituent assembly is now the Museum of the National Revival. There is concentrated essence of Bulgaria here.

The National Revival began in the 1830s and culminated in the recognition of Bulgaria as an autonomous province by the Great Powers in the Treaty of Berlin in 1878. It was all about being anti-Ottoman and pro-Bulgarian, about resuscitating Bulgarian national legends, national symbols, national pride. It was, owing to the Turks' bloodthirstiness, a dangerous cause to fight.

The museum is mostly a Revivalists' hall of fame, full of long Cyrillic captions and lithographs of grim-faced men with black moustaches. But there was colour in the uniform of a freedom-fighter (a killer of Turks). He wore an embroidered jacket cut like a toreador's, and a red sash, a black cap and moccasins. He carried a flintlock pistol, a dagger, and a sabre. You could see the fun of the revival in its accoutrements, but not in those who wore them.

Downstairs there was a traditional *slivova* still, shaped like an anteater but clad in metal and heavily riveted, like a tank on the Somme.

The Museum of the National Revival was empty bar me and its minders. Most Bulgarians had better things to do, like hassle me for dollars.

I ate fried aubergine with sour cream in a self-service cafeteria and put on shades to ride west out of town into the afternoon sun. At first I followed another *tranzit* route, the main highway between Sofia and the Black Sea. Turning off that highway was . . . well 'twas a blessed thing.

It was a warm night. The sun had heated the earth and the hills were quiet. As the sun went down it was possible to enjoy the long shadows cast by olive trees and walnut trees, instead of staring into the fireball. That is the difference between riding west and riding south. With no competing traffic I could take my hands off the handlebars and slalom down the hills.

Going up the hills was tough, however. At seven o'clock, with the monastery I was aiming for still an hour away, I passed the door of a bar in a village too tiny to be on the map. Passing such doors you get only the briefest glimpse inside, but long enough to hear the brittle beat from the cassette player and smell the burped air. I walked in and subsided in a corner with a pint of wine.

The walls of the bar were covered with posters of cosmonauts and Sam Fox, advertising Bulgarian Space Food. Old men in blue canvas came and sat at my table when all the others were full. They said nothing for about half an hour. Then they asked the who-what-where-why-when questions, in Bulgarian. I answered them, probably not in the right order. Word spread and I was invited to the bartender's table.

The bartender ran his show sitting down. He knifed the tops off bottles of Masteca aniseed liqueur and kept up a constant repartee with half a dozen cronies.

Someone who needed a crate of Masteca as a special favour

came and dangled a length of dirty industrial polythene in our faces. The boss granted the favour and took the polythene. He started tearing strips off it and eating them. He tore off a strip for me and instructed me to eat it. It was dry salted mutton, and tasted very good.

A man with sideburns and flared tracksuit bottoms took me to a friend's house. Outside it there was a chaos of vines, dung, dogs, geese, hay, and antique farming implements of wood and iron. On the inside the house was spick and span, controlled by women. They guided us into the dining room and brought food and *slivova*.

We watched a drama about Abraham Lincoln on the television, after which I was asked if I wanted coffee. No thank you. I shook my head. The women went away and ground the beans and made the coffee.

After coffee I was asked if I wanted to go to bed. Yes please. I nodded. Everyone relaxed and turned back to the television.

In Bulgaria a nod means no and a shake means yes. It takes a while to get used to this.

Half-way through the next morning, riding with a bad head and a soft front tyre, I came upon a fork in the road and a man standing on a bridge. To cross the bridge was to turn right and start climbing at once through a pine forest. To go straight on was to follow the river up its valley towards a beautiful dark blue mountain rising into a beautiful light blue sky. The map was no help. I asked the man on the bridge the way to Trojanski Monastery.

'You too! To the monastery, eh?' His name was Dmitrov. He pointed up into the pine forest. He stepped forward, having been leaning against the handrail of the bridge with his eyes closed, facing the sun and the blue mountain.

'Are you with the others?' he asked.

'The others? I'm on my own.'

'Yesterday two others came this way on bicycles. Dutch, they were, or Deutsch.'

'On their way to the monastery?'

'To sleep there. You can sleep there, very comfortable.'

'Were they interested in monasteries . . . *especially* interested?'

'Oh yes. They said they were very interested.'

'And their bicycles? What colour were they?'

'White, I think. Their bags were grey.'

'Yes, I think I know them. From Amsterdam, do you remember?'

'Amsterdam! Of course! You know them?'

'I think so. Their names are Eric and Rimkje. We met in Slovakia six or eight weeks ago.'

Dmitrov thought this splendid. So did I actually. I found myself thinking of Eric and Rimkje as old friends.

Dmitrov and I talked a little more, about Georgi Markov, the Bulgarian playwright killed in London by a compatriot with a poisoned umbrella, and about the lack of snow in recent winters, and global warming as the culprit, and Ecoglasnost as the team to put it right. Dmitrov was a handsome and alert old man who had retired to a house above the bridge. I wished him interesting encounters on his bridge during the rest of his retirement and hared off up the hill, salivating at the prospect of conversation with people who knew me, however slightly.

Eric and Rimkje had been at the monastery the previous night but they had already left. Three women sat in an ironing room beside the main gate eating bread and honey. They didn't know where the Dutch pair was headed next. I looked at the map and took pot luck.

At the end of the day I turned up a cleft in the Stara Planina towards Glozenski Monastery. The road climbed imperceptibly beside a lazy, glinting river. The river swung to the east. The road swung with it, and suddenly the monastery came into view, half a vertical mile up.

The road passed a marble mine. A batch of female marble miners in blue overalls was walking home and I asked them, in sign language, was it possible to get up there, up to the monastery? They shook their heads.

Was there absolutely no way ? Did *anyone* go up there? They shook their heads, smiling. Damn. It looked a fabulous place to spend the night.

I rode on . . . and remembered. A shake is a yes. They'd been saying yes. I turned round and found them doubled up laughing beside the road. Some had even had to take time out on their bums. OK, OK. I joined in.

They took me to the beginning of the road to the monastery and when I looked back they were laughing again, this time apparently at the idea of trying to get up there on a bicycle.

It did take some time – about three hours, mostly on foot, during which night fell and three wild boar engaged me in a bout of terrorize thy fellow rambler.

Some time after dark three young men from Sofia caught up with me. One of them was on the eve of his birthday. Another spoke some English. All of them wore sheath-knives on their belts. I wondered whether they were novice monks.

'Are there any monks at the monastery?' I asked.

'Tomorrow morning we go to the village to get hard drinks for my birthday friend.'

I tried again.

'In the monastery, are there any monks who live and work . . .?'

'I am sorry. I know only a few words of your beautiful language. Another friend, now in the monastery, he speaks fine English. Wait.'

The monastery stood on a flat rock protruding from a sharp, steep ridge which climbed like a missile fin to the foot of a cliff. The final approach had to be down a sloping aerial causeway the width of the track itself, with nothing but night falling sheer away on either side.

Steps were cut into the side of the flat rock, leading to a door which was opened for us. From here a dimly-lit tunnel, hewn through the rock, sloped up under the chapel into a tiny court-yard. Low white rooms with slate roofs formed three of its sides. The fourth side consisted partly of the chapel. Beside it, where there was no more rock to build on, the monks had built into space. There were steps down to washrooms and more steps up to a wooden gallery and two dormitories. These were occupied, though not by Eric and Rimkje, and not by monks.

'Hi. Howya doin'?'

The friend who spoke fine English introduced himself. He wore a US-Special-Forces T-shirt and a sheath-knife to beat all sheath-knives.

'Welcome to Glozenski,' he said, 'a place of adventures.'

Pink Floyd filled the yard from a battery-powered beat pumper on a table in the gallery. Five sullen young men sat round it drinking Ballantine's.

Across the yard an older man, half-priest, half-hippy, emerged from one of the low white rooms and signed me in.

'The Pope,' said the friend. 'He's in charge.'

He had recently taken up body-building. He worshipped Arnold Schwarzenegger, so I thought of him as Arno. Like Schwarznegger, he was basically a serious person – about body-building, about life. He was the son of a Bulgarian diplomat and had learned English at the American College in Athens. He looked twenty-five but was actually eighteen, and so were his friends.

There were two groups of youth up here, up here for nothing holier than a good time: Arno and friends, and the Ballantines crowd. They didn't know each other though they all came from the same suburb of Sofia. They regarded each other with the suspicion that comes of knowing enough to speculate.

I was drafted into Arno's team. He gave us a few minutes to wolf some bread and cheese, then led us back up the ridge into the night. We skirted the foot of the cliff and then descended again, down a gentler ridge to a saddle of grass where a lone shepherd had built a bonfire. We sprawled around it on rugs, drinking sweet red wine and watching orange sparks leap off the logs towards the brilliant milky way.

The wingtip lights of an airliner crossed the sky and I confess I thought of myself flying home. Not long now. Six months to Istanbul and three hours back.

There was a tomboy in the team, good-looking and no less good-looking for her combat jacket. She had come up earlier with Arno, but was not his girlfriend, exactly, so everyone performed a little. The less muscular boys told lewd stories, competitively. They laughed themselves hoarse and Arno became too embar-rassed to translate. Instead he told of his 'spooky feelings' in this place. He wasn't superstitious. He believed religion was a way of keeping stupid people down . . . but he still had spooky feelings in this place. He pointed across the chasm to the monastery, which was silhouetted against the stars. There had been a chapel on that rock for 750 years. When Vasil Levsky, the greatest freedom-fighter of them all, had been on the run from the Turks, the monks had hidden him there. And they had hoarded gold. Legend had it there was treasure in this mountain, and Arno believed it. Many had searched, all in vain, but Arno believed there was treasure in this mountain.

'I'm serious. This is not a normal mountain. For example, underneath us now, what do you think there is? Or under the monastery, or behind the cliff? I'll tell you. There are caves, hundreds of kilometres of caves. Oh yes. Tomorrow I will show you.'

He stood up and left the dome of light round the fire. He was gone for five minutes during which we finished the wine. Then he returned with a tree-trunk over his shoulder, exactly like Schwarzenegger in the opening sequence of *Commando*. He tipped it off his shoulder onto the fire and a plume of sparks went up. We applauded. Who needs lewd stories when you have muscles?

'Do you use steroids?' I asked.

'Yes,' said Arno.

'Really? You inject yourself for body-building?'

'Oh yes,' said Arno.

With the wine gone, the general laughter gradually died down and we turned briefly to politics. Someone named an extreme radical as the best politician in Bulgaria, and Arno said, 'I don't agree. That man said he will kill all sons of Communists. Well, my parents are Communists.'

Back at the monastery Arno and friends went to bed and I defected to the Ballantine's crowd for a nightcap. This group was older – in their early twenties – and vastly more cynical.

'You tell Margaret Thatcher there is no future for young people in this country. It's the worst place in Europe. The last stop. We want to escape – to Australia, Canada, New Zealand, America, Western Europe . . .'

'To do what?'

'Anything. Just to earn some money. Dollars, not leva.'

'If you had a visa, would you go tomorrow?'

'Yes. Right now if necessary.'

They were adamant. The best I could do was to say I was

enjoying being in Bulgaria, which elicited harsh laughter.

'Yeah. Enjoy youself. Enjoy your flight to London.'

The next morning I stuffed my front tyre with straw. It was continually going soft and I was almost out of patches.

The straw didn't work, however. About twenty miles from Sofia, beside some red volcanic rock, I felt the road coming through to the rims again. I applied my last patch to a tube already patched seven times, hoping it would hold. It did not.

A man rolled into view on a racer, the first racer I had seen in Bulgaria. He stopped. I returned to the road and asked if by any chance he had a spare tube I could buy. He had no tube, but he had some Tip-Top patches. Tip-Top were the kind I had. I splurged out about a litre of thanks, and barely noticed, while fumbling for vulcanizing fluid, that he had picked up the problem tyre and was running his thumb round its inside.

'Here,' he said, and placed my thumb where his had been. A single metal splinter about half the length of an ant had spiked its way through my entire stock of patches. I pushed the spike out with a tyre lever. The man smiled and we continued together towards Sofia.

A Hang-Glider's View

The man who had found the splinter in my tyre was ranked sixth in the Bulgarian national hang-gliding team. He had an aeronautical moustache – the winged kind generally seen under leather flying helmets – and he was lean, lean as a hang-glider, minimum disincentive to a thermal.

He was about thirty-five, self-effacing, tanned, divorced, and known as Bojidar. He apologized for the smog and bade me raise my eyes to Vitosha, the mountain that stops Sofia in its tracks along its southern side.

We coasted down the eastern end of the Sofia basin under a grid of power lines which disappeared into the smog ahead of us. The outermost ring of unfinished apartment buildings came into view, each chaperoned by its own tower crane. Sunday evening traffic streamed past, returning from weekends in the country. It had been hot. The Föhn Wind had been blowing from the south. Sofians had been taking advantage of it, using the last of their hoarded petrol, knowing the weather would break soon.

Bojidar told me to follow him and looked frequently over his shoulder to check I was in touch as he led us a dance along darkening back streets to the noisy old middle of Sofia.

He lived here with his sister and her small son Miroslav, a fair-haired boy with a sombre, oval face. The sister was a nurse. She was severe and beautiful and was wearing a short green dress. She smoked. She had everything in order in her ground-floor flat, which was central because she had to be near the hospital.

She managed to be efficient and languid at once. When we arrived she was washing Miroslav's hair. Shortly afterwards, food and drink appeared on a table in the sitting room and Miroslav appeared on the sofa with his head in a towel. Bojidar's sister was behind it all, in the bathroom, in the kitchen, across the table, yet in fact she seemed always to be there across the table in the short green dress, smoking.

A cousin who was a philology student arrived and was astonished to learn that I had not done drugs.

'What is the problem? They are not available in London?'

'They're available. You can get anything you want if you have the money.'

'Aha! You don't have the money!'

'I don't have much, but anyway . . .'

'You must try everything once, at least once,' he said, and we agreed to meet next day behind the university at half past one.

To judge from Bojidar's face I had been going up in his estimation during most of this conversation, but had plummeted at the end. Bojidar was an outdoors man. He hated the city but was tied to it by his work as a maintenance engineer on the tunnelling machines which were building Sofia's new metro. He got out of town whenever possible, usually to go hang-gliding.

He kept the city out of his dreams with cherished West German ear-plugs which he offered to lend me. I would be sleeping on the sofa and sleep was important; he had arranged to hand me over to Peter Popov, President of the Bulgarian Hang-gliding Association on his way to work next morning. That would be at seven o'clock, he said, 'because serious men stand up early'.

A Walking Tour

In the morning I walked with Bojidar along narrow streets to the National Library. The blue tint of early morning had replaced the orange tint of early evening. A good smell of autumn laced the air between the sooty buildings.

Peter Popov materialized out of a tide of sleep-walkers, and I noticed at once: he was white, but the ends of his fingers were dark brown. Something awful had happened. I braced myself. We shook hands. He apologized for his brown fingers. They had turned brown while gathering walnuts at the weekend.

Bojidar arranged an evening rendezvous and disappeared onto a tram.

We walked on up Ruski Avenue to 9 September Square and the charred heart of Bulgarian Communism.

9 September Square is formed by the Defence Ministry, the Georgi Dmitrov Mausoleum (containing Zhivkov's predecessor) and the Communist Party Headquarters.

'Not a pleasant place for Bulgarians,' Peter said.

V-shaped black smudges covered most of the walls of the Party Headquarters. Its insides had been badly damaged by arsonists two weeks before. The building was sealed off and under armed guard. Debate raged in the partially freed media about who was responsible for the fire. The Party (and the BBC) claimed it was a militant opposition group. But Peter said:

'Everybody believes the Communists burned the Party HQ themselves.'

They had done it, he said, to give the police an excuse to clear the 'City of Truth', a tent encampment which had filled the square since the elections as a continuous protest against the Communists' survival in power. The fire had started on the inside, Peter said. The flames were blue, indicating the premeditated use of special fuel. And the police had stood by while apparatchiks had walked out before the fire with the Party's photocopiers and everything else of value. It all pointed to the Party. Peter had seen the fire and was in no doubt.

The Party Headquarters is wedge-shaped and its thin end tapers as it rises to the inevitable red star. Overweight soldiers with desk jobs and medals on their breasts were walking into the Defence

Ministry with fat plastic briefcases. Peter touched my elbow to keep us moving. Not a pleasant place for Bulgarians.

We turned south down Vitosha Street.

Vitosha Mountain filled the middle distance like an opened fan. On the left a grand nineteenth-century government building had been gutted and turned into the Sheraton. On the right, further down, a crowd had gathered outside a bank and clerks were standing on boxes shouting numbers. It was 8 a.m., and foreign currency allowances of $30 per person per year were being handed out to applicants whose names had reached the top of some endless list. If you weren't there when your number was called, your name went back to the bottom.

The bank apart, Vitosha Street seemed to be in mellow mood; not much traffic, lots of strollers, busy cafés. I told Peter how well provided-for Bulgaria seemed after Romania. He explained that the absence of traffic was owing to an absence of petrol. The strollers were the unemployed. The cafés were busy because there was no coffee in the shops.

Bulgarians were used to being able to get everything they wanted in their shops. To be compared with Romanians, in terms of living standards, was humiliating.

We call them 'Mamaligari', said Peter, and I remembered Maria Elmano proudly dishing up mamaliga, a paste of ground maize, in her L-shaped kitchen in Sercaita.

We came to a large park containing the Palace of Culture, where on that day the Sofia branch of the Michael Jackson Fan Club was due to celebrate Michael Jackson's thirty-second birthday.

At the northern end of this park there is a very tall black monument commemorating the 1300th anniversary of the birth of the Bulgarian nation, which, according to the nation-builders, happened in AD 681 under Khan Asparoukh, the first Bulgar king to estabish himself south of the Danube. The anniversary was celebrated with great state fervour in 1981, and the monument is known by discerning Bulgarians, Peter said, as 'the biggest prick in Sofia'.

The lawns between the monument and the Palace of Culture were half dug up for the installation of fountains. It was a pre-revolutionary scheme, Peter said, perhaps for some forthcoming celebration of Zhivkov's long years at the national helm – he wasn't sure.

We walked among the cratered lawns and Peter described how institutionalized sycophancy makes dictators believe they are in some way blessed.

'You have heard of Georgi Markov?'

'Yes.'

'You know why he was killed?'

'For being a dissident?'

'As a birthday present for Zhivkov. He was stabbed with the umbrella on 7 September 1978, Zhivkov's birthday. It is true that the Russian poison in the umbrella took four days to kill him, but I am sure that Zhivkov understood the killing; he took it in the spirit in which it was intended. And on his seventieth birthday, what was the winning number in the National Lottery? It was 7-9-11, the day he was born.'

We sat down in a café and talked about hang-gliding. Peter cheered up. He took a paper napkin and drew on it the various types of course a tournament pilot has to fly. He explained about photographing landmarks to prove they have been covered. For the photograpy Peter had a Japanese camera, a Ricoh. The gliders which the team used were the latest kind, with narrow battened wings.

Then we walked north again to the headquarters of the Union of Democratic Forces on Dondukov Street. Here we met a man who kept us listening until the middle of the afternoon – so I missed my meeting at the university and never did do any drugs in Sofia.

Violet Tsekov and the Great Totalitarian Bribe

Dondukov Street was alive with shoe shops and taxis. We jay-walked it and presented at the UDF reception two Ecoglasnost names which I had been given in Ruse. They were met with blank expressions but Peter led on upstairs anyway.

The building contained parts of the Agrarian and Green Parties as well as Ecoglasnost – all came under the UDF umbrella. No big

Ecoglasnost names were present, and half the Greens were moving into other premises while the other half were at a parliamentary meeting. So we sat around. Peter told the Ecoglasnost secretaries that I was very influential back in London, and I bought an Ecoglasnost hat and T-shirt.

A poster urged us to 'Take a Bike to Ecotopia in the Name of European Youth Forest Action', and a lawyer-activist sat down briefly with us to say that emissions from the Giurgiu metals complex were if anything increasing. Then he had to dash off to be on television.

The Ecoglasnost rooms were filled with natural light from tall white windows. Bright young people bustled in and out in jeans. One of the secretaries experimented nervously with the new fax machine.

Into this benign confusion walked a man wearing a rumpled white jacket. His hair and stubble were grey. His jowls were slack. His teeth were browned by smoking and severely misaligned. His voice was deep and rasping like pebbles sliding around in the bottom of a plastic dustbin, or the voice-over in a commercial for moderately expensive quartz watches.

'Tsekov, Violet,' he said. 'I'm pleased to meet you.'

We went into a tall room and sat round a formica-topped table.

Tsekov had eschewed the limelight, but he had been in on Ecoglasnost from the beginning.

He worked for Ecran, the film studio, which seemed to have been allowed to survive for international PR purposes. 'Most of our films were never shown in Bulgaria,' he said. 'Just at international festivals, to show the world how open was the Bulgarian regime.'

But Ecran had persevered, and with renewed hope after Gorbachev's elevation to the Soviet presidency in 1985; he had endorsed for Soviet distribution an Ecran documentary about *War and Peace* which had been banned when first produced for having insufficient class-based content.

In Sofia Gorbachev's reforms spawned knee-jerk imitations. In July 1987 Zhivkov produced his *Conception on the Further Construction of Socialism in Bulgaria*, which has been described as 'a mesmerizingly wordy Bulgarian version of *perestroika*'. In view of Zhivkov's record of toeing the Moscow line (he had even asked

Khrushchev if Bulgaria might join the Soviet Union as its six-
teenth republic), this new Conception was to be regarded with
some scepticism. But it was a start, said Violet. 'And it all began
with Gorby.'

So it was that an Ecran crew, including Violet, went to Ruse in
September 1987. There had been a demonstration by a handful of
women against the chlorine gas from Giurgiu.

'We went to make one episode for a series on the changes in
Bulgaria. But we realized this was a whole film. These women
had been gassed for years. When they talked they began to cry:
"Our lives are passed, but we are doing this for our children and
grandchildren".'

'We understood that we could not stay indifferent. We realized
it is a crime to be silent. We went often to Ruse and became friends
with the women there. As soon as a rough of the film was ready
we invited the Ruse women to come to Sofia for three screenings.

'They came – of course they came – and the film showed
schoolchildren standing outside for a ceremony, using their red
school ties as gas masks against the chlorine clouds.'

Violet sat beside the table, resting an elbow on it, looking
sometimes out of the tall windows, sometimes at us. He described
another moment – 'a historic moment' – in the film; footage of the
third of three illegal demonstrations organized by the Ruse
women in 1987. It coincided with a visit to the city by a politburo
chief who had never in his long career (to the best of Violet's
knowledge) seen any evidence of opposition.

'Then, suddenly, he saw the slogans and the angry women. He
heard them shouting that their children were poisoned, that life
was intolerable in Bulgaria. And . . . his face. We filmed it. You
have never seen a face of such fear.

'Each night the cinema was completely full. After the screenings the Ruse women spoke to the audiences and the need for an
organization was clear – an organization to help them. Some
people wanted a general ecological organization. Others wanted a
Ruse Defence Committee, more specific. I was one of these.

'On the day of the third showing, 8 March 1988, the Central
Committee of the Communist Party vetoed our application to
found a formal organization. But we invited two hundred of the
Party élite to the film and many of them came. Five hundred

people came to the cinema that night. The foyer was full, the corridors were full, on the stairs, people were sitting.

'We offered a petition saying that our government should take action for the right of the people of Ruse to breathe clean air. Four hundred signed it. After the showing we held the first meeting of the Ruse Defence Committee.

'The next day the merry-go-round began. All the Party members who had attended the film were summoned and warned about "evil forces" behind it. They started tailing us – demonstrative tailing, so that you know you are followed. Also phone-tapping, and discussions with your boss. Secret reports were sent to the Party chiefs saying we were trying to organize a counter-revolution in ecological disguise.'

Violet spread his hands over the formica and leaned forward. 'And of course,' he said, 'in a way this was true. This was never a purely ecological movement. In a totalitarian state if a group is independent, it is political. So we can say that ecology was the form of the political struggle.'

(I was scribbling like crazy. Violet and Peter had an approving laugh about this. There was no doubt, though, that Violet was one of those who responds well to scribbling; he continued talking.)

By October 1989 the Ruse Defence Committee had evolved into Ecoglasnost, which had turned its attention to a plan to dam the River Mesta in the Rila Mountains south of Sofia. It was the rallying cry of the moment. For twelve days activists staked out the Crystal Gardens in the south of the city, collecting signatures for a new petition.

'The Party sent a brass band down there to drown the shouting of the Ecoglasnost people,' Violet said. 'But the crowds, they just thought "Wow! Ecoglasnost has an orchestra!".'

On 26 October forty members of Ecoglasnost were beaten up and arrested.

'That was the time when people made their choice. They didn't sign for Rila-Mesta. They signed to say "we don't agree, we want a change".'

On 3 November 5000 people attended an unmolested Ecoglasnost demonstration in Alexander Nevski Square. The bells of the

cathedral tolled and a petition with 11,500 signatures was delivered to the National Assembly two blocks away.

'It was the first mass public demonstration in Sofia. In the next
few days the opposition became truly a mass movement. It was
like an Indian summer. We expected a crackdown at any moment
but we didn't care any more.

'Then the 10th of November came, the day Zhivkov fell. We
didn't believe it. We ran into the street and I saw one of the Ruse
women in the crowd. She embraced me, she was crying. She said:
"I did not expect to live to see this".'

For Violet that day had been the high point. Then anti-climax had
set in, as it had everywhere from the Black Sea to the Baltic.

He believed there had been a chance that month to oust the
Communists along with their leader, as in other Eastern European countries. It had not been taken.

'The people are afraid,' Violet said. 'Totalitarianism is inside us
and totalitarianism means you aren't responsible for anything. It's
that responsibility we are afraid of. The Party does not need open
repression, because the power is still with them. Everybody had
something to lose. Totalitarianism oppresses people, and it bribes
them.'

The Union of Democratic Forces had been set up specifically to
defeat the Communists in the elections. It had failed; failed to
conquer the voters' fear of the unknown, and to out-bribe the
Communists. And now, having been united only in its opposition to the Communists, it was already breaking up. The Communists themselves would go eventually, Violet said. He stressed
'eventually'.

'The Party is like a huge dinosaur. It won't collapse, but slowly
it will rot.'

In the meantime it had changed its name, possibly set fire to its
own headquarters, and won a fair election.

'The Party is dead. Long live the Party!'

Violet stood up, shook our hands, and bared his brown teeth
for a deep and worldly belly laugh.

It was Bojidar's sister's birthday and she was preparing unhappily
for a birthday meal for some colleagues. She hated birthdays at the

best of times because of the extra queuing necessary to get anything special to eat. This time specials were off. It turned out that what she had intended to serve, including a cake she had baked herself, we had eaten the previous evening.

Peter, Bojidar, and I put some beer in Bojidar's Lada and drove to a northern suburb where Peter (who was divorced) was living with his mother in a flat with orange tiles in the lavatory and walnuts all over the kitchen floor.

Peter put an MTV tape into a video recorder he had bought on his way back from an international hang-gliding event. We drank the beer and ate salami and cheese and tried to ignore the mad psychedelic television screen. They assumed I liked it. I knew they assumed I liked it, and thought perhaps they liked it. In fact we all hated it. We got wise to this eventually and turned the television off. We filled the silence by discussing a terrifying new mind-over-matter pastime from the Orient. It involved jumping off tall buildings without parachutes. The idea was to stay close to the building and at the last moment change your downward motion into a horizontal, rolling motion by pushing out from the building with your legs. It was important to time that push absolutely right, said Peter.

The sport had been pioneered by two Japanese, a father and a son, but the father had died falling from a tall building without a parachute.

Ring Around Rila

The road and I had climbed considerably since Sofia, through genteel villa suburbs at the feet of Vitosha, past a reservoir for pairs and sculling, and up the bottom of a gorge lit by flaring Balkan maples.

Then the Iskar and the road had straightened out for a while, beside each other, under double avenues of chestnuts. It was one of those rare and priceless combinations of time and place and something else, when you just have to sing a bit of doggerel. Some might say the 'something else' is inner peace or self-knowledge. I would say it is having had enough sleep and food, and knowing there is no one within earshot.

Straight ahead, the Rila Mountains shrugged upwards like a rough clay sculpture of a rugby scrum. They are a knot of mountains rather than a straight line, and higher than the Tatras and the Fagaraş. They are higher, also, than Mount Olympus, although the Greeks once tried to make their mountain the highest in the Balkans by piling stones on top of it.

Grey-blue clouds were brewing in the veins of the massif, which filled an ever larger slice of the view with every chestnut tree that passed. Sofia was half an hour's drive back down the road; half a day by bike. But already the image of Peter Popov waving me away down Lenin Boulevard was blurred and distant. Our last conversation had been about a Nisa plastic carrier bag. I had said:

'She's been to London! I know that supermarket!'

'Probably not. It was a gift from someone else who went. When people go to the West they bring back plastic bags as gifts.' Then he had waved and waved till I was out of sight.

I had eaten in an expensive tourist fish restaurant in the gorge above the reservoir. The waiter had taken my order and had appeared in the window a few minutes later with a rifle. There was a fish pond out there. Bang. My meal had floated to the surface.

The chestnut avenues ended at the town of Samokov, where men drank, women queued for their evening cheese, and mountains filled the whole sky.

A sign said 29 kilometres from Samokov to Complex Maliovitsa, where I hoped there might be climbing boots for hire. The road slithered south-west into the mountains and was not much used at this time of year, the summer season having passed. The sides of the valley gathered round like night round a fire. The maples were more spectacular than ever, small and scarce among the conifers, but wearing all the colours of autumn at once; pale green on the lower branches and near the trunk, then yellow, orange, pink and scarlet up to wine-red at the top. By about eight o'clock the night had shut them out and there were only the silhouettes of pine trees against the moon.

Complex Maliovitsa is a cluster of amenities in cleared forest five and a half thousand feet up at the mouth of a hanging valley. The hotel was closed for repairs. The campsite was closed for winter. But a bar housed in a log cabin shed a little neon light on an expanse of knobbly, mutton-clipped grass. Inside, I joined two potato store-house builders from Dresden for *shopska* and meat. They said the Föhn Wind had blown itself out. The weather would break tomorrow.

The weather did not break. I slept in a low wooden building beside the bar and woke to a perfect morning.

The head of the hanging valley, three hours' walk away, was dominated by the rock summit cone of Maliovitsa peak. A mane of steep dry grass, encrusted with boulders, tumbled down from the rock to the treeline. At dawn there would have been mist in the trees, but I was up late.

The store-house builders had said there was no hope of finding boots up here. I walked across the mutton-clipped grass to the Central School of Alpinism and was shown to an Aladdin's cave of boots, rucksacks, ice-axes and skis. I chose a pair of steel-shanked leather boots and said I would be back in three or four days.

'Whenever,' said the man in charge. 'No problem.'

The mountains were almost empty. An hour above the complex at the end of a mule track a short, brown man with sinewy calves sat smoking in the sun in front of the old Maliovitsa refuge. From here the path narrowed to brown line, now picking a way up a broken granite step, now fading to a shadow along flat grass beside a peat-filtered stream.

By midday I was directly under Maliovitsa. By lunchtime, after a scramble round behind it, I was on the watershed. Moisture falling to the north would flow into the Black Sea; to the south, into the Aegean (but no moisture was falling).

In the last few steps to the ridge the view exploded around me. One moment it was the next tussock up the slope, three feet in front of my nose. The next, it was a hazy, heaving horizon, beyond God knew how many valleys, whichever way you looked.

Up here it was possible to get the measure of these mountains. They are not alpine at all, but more like Dartmoor on stilts. The tops are bald and windswept. The excitement comes in the wild plunging and rearing between them. The agent of vertiginosity may be a cliff, a waterfall, or forest so steep that the top of one tree is on a level with the scrabbling roots of the next. But above it all, the skin is smooth, the contours curvaceous. The Rila Mountains present a placid aspect to outer space.

Maliovitsa, for instance, is sheer on its north face, but accessible from the south by a gentle grass ramp. I heard a shout on the wind and turned to see two figures up there. They waited as I approached along the ridge, and we took each other's pictures.

They were officers of the Bulgarian Air Force, flight engineers attached to squadrons of Mig 21s, 23s and 29s in Burgas on the Black Sea coast. They were in their mid-twenties. Russian binoculars and Carl Zeiss cameras hung from their shoulders in

leather cases. They wore spotted handkerchiefs as cravats and
were on a week's leave, staying at the Rila Monastery.

I asked which way to the monastery from here and they pointed
to its roof, a thick red border holding back the forest round the
four sides of a great courtyard. It was a vertical kilometre below
us.

There was a short way down, which they took, and a long way
down, which I took. But I went as fast as I could, with their
parting words echoing in my head:

'If you are at the monastery at nineteen hours we can eat
together. The best fish in Bulgaria.'

I walked into the courtyard, blistered and knackered, exactly as
the clock struck seven.

Rila Monastery symbolizes Bulgaria, Bulgarian history, Bulgarian nationalism, and Bulgarian resistance to the Ottoman yoke. It
is nearly a thousand years old. It is breathtaking to look at, yet
relaxing and actually satisfying to walk round. All tour buses go
there (avoid high season). All Bulgaria brochures feature it. The
road is smooth. The air is clean. The fish is good. The flagstones
are cool for pummelled feet. The wooden galleries give sump-
tuous views of the mountains, and shade wherever the sun is.

There is a wonderful description of the monastery, and of a visit
to it by a Patriarch in a Mercedes, by Brian Hall in *Stealing From A
Deep Place*. And Nagel no doubt does a thorough job on icons,
frescoes and foundations. I don't. I was famished.

The flight engineers appeared at the eastern entrance to the
courtyard, showered and changed. One of them had a new
Moskvich coupé in which we rolled down the valley a little way
to the fish restaurant.

The restaurant had satellite television and we got drunk watching big names and classic videos on MTV Europe. Paul McCart-
ney sang 'There Couldn't Be A Better Moment'. John and Yoko
sang 'Just A Jealous Guy'. Brian Ferry sang something. The fish
was grilled trout, so grilled that the bones and fins crunched in
your mouth.

Only one of the flight engineers talked. His name was Robert.
The other just drank. Robert asked where Farnborough was and
said a Mig 29 had been to the air show there.

'And to Paris,' I said. 'It crashed.'

'Pilot error,' said Robert quickly.

The meal began with a bottle of *rakir*, continued with a bottle of wine each and ended with another bottle of *rakir*. At the end Robert asked:

'What is the English for *waffen*?'

'Firearm, gun,' I said. 'Why?'

'Oh, nothing.'

'Do you have one?'

'Yes.'

'Here?'

'Yes.'

He eased the muzzle out of a leather bag on the seat beside him. It was strangely terrifying.

'I am an officer,' he said.

At this point the silent one excused himself. He didn't come back. When Robert and I went outside the Moskvich was gone, with my rucksack in the boot. I'd been stung, but was too drunk to panic.

I leaned against the wall of the restaurant watching Robert's leather bag.

'Where has your friend gone?' I asked.

'He likes to drive when he drinks *rakir*. He is a good driver.'

'I think my rucksack is in the car.'

'Yes, and mine.'

I continued watching the bag. Robert showed no sign of opening it. Time slowed down as I tried to sieve the treacly alcohol out of my head. Suddenly the Moskvich was back, its headlights shining in my eyes. The silent one was raving to Robert about its engine. My pack was out of the boot and on my back. I was following Robert down through a field towards the river. I was on my back in my sleeping bag, conscious of the stars, then . . . then I was hot, with a dry mouth and a full bladder and a bad head, awake in the morning sun.

Robert and friend had to return to Burgas. I promised to look them up when I got there and walked back up the valley, past the monastery, to a forest clearing called Partisanska Polana.

Partisanska Polana . . . it was not difficult to picture the parti-

sans here, in their moccasins and sashes, plotting vengeance on a
turncoat, or a raid on a sultan's caravan. They would descend like
Assyrians, like the wolf on the fold. Should the Turks send a force
up to flush them out, sentries on crags above the road would give
the *qui vive?* and the partisans would vanish over the high passes,
to Maliovitsa, to Musala, to the Mesta.

I vanished over a low pass, hobbling as yesterday's blisters
rubbed raw. I looked back, and the hideout was lost in a great
bowl of pine trees. Somewhere up ahead in the bleak core of the
mountains there was another refuge. I reached it at dusk having
passed no one since the monastery. The refuge sat on a shelf
between two lakes in a stark grey cwm. There were at first no
people and no lights. Then a crew of workers appeared, walking
up from the lower of the two lakes, preceded by the sound of their
own weary banter. One of them climbed a pole, and lights came
on. A stove had been burning all day in the kitchen and the
warmth was welcome. So was pea and trotter soup from the urn
on top of the stove. I shared the workers' table and their dormi-
tory, but hardly their conversation; my contribution consisted of
trying to explain the meaning of 'road' as in Main Road and 'lane'
as in White Hart Lane. The English football league is avidly
followed in Bulgaria.

Cold rain drove into the cwm in the morning. This time the
weather really had broken. The workers advised returning to the
monastery, but I was hoping to complete a circuit without
retracing my steps.

Reassuring the anxious foreman with bold claims about my
experience of mountains I set off up the side of the cwm with a
plastic sack over my head. I was wearing shorts but was warm
from breakfast by the kitchen stove. I had a map and thought I
knew where I was going.

The plan was to drop down into the next valley as soon as
possible and follow the stream in the bottom of it all the way to
the Maliovitsa road, about twenty miles away. However, the path
soon disappeared into cloud and the rain turned to snow. The
snow got harder, settling quickly. Steadily the cold moved in
towards my teeth and bones. I abandoned the path, which was a

mistake, and had to climb slowly down a slope of giant boulders, at the bottom of which, still in cloud, I realized I was lost.

Three hours later I reached a dam holding back billions of gallons of rain and melted snow. Beside it stood a hut, one moment lost in cloud, the next commanding epic views down the deserted valley. A dog was lying in the doorway. I leaned over it and knocked. The door was opened by a giant in an orange jersey; a policeman trying to tell me I was trespassing. Two colleagues appeared in uniform behind me. One was stick-like, the other more of a blob. The Blob ushered me in. There was a hallway, then a room containing three beds, a stove, a green metal cupboard and a table. The Blob sat me by the stove and signalled for me to hang my frozen clothes above it. The Giant poured me a mug of Imperial American Whiskey and asked for my passport. The Stick poured some whiskey for himself and turned up the volume on the radio.

The reservoir and its catchment area were out of bounds because they supplied Sofia with water. (I twigged. This must be the valley of the Iskar. I also registered how easily I could have poisoned all of Sofia by now.) When the Giant was satisfied that I meant the water no harm he handed back my passport and accepted an invitation from the Stick to dance. They kicked back the beds, stood side by side facing the cloud-filled valley, and waited solemnly for the right point in the music to come round again. It was siren music, the kind which, seamlessly, can fill a whole Bulgarian wedding day. The Stick looked over his shoulder and lamented with the most eloquent of drunken gestures that there were no women up here to dance with . . . or to fuck. They started. Boy, could they dance. The Giant was light on his feet and possessed by the rhythm. The Stick began to ripple, more like a whip, and his adam's apple shuttled up and down in his throat. The Blob sat in the corner laughing. The Stick was up on the beds now, all three of them at once, stooping under the ceiling and flicking out his boots like a Cossack. The Blob was on his feet too, stamping them into the floorboards, thumping the table, thumping the air.

They paused to ladle out soup. As we ate it the Stick stood up, opened the window and fired six rounds from his pistol into the cloud. The other two admonished him. The Stick fell back onto a bed and clicked off the magazine to count the remaining rounds. He handed me one.

'Souvenir?' I asked. No, he said. They all had to be accounted for.

But the Stick did not wish to appear ungenerous. He took a heavy bunch of keys off the wall and opened the green metal cupboard. Inside, at the back, there was a rack of automatic rifles. In front of them were two machine guns with curving magazines, a box full of handguns, and a long green canvas bag. The Stick took one of the machine guns, pulled out a shoulder brace, released various safety catches and shouted excitedly at me to pull the trigger. The barrel was pointing out of the window. I pulled, once, very quickly. Two ear-splitting bangs. Two empty shells hit the ceiling. The trigger guard bounced back and numbed my thumb. I was impressed – no hiding that. The policemen were delighted.

'Kalashnikov?' I asked.

'Kalashnikov. AK-47.'

The Stick was on a roll now. He put the machine gun away and hefted out the green canvas bag. The Blob closed his eyes and put his face in his hands and went out into the hallway and paced around a bit. By the time he was seated again in his corner the Stick had unzipped the bag and was putting together the kind of thing used by the Mujahidin to seal off entire fiefdoms in the Hindu Kush.

When assembled it was about five feet long with an A-frame support under the barrel. He rested the support on the window sill and went back to the cupboard for the ammunition box, but was too drunk to fit it. The Giant helped him. Then the Stick, lying on the bed beside the gun, released the safety catch and yanked back a slide which put the first round in the breach. He motioned for me to fire. I squeezed the trigger, holding it for an instant, and my three rounds were embedded half a second later in a tree across the valley. Three was not enough for the Stick. He rolled over on top of the gun and his whole body tensed. Seventeen more rounds sprayed into the cloud in a couple of mad seconds. Empty casings spat and bounced round the inside of the hut. The Stick rolled back with a manic look in his eyes. Then silence returned, sweet and ringing, and he reached over and shook my hand. It was mighty reassuring to see him count the empty shells and take the gun apart and clean it. Meanwhile, the Blob used sign language to indicate that one bullet from this gun would get through a brick wall and still make a hole in a body the size of a large loaf of bread.

I was warm now and had to be going. The Blob told me the way to the Maliovitsa road and gave me a bunch of grapes. The Stick grinned goodbye from behind his heap of lethal Meccano. The Giant came with me to the door, and asked me not to tell anyone about the firepower demonstration. He touched his shoulder; it would cost him his epaulettes.

Two hours further on another policeman tapped on the window of his cabin and asked if I'd heard gunfire at the dam. Gunfire? None of that, but some colleagues of his had been extremely kind. Soup, whisky, a stool by the stove . . .

This one was not to be out-hosted. He invited me in to smoke and play chess. The cigarettes were lit on an electric heater because he had no matches.

'No matches,' he said. 'No food, no drink, no money, Bulgaria kaput. But the police are OK, yes?'

'Definitely.'

'You talk to Iron Lady. Tell her Bulgaria needs food and money.'

He had me checkmate in about a dozen moves. It was raining again outside, vengeful rain making up for time lost to the Föhn Wind. I didn't fancy the remaining two hours' walking to the Maliovitsa road, but they had to be done.

At exactly that moment a stray bus appeared outside, trying to get to Maliovitsa. The policeman promptly commandeered it for me. Inside an hour I was back in the bar across the mutton-clipped grass being thwacked round the shoulders by the Dresden potato-store-house builders.

Home Straight

On 3 October I wrote in my diary: 'Germany is re-unified today – they are having a concert in the Schauspielhaus to celebrate – and it seems ordained that this trip should be coming to an end. My toothpaste from Budapest is nearly finished. The zip on my handlebar bag is going. The stick fell out of my deodorant last night.'

That evening my water bottle was filched from outside the restaurant in a mining town in the mountains near the Turkish border. And the next morning, my last in Eastern Europe, I heard metal on metal when I tried the brakes, and knew the blocks were through.

So the signals were there. It was in the tea-leaves. I must have got the tempo about right.

In fact the tempo quickened after Maliovitsa, as apparently it does when a horse turns for home. My balls disappeared on the fast sub-zero descent from the complex to Samokov. It was a Saturday morning and industrious families were out among the cedars in the bottom of the valley, gathering wild mushrooms. These people were well-wrapped against the decisive seasonal cold, but my balls had only lycra and were being freeze-dried through it, so they snuck indoors; took the body-heat option reserved for exceptional circumstances.

I managed to be alone with *Don Giovanni* and a warm air blower in a roadside café for half an hour, thrusting fingers down

my shorts to act as tent poles and create the right ambiance for
testicular re-entry. They eventually emerged. I continued to the
ski resort of Borovets, humming the joys of fertility.

Thousands of British schoolchildren learn to ski in Borovets
every year, and there is draught McEwan's for their teachers at the
Golden Lion English Pub in the basement of one of the mass-
produced pyramidal hotels which rise from the trees on the north
flank of Musala Peak and earn much-needed dollars for the
Bulgarian government. I did not tarry for the McEwan's. Instead
I nearly killed myself freewheeling away from Borovets towards
Plovdiv and the Black Sea.

Anxious not to use my worn brakes, I tried swinging across the
road when approaching hairpins in order to take them wide,
without slowing down. On one sharp right hander I met a Lada
coming the other way and missed it – wincing at the Dopplerized
sound of its horn – by the width of a pannier.

There was a wonderful view from this road. It led out of the
hard-cash space-station created for Western skiers in the mountains, down into a land of dung and apples. The relentless
coniferous forest of the previous few days gave way to rough
pasture and odd squares of orchard. The road surface became
cracked and believable. At the bottom of the freewheel, at a T-
junction with the main Sofia-Plovdiv road, I saw my first sign to
Istanbul.

Plovdiv

The Plovdiv International Industrial Goods Fair was in progress.

My guide was a young man named Pavel with whom I had
watched an Agatha Christie film the previous night and in whose
sister's bed I had slept, without the sister. Pavel was sixteen but
could have passed for twenty-two, not by dint of hairiness or bulk
but by his air of sharp sophistication. He wore fashionable
Western clothes; docksiders, ochre baggies, polo shirts and
assorted California-motif tops – some zippered, some with turtle-
necks. And he spoke excellent English, having come eleventh out

of 'oh about a thousand' in the competitive entrance exam for Plovdiv's English-language secondary school.

Pavel was not actually interested in the Fair. He was doing right by his parents who had brought us together having met me in a restaurant. I could not generate much interest either, not being a potential buyer of wide-bore drill bits or frankfurter-smoking machines. Neither of us let on to the other that we might be bored, but neither held the other back. We moved quite fast.

It was depressing. Hundreds queued for Federal Republic of Germany carrier bags to stuff with leaflets about pesticides and optic fibres – or just to have the carrier bags. Renault 5s made under licence in Iran won dreamy caresses. A pair of Italian motocross bikes reclining in a chrome-scape of espresso machines drew groans of consumer frustration. The crush round the Mercedes stand was impenetrable and sinister.

The giant Soviet pavilion emitted a continuous English commentary on ammonium compounds and electric hoists available through Gosplan. But the big story of the 1990 Fair was that half the Soviet pavilion had been taken over by the Bulgarian private sector. It was more a symbolic than a substantive takeover. On show were two baths, some frocks, a selection of crow-bars, four kinds of coal arranged on fast food trays, and a prospectus produced by a rubber-washer specialist, but no rubber washers.

Most exhibits in the fair prompted in their beholders craving, indifference or incomprehension. The only one to elicit something from near the positive end of the range of human emotions was an episode of Benny Hill; English TV comedy with Bulgarian subtitles being offered as a Polish export on a Japanese television. Pavel and I tittered with about fifty others for a bit, then left the Fair.

Outside the turnstiles scores of anxious people were soliciting addresses.

'They are playing Jackpot,' Pavel said. 'They want to make a million dollars.'

A chain-letter craze was sweeping Plovdiv, which had not heard of chain letters until the current economic crisis. By sending money to an address three or four places up a list to which they then added their own addresses, penurious Bulgarians could guarantee themselves a fortune in the post within a week or two.

'It doesn't work,' I said. 'It's crazy.'

'No, it works. With Jackpot you can make a million dollars in three weeks. If you don't have dollars you can play a leva game.'

'Why trust the people below you in the chain to send you money?'

'My father started one week ago and already he has a hundred and sixty dollars. I am playing five games. I am waiting for the money now.'

He hailed a taxi. The driver was involved in a chain-letter run by 'MIF Technical Development Collective Firm', whose letter claimed to be quoting Jesus when it said: 'If you have got two shirts, share one with your neighbour'.

When we got to Pavel's apartment building he went straight to check the post. Nothing yet. He lost his cool for a moment and hit the metal box with his fist. Then he smiled. 'It will come,' he said. 'I know it will come.'

Two days later I smelt the sea. It had been easy riding down the wide spatula of agricultural land which separates the Stara Planina from the Rodopi Mountains in the south.

The mountain weather kept to the mountains, and over endless hectares of vines and peanut plants empty skies let through all the heat the autumn sun could throw down. Schoolchildren lolled through the afternoons wherever there was shade, instead of helping with the harvest.

The sea smell wafted first off a lagoon, south-west of the Bay of Burgas. Then it came stronger. A breeze carried it up from the port to a hill behind the city, from where you could see the whole bay and its cliffs, and cargo ships waiting for cranes, and the long blue horizon.

I found a hotel room in a fishing village on a headland twenty miles down the coast, then got a bus back into Burgas and phoned Robert the flight engineer. Robert was out drinking but his silent friend was in the flat they shared on base, in bed with his girlfriend. He answered the phone. He would send Robert to me.

Robert found me on the terrace of the Hotel Brig by the bus station.

'AM I GLAD TO SEE YOU!' he said.

I said I was glad to see him too, and we went and ate *calamari* in a

fancy fish restaurant a few blocks inland behind the opera house.
Robert had been drinking because he was on edge, and he went on
drinking. His Mig 29 was going up the next day and if anything
went wrong with it he would go to jail. The thirty-million-dollar
plane was his sole responsibility. It was the same before every
training flight, three or four times a week; he couldn't sleep.

He wanted to work for the RAF, or better still British Airways.
I said I'd ask around. Mig expert seeks work in NATO . . .

'Have you seen *Top Gun?*' I asked.

'Three times. Some of my friends study it for their diploma.
Those planes are F-14s adapted especially for aircraft carriers.
Also, in the training flights, Intruders and A-7s.' Others of his
friends had studied the use of Harriers in the Falklands War. For
his own diploma Robert had specialized in F1-11s and their
bombing raid on Tripoli in 1986.

He had a room in town as well as on base. We went there to
listen to Mussorgsky and drink rum. For some time forked
lightning had been playing across the sky and a wind had been
picking up. Now rain started and the power went off. Robert lit a
candle and showed me a computer print-out of the *Kama Sutra*
and some soft porn called *Bedside Companion* which friends who
worked for Balkan Airways had obtained on foreign stopovers,
'to improve the English'.

It was two in the morning. I left Robert to his pre-flight vigil
and took a taxi back down the coast road to the fishing village on
the headland. The windscreen wipers worked like desperate
pump hands and the driver craned forward the better to see
through them. By now the rain was falling so fast that it stood on
the road in long strips which hit the bottom of the car like a
timpani roll.

The storm continued throughout the next day but I set off all the
same. The wind was northerly – Russian, therefore – and Bulgaria's famous Black Sea sands were deserted, beaten flat by the
breakers and the rain.

The road passed through 'Duni', a Three Star Holiday Village
with tri-lingual signs detailing prices per half hour for pedalos,
windsurfing and water-skiing. The village mascot was a pelican.
The beach umbrellas were all up-ended and the lifeguard's tower

looked to be on its way down too. The hire shops and bars were battened down but the wind had still ripped holes in their thatches.

In the middle of the afternoon I reached a sign saying Istanbul 334 km. I took off my shoes to wring out my socks, then followed the sign inland, climbing steadily for about three hours into unnamed and uninhabited mountains. The rain never let up. It was spectacularly indoors weather.

The frontier post was on a major watershed. From here it was downhill all the way to the Bosporus, but my brakes had gone and I would be unlikely to get there alive without them. There was no real option. I walked over to a Romanian tour bus waiting to be searched by Turkish customs, and asked the driver if he had room for a bike and a body as far as Istanbul.

'You are going to Istanbul?' he asked.

'If possible.'

'WE are going to Istanbul! Come on, come on!' And it was done. My steed was shoved in among the jerry cans and by suppertime I was staring dumbly at a moonlit Sea of Marmara.